Truth *And Social Science*

Truth *And Social Science*

From Hegel to Deconstruction

ROSS ABBINNETT

SAGE Publications
London • Thousand Oaks • New Delhi

SAGE Publications Ltd
6 Bonhill Street
London EC2A 4PU

SAGE Publications Inc.
2455 Teller Road
Thousand Oaks, California 91320

SAGE Publications India Pvt Ltd
32, M-Block Market
Greater Kailash – I
New Delhi 110 048

British Library Cataloguing in Publication data

A catalogue record for this book is available
from the British Library

ISBN 0 8039 7592 9
ISBN 0 8039 7593 7 (pbk)

Library of Congress catalog card number 97–062127

Typeset by Mayhew Typesetting, Rhayader, Powys
Printed in Great Britain by Redwood Books, Trowbridge, Wiltshire

Contents

Acknowledgements

I would like to dedicate this book to my mother and father, for all their long years of hard work and support. And to Siân Davies for all that she has given me in the short time I have known her. I would also like to extend my thanks to my former colleagues at the University of Portsmouth – Professors Tester, Shilling and Smart – for all their efforts on my behalf. Thanks are also due to Chris and Robert Rojek for their help in getting the book into production.

Introduction: Idealism and Social Thought

Hopefully, this book has not turned out to be an attempt to specify the nature of a 'social science' as a discrete analytical project, with its own irreducible standards of truth and validity. What I have tried to do – and obviously the degree to which I have succeeded is a matter of critical judgement – is to show that the concept of 'truth' is fundamental to the ideas of community, identity and subjectivity which have shaped the discourse of the social sciences in general, and sociology in particular. Truth, I will argue, is an historical construction, whose acknowledgement is originally inscribed in the relations which constitute human sociality – or what I, following Hegel, will call ethical life.[1] Thus, presenting the forms, relations and institutions through which truth is constructed within particular historical configurations of sociality is not something which ought to be reserved for a 'universal' and prescriptive philosophy of science. Karl Popper's attempt to determine the limits which scientific methodology places upon social explanation, for example, ends up by excluding every reconstruction of ethical life which does not acknowledge the reflective/critical individual as its origin and aim.[2] Famously, Marx's historical materialism and Freud's theory of repression are ruled out of court, on the grounds that what cannot be 'objectively' falsified (i.e., what is not believed 'hypothetically') is, by definition, 'pseudoscientific', and the ally of social and political irrationalism. My claim, however, is that the historical determination of truth within the 'substance' of ethical life demands that we acknowledge the relationship of self-consciousness (subjectivity), to the 'objective' structures in which its activity is situated (economy, state, culture, etc.). Such a recognition, I will argue, is possible only through rational reconstructions of a collective, socio-historical 'fate'.

This relationship of history, rationality and truth is crucial to understanding what is at stake in sociological theorizations of modernity. The conception of ethical life – or *Sittlichkeit* (from the German *Sittlich*, which makes an explicit identification of the ethical with the customary, the public, the communal) – that is deployed throughout the structure of the book articulates the fundamental themes of Hegel's speculative idealism. For Hegel, the concept of 'humanity' emerges with self-consciousness; and self-consciousness is originally, and by definition, implicated in the structures and relations of ethical life. Consciousness, in other words, only becomes self-consciousness when it is recognized by an other. This is important because the beginning of the *Phenomenology of Mind* has to provide a credible account of the transition from conscious instinct (primarily the desire to consume) to the establishment of a recognizably ethical life.[3] What emerges from this transition is a moment of absolute domination: the slave's unreserved obedience to a master, who has (phenomenologically/historically) vanquished him in a struggle for recognition. The important point here is that although the original moment of sociality is founded upon violence and the fear of death, its history discloses a development which exceeds the simple perpetuation of fear. The relationship which is established between master and slave – one of unquestioning service and noble obligation – produces a universal transformation of self-consciousness through the activity of the slave. In order to understand the history of ethical life, therefore, we must acknowledge that the 'objectivity' of social relations (even within this mythology of absolute domination) is never given independently of self-consciousness. Ethical life is 'actual'[4] only in so far as it includes the formation and activity of those who participate in its 'substance'. From the beginning, therefore, human subjectivity is confronted by structures, relations and institutions which appear as (true, rational) determinations of its historical fate. I will argue that the project of social scientific explanation, should be understood in terms of this recognition. For it is by postulating the conditions under which self-conscious subjects must act (i.e., the conditions under which they recognize themselves and others) that it is possible to judge the concept of 'modernity' in its relation to ethical substance.

In a sense, then, the book is an attempt to expound the nature (and the possibility) of this judgement; that is, to expound the relationship of sociological conceptions of community, identity, subjectivity and totality to Hegel's speculative conception of *Sittlichkeit*. In his introduction to the *Philosophy of Right*, Hegel famously remarks that 'What is rational is actual and what is actual is rational'.[5] This proposition is frequently read as the assertion of an historicist necessity: human consciousness, and the relations through which it has evolved, are immanently rational; and so 'history' is, in the end, the process through which ethical life achieves coincidence with its concept (i.e., the absolute mediation of self-conscious subjects). Yet Hegel makes it clear in both his logical and phenomeno-logical dialectics that the concept, or 'truth', of *Sittlichkeit* cannot be disintricated from its secular history: for the actuality of ethical substance is always 'rationalized' through contradictory and conflictual determina-tions of 'the good'.[6] What needs to be clearly understood is that Hegel's remarks about 'Absolute Knowledge'[7] and the dialectical necessity of the 'Notion' do not entail an 'end' to history, in which the concept of ethical life would finally make its earthly appearance. Speculative thought is founded upon the essentially tragic – although far from despairing –

recognition that the secular (the finite, the limited, the contingent), while it is irreducibly 'rational' in its constitution, always remains inadequate to the categories of pure speculative necessity (the infinite, the spiritual, the *causa sui*). The relationship between Hegel's idealism and the 'substance' of modernity, therefore, is not determined by a desire to make the city of God from the ruins of humanity. Rather, his philosophy demands acknowledgement of the aporias and contradictions inscribed in ethical life; for however 'rational' the totality might be, its ('objective') differentiation will always determine the necessity of reflection and critical judgement.[8]

A couple of points need to be clarified here. I began by suggesting that speculative idealism is marked by a particular account of the relationship between self-consciousness and the forms and institutions of human sociality. For Hegel, the autonomy of the subject must be understood in terms of the objective/existent conditions of its activity. The critique of Kant's doctrine of morality presented in the *Phenomenology of Mind*, for example, is concerned to show that in conceiving its formal independence as the absolute ground of moral action, rational subjects become increasingly complicit with the utilitarian (atomistic, self-seeking) demands of civil society. The particularization of work, satisfaction and desire inscribed in bourgeois property relations, in other words, is reinforced by Kant's presentation of the moral will as transcendent of all secular (finite, self-interested) motivations. For where it is the will of the isolated individual that is conceived as the arbiter of moral action, particular interests appear as if they are identical with the universal good.[9] Critical morality, then, postulates a certain 'abstract' relationship between the reflective subject and the substance of social and political life; a relationship which acknowledges neither the conditions of its own possibility, nor its participation in the 'fate' of modern self-consciousness (the loss of ethical mediation, the dominance of abstract individualism, the 'irony' of the self in its relation to the law).

This account of the relationship between Kantian moral consciousness and the constitution of modernity points up a number of distinctively 'speculative' ideas. Hegel's idealism demands that philosophical thought should be recognized as more than a purely analytical exercise, which remains distinct from, and irrelevant to, the constitution of community. The distinctions – between reason and existence, concept and intuition, autonomy and inclination – which are posited in Kant's critical philosophy, for example, have participated in the formation of modern ethical life. For it is through the formal necessity of the categorical imperative that the egoism of the abstract 'personality' achieves its moral sanction. Hegel's critique of Kant, therefore, is not an attempt to 'refute' transcendental idealism in a narrowly analytical sense. Rather, it is woven into the logical and phenomenological dialectics through which the history of modern social, ethical and political life is articulated in Hegel's social, ethical and political thought. What is important for Hegel is the recognition that Kant's critical philosophy has a history, and that as such, the emergence of practical/reflective autonomy into *Sittlichkeit*, demands that 'we', as speculative thinkers, judge its relationship to modern forms of legality, autonomy and self-recognition. What ought to concern us, in other words, is expounding the complicities that emerge between 'abstract' philosophical categories (categorical imperative, reflective judgement, practical autonomy, etc.), and the distinctive forms of coercion, domination and violence which afflict modernity.

One of the fundamental issues that will inform my account of modern social theory, is the question of the origin, the beginning. Within speculative philosophy, Kant's idea of moral autonomy is conceived as proceeding not from the self-consistency of the good will, but from the increasing antagonism of civil society. It is acknowledged as having a certain complicity with the reflective, self-seeking ego,[10] and with conflicts determined by its activity. The a priori necessity of practical reason, in other words, is disclosed as an 'abstract' construction whose significance must be understood in terms of its relationship to the 'objective spirit' (law, state, civil society, etc.). Why, then, is this significant to modern social science and social theory? Well, Hegel's account of Kant's philosophy makes it clear that the categories through which subjectivity, identity and community are expounded, retain a kind of historical potency. Indeed, the critique of Fichtean philosophy which Hegel pursues in *The Science of Logic* attempts to show that the oppositions of subjective idealism are capable of becoming even more ethically and politically abstracted than in their originally Kantian form.[11] I will argue that it is this Kantian potency, with its attempts to determine the legislative domains of knowledge, freedom and morality, that lies at the foundation of 'modernist' social thought. And that it is also possible to recognize the influence of a certain Kantianism in the 'poststructuralist' conceptions of ethics, community and identity I will examine.

Beginnings, introductions and prefaces are notoriously difficult, not just from a literary or pedagogical point of view, but because they raise fundamental questions about the nature of the origin, the construction of the 'given', and the relationship of modernity to its future. The prefaces and introductions which Hegel wrote to his substantive works, he was at pains to point out, were always at odds with their content. For speculative philosophy demands that the necessity of its transitions is conceived through the concrete historical content of ethical life. We must recognize, in other words, that the dialectical necessity that Hegel expounds in the Preface to the *Phenomenology of Mind* appears as a kind of scholastic determination to abstract the 'rational' from the violence of human history. This is only because it is a pedagogical exercise, designed to orientate the reader before his or her entry into the 'historical time' of Hegel's exposition. The point, then, is that an introduction must be understood as abstracting speculative categories – negativity, spirit, subjectivity, self-consciousness – from the content in which they are embedded. Thus, if the project of the book is understood as an attempt to discern the persistence of Kantianism in 'modernist' social thought (and to suggest that judging its reproduction in determinate social paradigms bears upon the recognition of ethical substance), then the following account of Kant's critical philosophy should be read only as an attempt to outline the guiding thread of my exposition.

Put very briefly, Kant's philosophy articulates three exclusive domains of transcendental legislation: knowledge, freedom and judgement. The first of these legislative domains is expounded in the *Critique of Pure Reason*. Here Kant attempts to set out the transcendental (a priori) conditions which determine our experience of an 'external' world of objects. His argument is that the mind does not simply receive impressions – or what Kant terms 'intuitions' – from a realm of empirical objects; rather, it actively constructs those intuitions into a causally interacting totality of bodies in space and time. Thus, a science of physical objects (i.e., the mathematical postulation of universally necessary relations between particular events) is possible only because the categories of the human understanding (*Verstand*) are demonstrably apodeictic. I will suggest that this kind of argument – in which the inner-articulation of a given totality is re-presented as explaining every 'contingent' phenomenon – is deployed, differently, in the two classically modernist forms of structuralism: Marxism and functionalism.

The second legislative domain which Kant sought to determine within the critical philosophy is rational autonomy. For Kant, the external world is determined by the category of efficient causality: every event in space and time has a cause which immediately preceded its occurrence. The trouble with this account of experience is that it leaves no room for moral autonomy. If the first *Critique* were presented as a comprehensive account of reason's legislative power, then every action would have to be referred to an external, 'heteronomous' cause (self-seeking desires); and the 'ethics' of human sociality would have to remain obedient to Hobbes's principles of rational domination. Kant, however, maintains that human subjects are capable of determining themselves independently of the desires and inclinations of their 'phenomenal' existence. For Kant, we are all capable of moral actions because, as rational subjects, we are all capable of recognizing when our actions contradict the respect which is due to all rational beings. For example, I should not kill to secure my own advantage because if killing were adopted as a universal 'maxim' of action, there could be no ethical life, no property and no civil society. Kant's moral philosophy, therefore, attempts to determine the categorical imperative ('Act only according to that maxim by which you can at the same time will that it should become a universal law')[12] as the expression of the (good) will's formal consistency with itself; a consistency which places the rational subject beyond the heteronomous demands inscribed in contemporary social, ethical and political institutions. I will claim that this Kantian primacy of practical reason has provided the foundation of modern 'cognitive' sociologies – particularly the work of Max Weber and Jurgen Habermas.

Finally, Kant's *Critique of Judgement* deals with the relationship between the legislative domains of practical and theoretical reason. Within the boundaries circumscribed by my exposition of community, modernity and ethical life, the most important thing to emerge from Kant's remarks on aesthetic and teleological judgements is the role he attributes to feeling in the reception of the unity of practical and theoretical reason. For although we cannot 'know' that the world of phenomena is the expression of an uncontingent, self-determining intelligence (God), certain appearances produce a 'sensation' (awe, inspiration) which stands in the place of such knowledge. This redetermination of the (practical and theoretical) faculties in the presence of the sublime is one of the central themes in Lyotard's reading of Kant. Indeed, the general possibility of judging 'without a concept' is variously explored in the work of Derrida, Foucault and Lyotard. I will return to this in a moment.

I have already said that this book is an attempt to expound the relationship of sociological conceptions of community, identity, subjectivity and totality to Hegel's idea of *Sittlichkeit*. This relationship, I will argue, takes the form of a judgement in which the categories of theoretical explanation are conceived as theoretical reconstructions of the substance of ethical life. Each of the competing paradigms, through which the project of a sociology is determined, represents an abstract identification of 'rationality' and 'totality'.[13] Marxism, for example, postulates the negative structure of capitalist relations of production as the final determinant of moral, religious and political ideologies. For Habermas, on the other hand, the structures and institutions of society must be understood as structures of communicative action. And so the 'rationality' of the 'life world' is presented as a constantly redetermined demand for dialogical consensus. Such examples do, of course, require detailed elaboration. However, if it is allowed that Marx and Habermas's ideas would at least be recognizable from these descriptions, then it is possible to make a fundamental point. Namely, that each paradigmatic form is 'abstract' in the sense that, while it does disclose something essential about the nature of modernity, this disclosure is always limited and exclusive. The judgements that we, as speculative philosophers, must make therefore depend upon our recognizing the Kantian oppositions inscribed (and re-inscribed) in different sociological/social scientific paradigms. In a sense, these paradigms are the forms in which the substance of modernity becomes reflective; they specify the contradictions, aporias and complicities through which the 'concept' ethical life (the idea of universally mediated freedom) has determined itself.

Ultimately, my account of the project of a social science is an attempt to set out its relationship to the kind of speculative judgement which is expounded in the 'Doctrine of the Notion'.[14] What Hegel attempts here, is to show that in order to 'judge' adequately the connection between an object and its attributes, it must be recognized that what is 'essential' to its being is not accidentally conjoined with it. Thus, the universal qualities of humanity (subjectivity, self-consciousness, autonomy, etc.) must be acknowledged as essential to its concept/idea, even if the 'actual' conditions under which it exists – the contemporary form of ethical life – does not express that universality. Speculative judgement of *Sittlichkeit*, therefore, requires (and reproduces) the discourse of abstraction; for it is only through the oppositions inscribed in 'modern' theoretical paradigms that it is possible to recognize the idea of rationally mediated autonomy.

It is this relationship between the discourses of abstraction and the logic of speculative judgements that I will try to defend against post-structuralist critiques of subjectivity, community and ethical identity. Again, the constraints of an introduction will not allow me to describe the detail of the positions which Foucault, Lyotard and Derrida occupy with respect to Hegel. However, I will argue that a claim such as Derrida's – that Hegel's philosophy cannot take account of the dispersal that its formative categories presuppose, and that, as a result, speculative history articulates a violent suppression of (racial, sexual, cultural, etc.) difference – fails to acknowledge that the law of dialectical (or rather 'speculative') transition is not expounded as 'present' in its historical determinations. Rather, it is recognized through the necessity of judging forms of abstraction, whose ideals of legality, freedom and community promise comprehensive solutions to the contradictions of modernity. I will return to these themes of violence and rationality in the concluding chapters.

Notes

1. See especially Hegel's *Philosophy of Right*, trans. T.M. Knox, Oxford University Press, 1967b, paragraphs 142–57.
2. For a detailed account of Popper's ideas on the relationship between metaphysics, critical thought and political freedom, see *The Open Society and Its Enemies* (1966) (volumes one and two).
3. G.W.F. Hegel, *Phenomenology of Mind*, trans. J.B. Baillie, Harper & Row, 1967a, pp. 228–40.
4. Hegel, *Hegel's Logic: Encyclopaedia of the Philosophical Sciences, Volume One*, trans. W. Wallace, Oxford University Press, 1982, pp. 200–22.
5. Hegel, *Philosophy of Right*, p. 10.
6. Hegel, *The Science of Logic*, trans. A.V. Miller, George Allen & Unwin, 1969, pp. 818–23.
7. Hegel, *Phenomenology of Mind*, pp. 789–808.
8. Hegel, *Science of Logic*, pp. 824–44.
9. Hegel, *Phenomenology of Mind*, pp. 615–27.
10. Hegel, *Philosophy of Right*, pp. 75–105.

11. See 'The Doctrine of Essence', in Hegel, *Science of Logic*.

12. I. Kant, *Foundations of the Metaphysics of Morals*, trans. L. White Beck, Macmillan, 1985, p. 39.

13. For the original 'modernist' formulation of the idea of a 'paradigm', see T.S. Kuhn, *The Structure of Scientific Revolutions* (1970).

14. Hegel, *Science of Logic*, pp. 622–61.

1

The Rational and the Social

It is in the Preface to the *Philosophy of Right* (1967b) that Hegel makes what is perhaps his most infamous assertion: 'What is rational is actual and what is actual is rational'. On this conviction the plain man, like the philosopher, makes his stand, and philosophy starts its study of the universe of mind as well as the universe of nature'.[1] What Hegel's statement appears to assert is a relationship of identity between being and reason which is inscribed in all natural and historical forms; and that this relationship gives absolute sanction to the 'modern' form of political authority set out in *Philosophy of Right*. The consequences of reading Hegel's Preface as stating an immanent identity of being and reason are not difficult to identify: they are repeated, differently, in all Marxist, humanist and poststructuralist objections to speculative idealism. First, there is the claim that Hegel's philosophy presupposes an original human essence, whose development towards self-recognition is the true cause of historical progress. Secondly, Hegel's concept of absolute knowledge is presented as implying a *condition* in which all subjective forms of desire, reflection and activity would find universal satisfaction. Thirdly, it is supposed that every form of difference – race, class, gender, nationality – is suppressed by Hegel's assumption of an immanent–historical identity among self-conscious subjects. Finally, there is the suspicion that Hegel's account of the 'end of history' – i.e., the end of unrecognized contradictions within ethical life (*Sittlichkeit*) – can only mean the suppression of moral 'autonomy', whatever form this might take.

What I have presented above are the precepts of a general deter- mination to read Hegel's thought as a metaphysical system, in which every event, category or form determines its truth in relation to the (totalized) totality of ethical life/absolute knowledge. This determination entails a generic understanding of Hegelian social and political thought as the articulation of a violent rationalism (*logocentrism*), which sup- presses a more natural or more creative or more ethical spontaneity of human thought and action. Karl Marx's critique of Hegel's political thought is founded upon his rejection of the latter's attempt to recognize and mediate the antagonisms of 'bourgeois' self-seeking. Marx conceived capitalist civil society as the complete negation of 'natural' creative autonomy, and, as such, proposed that it is only through the revolutionary critique/destruction of private property that humanity can liberate itself from a merely 'ideological' critique of social relations.[2] Emmanuel Levinas's account of the 'logocentrism' which afflicts Western philosophy in general has attempted to show that the ethical commandment is a moment 'infinitely' reinscribed in the face of the other, a moment which cannot be 'substituted for' by the categories of rational 'totality'.[3] Jean-Francois Lyotard and Jacques Derrida, in different ways, regard the conflation of community, substance and identity in *Sittlichkeit* as violence against the unforeseen, unrealizable 'difference' of the other.[4] All start from the premise that Hegel's conception of community is blind to the restrictiveness of its presuppositions – the 'necessity' of bourgeois property relations or the historical substantiation (*Bildung*) of ethical necessity, or the primacy of knowledge/cognition over 'difference' – and that this blindness determines and legitimizes an inherently violent concept of political authority.

For us, then, the primary issue which emerges from the general precepts of anti-Hegelian thought is the compatibility of social scientific forms of explanation with a speculative approach to ethics, politics and justice. Hegel's assertion of the identity of being and reason in the Preface to *Philosophy of Right* seems to imply that once absolute knowledge is inscribed in the substance of ethical life, the transparency and universality of all individual motives and satisfactions will be such as to remove opposition and conflict. Given such an a priori determination of the fate of self-conscious humanity, it would certainly be difficult to see how the contradictions Hegel sets out in the *Phenomenology of Mind* (1967a), could be understood as anything other than the preordained stages of a transhistorical necessity. The problem with developing a speculative approach to social explanation, therefore, appears to be the resistance of Hegel's thought to the uniqueness of socio-historical forms, to the 'difference' which emerges within them, and to the violence, injustice and domination which inhabits the structures of modernity. It is against the background of this supposed resistance that I must understand the relationship between Kant's critical philosophy and the development of a social science. For unless we are able to establish why it is Kantian and not Hegelian thought which has been the primary influence on social explanation, and how this influence has limited the recognition of community, identity, difference and justice, a speculative social science could only reproduce a set of fixed presuppositions about the nature of ethical life.

My argument, therefore, will attempt to show that the generic objections to Hegel's philosophy have significantly misrepresented the 'speculative' nature of his social and political thought, and that his account of the relationship between 'modernity' and its theoretical recognition remains open to the violence (exclusion, suppression, misrecognition) determined (and re-determined) within ethical life. The idea

of a social science I will develop, then, is dependent upon three fundamental claims about the nature of human sociality, modernity and critical
recognition. (1) There is an essential link between the constitution of
'modern' social and political life (citizenship, civil society, sovereign
individuality etc.) and the transcendental categories of 'reason', 'understanding', 'autonomy' and 'judgement' deployed in Kant's three *Critiques*.
Critical philosophy, in other words, is the 'reflection' of difference and
diversity within modern ethical life. (2) The philosophical foundations
of modern social science are located in the oppositions (autonomy–
heteronomy, concept–intuition, noumena–phenomena, reason–understanding) posited in Kant's account of theoretical, practical, teleological
and aesthetic judgements. The 'classical' forms through which I will
characterize the project of a social science (Marxism, functionalism, action
theory and their variants) all reproduce Kantian ideals of synthesis,
identity and agency. (3) It is only through these 'reflective' conceptions of
ethical life that it is possible to re-cognize the 'idea' of sociality. For
although none of them is able to give a comprehensive account of
modern ethical life, it is through the (hierarchical) categories and oppositions they deploy that the possibility of community/mediation is
thought. A speculative social science, therefore, is concerned with thinking the concepts of justice, identity and inclusion through the discourse of
abstract separation and difference.

Kant and the origins of social science

In the introduction, I attempted to set out the fundamental questions
with which a social science is, in general, concerned – that is, the nature
and extent of inequality, the possibility of social justice, the construction
of social difference, and the inclusiveness and exclusiveness of social
relations. The generic conception of Hegel (as an abstract rationalist) that
I have attempted to construct is obviously resistant to this idea of social
science as an ongoing 'critique' of ethical life and its institutions. For it
presents speculative idealism as a system in which 'difference' (race,
gender, class or nationality) can always be recognized as identity; where
'otherness' (the excluded, the unrecognized) is always mediated within
the 'same' (spirit and its categories); and violence and domination are
always productive of higher, less contradictory forms of ethical life.[5] In
order to conceive the possibility of a 'non-totalizing' social science,
therefore, it is necessary to specify precisely the relationship between
'abstract' (Kantian) and 'speculative' (Hegelian) idealism. I have claimed
that the concepts of identity, autonomy and synthesis deployed in Kant's
critical thought are: (1) originally related to the constitution of modern
'differentiated' relations; and (2) the presupposition of 'social scientific'
forms of explanation. My argument is that the discourses of a social
science reproduce the idea of ethical life as an 'abstract' totality: each

prioritizes one 'synthetic' element (productive activity, functional interdependence, etc.) without being able to account for the universal
'conditions' in which that synthesis takes place. It is Kant's 'abstract'
idealism, therefore, which is the *condition* of a speculative social science;
for it is through the reproduction of (modern) separation and difference
that the 'idea' ethical life (its mediations, contradictions, etc.) is 'thought'.

In his essay 'What is Enlightenment?',[6] Kant attempts to expound the
historical and political consequences of endowing the individual subject
with a capacity for absolute rational self-determination. His aim is to
show that by daring to use their 'sovereign' intelligence, individuals can
sustain a critical (and non-violent) relationship to the institutions that
govern them, and that, consequently, the authority of these institutions
should always remain open to – although not dominated by – reason's
'practical' independence. Kant's notion of 'Enlightenment', therefore,
opens the theoretical discourse of modernity through the postulation of
four basic tenets: (1) the situation of the autonomous individual subject
at the centre of moral, political and social thought; (2) a belief in the
infinite capacity of reason to refine and improve social and political
institutions; (3) a commitment to displace 'irrational' superstitions,
traditions and religious doctrines; and (4) a belief in the rational order
and intelligibility of natural and social phenomena.[7] What is important
to remember here is that the critical relationship which autonomous
subjects ought to maintain to civil community is founded on the fundamental determining principle of Kant's philosophy: the primacy of
practical (moral) over theoretical (cognitive/instrumental) reason. The
freedom with which the Kantian subject responds to the domination of
civil institutions, in other words, is originally (a piori) rational: it is the
recognition of 'ends' universally consonant with individual self-
determination.

In common with all Kant's post-critical writings on history and
politics, the essay on Enlightenment presupposes his three 'critical'
works: the *Critique of Pure Reason* (1982a); the *Critique of Practical Reason*
(1956) and the *Critique of Judgement* (1982b). The individual's 'rational'
relationship to the institutions of ethical life, and the open/indefinite
idea of historical progress sustained by this relationship, must be
understood within the structure of 'transcendental' faculties which unify
and differentiate human experience (i.e., theoretical, practical and reflective judgement). I will argue that social scientific forms of explanation
are characterized by their re-presentation of the categories through
which Kant determines the concepts of progress and modernity. Each
'paradigm',[8] in other words, attempts to explain the development,
cohesion and negativity of (modern) ethical life by postulating the
priority of one particular element within the totality. Thus, the idea of a
social science emerges with the differentiation of explanatory forms
which: (1) have rejected the ideas of unity, identity and progress inherent
in Kant's notion of 'history'; and (2) reproduce the 'legislations' of

transcendental reason (understanding over intuition, reason over desire, judgement as the faculty of unity) as independent powers within ethical life. I must, then, give a preliminary account of the concepts, relations and ideals determined within the critical philosophy, and of their relationship to social scientific forms of explanation.

Kant's critical philosophy is an attempt to set out the a priori conditions which govern human experience. For Kant, the concept of 'experience' is not restricted to our representation of the external world, but includes, as accomplished 'facts of reason, moral autonomy and aesthetic sensibility'.[9] The three *Critiques* therefore constitute a comprehensive account of cognitive knowledge and its relationship to moral, aesthetic and natural 'finality' (purposiveness). Kant's first *Critique*, the *Critique of Pure Reason*, attempts to show that knowledge as such (i.e., cognition of the external world) is possible only through: (1) the 'representation' of chaotic sense data through the 'modes of intuition' (space and time); and (2) the understanding's organization of these representations into a realm of causally related 'objects'. This spontaneous organization of sense impressions springs from what Kant considers to be the a priori conditions of external experience: the formal categories of causality, reciprocity, substantiality, etc., through which the realm of 'phenomena' is constituted. It is only by limiting these categories to their proper 'sensible' objects that we are able to avoid the illusions of pure reason (God as the 'first cause' of the universe, time as a form independent of, and prior to, spatial events, etc.), and remain within the realm of legitimate 'knowledge'.

The *Critique of Pure Reason*, therefore, inverts the 'empirical' relationship of cognition and objectivity in which the subject passively receives knowledge through sensory affection.[10] For Kant, knowledge is constituted through the understanding's organization of spatio-temporal intuitions into a realm of objects governed by efficient causality. We cannot know the nature of 'things-as-they-are-in-themselves', for knowledge as such is regulated by the categories of the understanding (*Verstehen*). Thus, we cannot 'know' God, or the ultimate nature of reality (the being of the 'noumenon'), but we can have a science of physical objects causally interacting in space and time.

What is important here – and this will become clearer when I come to look at structural explanations in more detail – is the notion of 'exteriority' which is articulated in the first *Critique*. For Kant, it is the a priori concepts of the understanding which organize sense impressions into a unified realm of appearances. This spontaneous work of the mind cannot be known in the way that phenomena are known; rather, its necessity is inferred from the accomplished fact of our experience of objects in space and time. Kant's account of external experience therefore posits a constitutive priority of the understanding (mind, discursive spontaneity) over the 'content' which is given through the modes of intuition. It is this external relationship of a non-universal content (the particular, the discrete) to the universal (legislative, necessary) conditions of its realization which is reproduced in structural explanations of 'society'. Durkheim, for example, claims that it is only through the existence of social institutions as 'external facts' that the individual is capable of anything more than violent and destructive egoism. Wrong and evil are understood as the residue of a pre-social individualism which periodically threatens the 'unity' of the collective.[11] Marx, on the other hand, attempts to expound the (universal, structural) truth of capitalism as the progressive alienation of humanity's 'natural' productive essence.[12] Both forms of explanation, I will argue, fail to recognize the violence inherent in reducing the individual to a form exclusively determined by the external/independent necessity of 'structural' causes.

Kant's second *Critique*, the *Critique of Practical Reason*, is concerned with the human subject's capacity to act freely in the world. As we have seen, the first *Critique* sets out the a priori conditions upon which a science of physical objects is founded. Kant's claim is that if it is possible to give a comprehensive account of the type of understanding which generates experience of phenomena, then the transcendental conditions of a science of efficient causes will have been established. Phenomenal events, in other words, are always determined by spatially discrete and temporally precedent conditions. Thus, the fundamental question which Kant attempts to answer in the second *Critique* is how it is possible for human subjects to act autonomously when the phenomenal world, of which they are a part, is exclusively determined by external causes? Or put another way: how is reason able to determine itself independently of the appetites, pleasures and satisfactions which are rooted in the body of the rational subject?

Kant's attempt to resolve the apparent contradiction between a deterministic–scientistic account of the phenomenal world and the possibility of 'free' human action involves three related elements. The first of these is the formal negativity of reason. Human subjects do not simply respond to the appetites and aversions (inclinations) which constitute their bodily/phenomenal existence. According to Kant, rational self-awareness always and necessarily intervenes between the experience/ feeling of desire and its actual fulfilment. This negativity in relation to the world of phenomenal causes is the 'fact' upon which Kant founds the 'practical' power of reason.[13] The second element which can be identified in the critical ethics is Kant's attempt to generate a positive moral necessity from this 'negativity' of rational self-awareness. For Kant, the capacity of the human will to recognize its inclinations as non-rational (and therefore non-human) places it under an obligation to act in accordance with the demands of practical reason. These demands take the form of 'categorical imperatives', which command obedience under all possible circumstances and conditions. Kant offers the example of keeping a deposit secretly entrusted to me by someone who has since died. Expediency demands that I increase my personal fortune by keeping the deposit. Practical reason, however, demands that I return the deposit to its rightful beneficiaries, for if the practice of fraud were adopted universally, the institution of property would cease to exist. Kant's position is that one should always act as if the principle ('maxim') of one's action were a law for a community of autonomous individuals. Where this is demonstrated to be impossible by the principle of 'universalizability',[14] one's action has no moral content, and is determined purely by self-interest. The final element of Kant's critical ethics is the idea that by adhering to the moral law, each individual determines him/herself as a member of a republic of free individuals, each of whom is respected as an end in him/herself. As the realm of absolute 'ends', this republic is governed not by the particular desires and satisfactions of civil community, but by the 'free' causality of the rational will.

If we return to the concept of 'public reason' deployed in 'What is Enlightenment?', it becomes clear Kant's notion of rational, non-violent criticism presupposes the exteriority of the individual subject and civil community posited in the second *Critique*. Public reason, as a critical instrument, should always be ranged against what Kant conceives as the 'heteronomy' of civil institutions, that is, against their necessary contradiction of the 'ends' truly consonant with human freedom – universal recognition of 'legitimate' ownership, of the procreative end of sexual difference, of human life as an absolute end in itself.[15] This radical opposition of 'free' causality (autonomy) to the institutions of civil life (heteronomy) is important for two reasons. First, it appears to provide a rational account of socio-historical progress which does not fall into the Hegelian trap of making societies bearers of a transhistorical necessity (i.e., the necessity of spirit's self-recognition). Secondly, Kant's idea of moral autonomy provides the foundation for a type of social critique in which the 'subject' is distinguished by its original capacity both to constitute and criticize the social relations in which it participates. Weber, for example, understands the concept of voluntarism (agency) as a spontaneous capacity of the subject to give 'meaning' to the social relations in which it is historically situated. Accordingly, his account of the emergence of a capitalist economy from feudalist productive relations stresses the role of Protestantism – or more precisely Calvinism – in forming the normative attitude of bourgeois asceticism.[16] Habermas, on the other hand, attempts to reconstruct Kant's idea of universal ends through a communicative concept of reason. Language is conceived as a pragmatic form which springs from the original necessity of articulating the shared/intersubjective nature of experience. Thus the history of 'the social' is presented as the history of a public sphere – the life world – whose essential necessity is the clarification of the motives, intentions and purposes of 'modernity'.[17]

I will examine these social scientific accounts of voluntarism and autonomy more fully in Chapter 3. However, the Kantian origin of this type of social critique has already raised fundamental questions about the relationship of the individual subject to civil community. First, there is the problem of conceiving the human subject as a form originally transcendent of the objective determinations of modernity (law, productive relations, the state and its authority). If, to take Habermas's argument, the original end of language is dialogical consensus, does this not presuppose a transcendental relationship of language to the objective forms (work, satisfaction and desire) whose 'necessity' it seeks to clarify? Secondly, there is the problem of 'negativity', or the subject's lack of positive satisfaction in the institutions which constitute its social existence. Habermas's idea of communicative reason seems to posit 'consensus' as an abstract form beyond the subject's concrete historical formation, while Weber's account of modernity describes the failure of normative spontaneity to survive the demands of bureaucratic rationality. The power of Hegel's notion of ethical life (*Sittlichkeit*), I will argue, is its account of the relationship between self-conscious subjects and the 'objective' categories through which their self-recognition is mediated. The law, political authority and productive relations, in other words, are all 're-presented' through the forms of subjectivity which they open (i.e., creative servitude, negative freedom, morality, conscience, etc.), but which they cannot completely subordinate or control. Thus, the 'substance' of ethical life – its contradictions, mediations and negations – is inscribed in this reciprocal relationship between subjectivity and its objective forms.[18]

Kant's *Critique of Judgement* is the completion of his philosophy of subjective faculties. The realms of theoretical and practical reason which he delineates in the first and second *Critiques* posit distinct a priori relations between reason (*Vernunft*) and understanding (*Verstand*): the proper object of reason is the faculty of subjective desire, while the understanding is legitimately used only in the cognition of phenomena. It is this independence of practical and theoretical faculties which constitutes the necessity of a critique of 'reflective' judgement,[19] for neither reason nor understanding can produce 'unity' within the experience of the subject. The determinate judgements which proceed from the understanding and the moral will cannot sufficiently reduce the contingency which follows from their 'legitimate' establishment. Both practical reason and cognitive understanding retain an 'exteriority' (the body of the self and the other as sources of desire, the heterogeneity of local laws, the obscurity of the universal in its empirical forms) to which their particular legislative powers are opposed.

The cognitive understanding is expounded in the first *Critique* as the condition of phenomenal experience as such, while the second Critique expounds the conditions under which the idea of freedom can become regulative of the faculty of desire. Neither of these faculties unify the activity of reason with its object. The understanding cannot determine the occurrence of 'each particular thing in nature': its laws are formally universal, and always require cognitive articulation in the contingency of

phenomenal events. Practical reason, on the other hand, can only determine the concept of autonomy in relation to particular empirical desires;
it cannot realize its necessity in the realm of phenomena. Thus, for Kant,
reflective judgement is the faculty through which the critical subject
posits the unity of freedom and nature as an unconditional necessity.[20]

Kant's critique of this unifying activity is an attempt to establish a
principle by which experience can, in the absence of determinate concepts, represent the universal conformity of nature to the faculties of
cognition. The a priori necessity at stake in Kant's third *Critique*,
therefore, is the capacity of the subject to proceed from the immediate
singularities of cognitive experience to the reception of a non-cognitive
universal in which contingent forms appear as necessary. It is through
this 'reflective' judgement of appearances as expressing the purpose of
an infinitely self-determining intelligence (God) that theoretical reason is
ultimately validated as a unifying form. For it is only if the contingency
of the 'empirical' laws which are licensed by the understanding is
governed by a unifying principle that it is possible to maintain the
transcendental necessity of the categories – substance, reciprocity, causality, etc. Kantian aesthetics and teleology, then, are founded upon non-
cognitive (subjective) disclosures of nature as a rational totality. And so,
by presenting appearances under the 'final' principles of freedom and
purposiveness, reflective judgements disclose a ground of possible
empirical laws which is neither a concept of nature nor of freedom, 'but
a unique (subjective) principle of unity'.[21] For Kant, in other words,
judgements of beauty, sublimity and (natural and ethical) finality all
refer to the 'unity' of practical and theoretical legislation – that is, to the
unrepresentable 'idea' of nature as a whole.

That the power of judgement constitutes an independent faculty,
therefore, is vouchsafed by the necessity of purposiveness to a unified
cognitive experience. For without judgement's 'reflective' attribution of
an aesthetic or teleological finality to particular representations, the
realm of appearances determined by understanding and intuition alone
would present 'an endless multiplicity of empirical laws, which are yet
contingent so far as our insight goes, i.e., cannot be cognised a priori'.[22]
Kant's idea of reflective judgement, however, is related to the objects of
cognitive experience only as a moment of individual attribution. The
idea of 'finality' through which empirical appearances are unified (i.e.,
the idea of nature as a rational whole) cannot be represented through
universal concepts, for aesthetic and teleological judgements of such a
unity are always subjective, particular and cognitively unrepresentable.
For Kant, then, the a priori association of the idea of finality with the
faculty of judgement is a *subjective* necessity determined by cognition's
inability to realize its own principle (i.e., the universal conformity of
phenomenal experience to law). And so it is precisely the unrepresentability of the 'object' of judgement (the idea of totality) which constitutes
its transcendental necessity for cognitive experience.

The substance of Kant's *Critique of Judgement* is concerned to establish
the independence of two distinct moments in which this unrepresentable
unity is manifest. In the first of these moments, the aesthetic (which Kant
divides into the 'Analytic of the Beautiful' and the 'Analytic of the
Sublime', according to the 'artistic' or 'natural' production of 'disinterested' pleasure), it is the independence of the formal representation of
the object from the desire 'to use it for the purpose of cognition' which
constitutes the subject's discrimination of finality.[23] The feeling of
pleasure which is coupled with such a representation does not derive
from the possibility of subsuming the immediate apprehension
(intuition) of the object under a particular concept. Taken in general
therefore, Kant's idea of aesthetic experience attempts to establish the
reality of a pure, disinterested form of affection. His account of the
relationship between aesthetic judgements and the faculty of 'pleasure
and displeasure' maintains that if the object represented in imagination
expresses a unity of understanding and intuition, then this representation
must be regarded as ultimate, or 'final'. When the form of an object
occasions pleasure merely through 'reflection' upon it, that is, independently of cognitive or moral concepts, the pleasure resulting from this
representation is for Kant both subjective and universal. The possibility
of aesthetic affection is grounded in the faculties of human cognition,
although its occasion is always a matter of particular reflective
judgements.

Teleological judgement, or the 'logical representation of finality in
nature', on the other hand, is not concerned with the immediate apprehension of finality in the form of the object.[24] The empirical ground of
this moment of reflection belongs to the theoretical part of philosophy,
for the determination of an object as embodying a 'natural end' requires
the subsumption of particular instances under a general concept. Teleological finality is not conceived through a principle independent, a priori,
of the aesthetic. For although its judgement does not immediately discern
the unity to which 'pleasure–displeasure' is responsive, the concept of a
natural end organizing the contingency of appearances depends upon
the reception of empirical multiplicity as unified in its form. It is the
same subjective a priori principle which produces the judgement of taste
that prepares the understanding 'to apply to nature the concept of an
end (at least in respect of its form)'.[25] Teleolgical judgement, in other
words, reduces the contingency of particular appearances through
reflection on their formal finality, and it is this subjective apprehension of
unity which contributes to the understanding's cognitive determination
of objects.

For Kant, then, reflective judgement is the faculty through which the
legislations of reason and understanding are conjoined, without either
losing their independence or integrity. Theoretical cognition of nature
determines a boundary between the 'sensible' world of conditioned
appearances (phenomena), and the 'supersensible' world of 'things-as-

they-are-in-themselves' (noumena). It is this boundary which is pre-supposed by Kant's critical ethics: moral actions are expounded in the second *Critique* as practical reason exercised against the external (hetero-nomous) causality of the phenomenal world. The faculty of judgement, by its attribution of aesthetic or teleological finality to cognition, pro-duces a 'subjective' mediation between the realms of practical and theoretical reason. For by discerning a formal unity of cognition with its objects, reflective judgements provide the 'supersensible substrate' entailed in Kant's doctrine of experience (i.e., the realm of uncontingent, universal laws) with a 'determinability' that presents freedom as the finality manifest in nature.[26] The demand that 'causality by freedom' (or the 'nominal' spontaneity of the will) ought to be able to take effect in the world, therefore, is met, albeit subjectively, by teleological and aesthetic judgements of finality, for the reflective attribution of pur-posiveness to nature constitutes its apparently contingent particular laws, into a self-determining totality. Ultimately, it is the subjective, unrepresentable idea of God (as substance, integrity, intellect) which guarantees the unity of reason and understanding, while leaving them 'objectively' unreconciled.

The bridge that Kant constructs between cognitive understanding and practical reason in the third *Critique* is merely subjective: it is 'felt' rather than 'known' by those beings who possess the faculties of critical reason. The realms of 'freedom' and 'heteronomous causality', in other words, remain objectively opposed, and the exercise of moral will, an act of self-denial beyond mediation with the institutions (and satisfactions) of civil community. The *Critique of Judgement* sanctions pleasure/satisfaction only in so far as its 'object' is pure, 'unrepresentable' finality; and such satisfaction – in the beauty of art, or the sublimity and purposiveness of nature – is, for Kant, always beyond the inclinations and desires constituted in actual social relations. This radical separation of will and practical reason from the 'objective' forms of ethical life (law, work, satisfaction and desire) is crucial to my account of the relationship between reason and the idea of a social science. For Kant's notion of reflective (non-cognitive) judgement can be read *either* as signifying the end of reason's 'substantive' formation of human subjectivity, *or* as an abstract recognition of ethical life (*Sittlichkeit*) as the bearer of formal/legal acknowledgement among sovereign individuals. I will argue that Kant's 'reflective' abstraction of the law (or legal recognition) from the concrete historical forms in which it is inscribed[27] points to the necessity of acknowledging the 'formative' powers of productive relations, instrumental reason, functional interdependence, systemic organization, etc.

My fundamental speculative claim is that the idea of a social science depends upon the recognition of human subjectivity as an historical form. Its self-recognition must be understood as mediated by, and constitutive of, the social forms and relations which it inhabits. This claim is founded on the critique of Kant – and 'abstract' thinking in general – which Hegel develops in his three major works: *Phenomenology of Mind*, *The Science of Logic* (1969) and *Philosophy of Right*. As I have said, however, the relationship of Kant's reflective judgements to the 'legitimate' difference of practical and theoretical cognition has also been read as the end of reason's capacity to (pre)determine 'difference' in general. Specifically, the reading of the 'Analytic of the sublime', which Jean-François Lyotard presents in *The Differend* (1988a) (and develops in his *Lessons on the Analytic of the Sublime* (1994)), claims that the sensitivity to the sublime which Kant presents in the third *Critique*, discloses a moment of 'affection' which cannot guarantee 'freedom' and 'cognition' as the 'realms' of two transcendentally autonomous faculties (reason and understanding). For Lyotard, the feeling of 'agitation',[28] which Kant attributes to the sublime 'unrepresentability' of nature as idea (i.e., as a self-determining totality), must be recognized as the ethical demand which arises from every hierarchical formation of difference (or rather from the spontaneous emergence of 'differends'). The notions of community, collective identity and substantive self-recognition, whose necessity my speculative reading of Kant will attempt to disclose, are, for Lyotard, dispersed throughout a 'social bond' which comprises no more than an aggregation of different 'genres of discourse', all of which have their own untranslatable rules of phrasing, formation and conduct. As we will see in Chapter 5, Kant's conception of reflective judgement, for Lyotard, gestures towards an ethics and politics in which each is responsible to 'phrase' the unforeseeable/unforeseen difference ('differends') which plays around the frontiers of 'heterogeneous' discourses.

This rejection of Kant's claim that reflective judgement is a 'faculty' related a priori to (and regulated by) practical and theoretical cognition determines the anti-Hegelianism of *The Differend*. For Lyotard, 'post-modernity' is chacterized by the absence of mediation between the discourses which have displaced the authority of communitarian/civic institutions.[29] It is this 'absence' which Lyotard attempts to trace throughout Kant's critical philosophy: that is, in the exchanges between sense data and understanding in the first *Critique*, between practical reason and desire in the second *Critique*, and the 'affective' responses of the subject to the finality of nature in the third *Critique*. For Lyotard, then, Kant's account of aesthetics and teleology discloses the dispersal of ethical obligation; for in the absence of conceptual/cognitive discourse (understanding and practical reason), 'the subject' must judge a particular instance (of beauty, sublimity or purpose) which is presented to it only as affection ('agitation' of the faculties of reason and under-standing). The *Critique of Judgement*, in other terms, is presented as narrating the end of a transcendental 'I' which is cognitively assured of the 'truth' of its experience and moral agency. After Kant, according to Lyotard, we are left only with the necessity of judging wrong and injustice in the absence of 'metaphysical' conceptions of community and identity.[30] Thus, Hegel's presentation of critical philosophy as essential to the 'idea' of modern ethical life (*Sittlichkeit*) is understood by Lyotard as suppressing the marginal, interstitial moments in Kant, which gesture towards non-conceptual/non-totalizing judgements of difference.

If speculative thought is to provide the foundation for the 'idea' of a social science, therefore, I must be able to give an account of ethical 'substance' (i.e., sociality, community, civil association) which: (1) acknowledges the Kantian oppositions of concept and intuition, morality and desire, autonomy and heteronomy, as both essential and inadequate to notion of 'modernity' (differentiation, recognition, mediation); (2) retains an 'openness' to the contradictions determined within it – and to the impossibility of suppressing its 're-fomation'; and (3) does not reduce difference to the predetermined moments of a transhistorical necessity. Thus, it is the social, ethical and political consequences of Hegel's critique of Kant that I must attempt to specify.

Hegel's concept of ethical life

The main purpose of this section is to set out the fundamental principles of Hegel's notion of ethical life (*Sittlichkeit*) and to establish how this notion informs the critique of 'modern' and 'postmodern' social theory developed in the following chapters. So far I have tried to show that the notions of theoretical and moral necessity that are set out in Kant's first and second *Critiques* provide the foundations for structural and voluntarist sociologies; and that the idea of reflective judgement articulated in the third *Critique* has influenced the poststructuralist rejection of transcendental legitimation/necessity. I have also suggested that the 'use' to which Kant's philosophy is put by modern and postmodern social theory is problematic, that is, that generically, this 'usage' fails to recognize the ideas of reconciliation and re-formation (of ethical life) immanent in critical ethics, epistemology and aesthetics. A speculative approach to the concept of a social science, therefore, must start by making explicit the contradictions and aporias which inform Kant's account of autonomy, modernity and 'Enlightenment'.

Hegel's *Phenomenology of Mind* is, above all, a critique of 'abstract' thinking. It is an attempt to show that the historical forms and structures through which self-conscious subjects recognize themselves are never timeless or absolute, and that the distinctions between 'self' and 'other' that are sustained in these forms always reproduce contradiction and misrecognition within ethical life. Kant's concept of 'Enlightenment', for example, attempts to set out the limits within which rational criticism and non-violent re-formation of the civil community ought to take place. His understanding of the relationship between morally autonomous individuals and the demands constituted in their social relations postulates a separateness of subject and object (of necessity and its re-presentation) which perpetuates an abstract, unmediated conception of the law. The ethical questions by which I have sought to characterize the project of a social science (the nature of inequality and injustice, the social construction of difference, and the inclusiveness and exclusiveness of social relations and institutions) therefore are conceived as necessarily related to the a priori conditions that govern human experience – the estrangement of cognition from 'things-as-they-are-in-themselves', the primacy of abstract moral spontaneity, and the 'aesthetic' indeterminacy of mediation between the realms of 'autonomy' and 'heteronomy'. Within the terms of Kant's idea of Enlightenment, then, difference, inequality and injustice can be acknowledged only in so far as they infringe the formal 'legal' recognition of morally autonomous individuality. The concrete forms of work satisfaction and desire, which constitute the civil community, must always be recognized as 'heteronomous' with the universal ends of the moral law – even if the 'reflective' judgement of these forms seeks to include them within the rational progress of humanity.[31] Within the Kantian system, in other words, 'the law' is always an abstract demand: its recognition of the 'self' in its relations to the 'other' cannot acknowledge the formation of subjectivity within its historical context.

In general, the critique of Kant developed in Hegel's *Phenomenology of Mind*, discloses the contradictions which result from the (a priori) separation of the subject from the conditions of its formation. Hegel's expositions of 'Pleasure and necessity', the 'Law of the heart' and 'Virtue and the course of the world' (reason); and the 'Beautiful soul' and 'Evil and forgiveness' (spirit),[32] in other words, develop the *historical* consequences of positing the autonomy of the individual as separate from the 'substance' (totality) of ethical life. The logic of this development is that the forms of subjectivity and objectivity which appear within *Sittlichkeit* are sustained through a reciprocal relationship: the subject's 'moral' representation of the conditions in which its activity takes place is inevitably 're-formative' of those conditions. We have seen that, for Kant, practical and theoretical reason are forms which, if employed properly, provide the subject with 'transcendental' guarantees for its knowledge and moral activity. For Hegel, on the other hand, the relationship between 'objectivity' (contemporary productive, political and religious relations) and its 're-presentation' cannot be confined within the limits that transcendental reason attempts to establish. In attempting to determine itself independently of all temporal satisfactions, the moral subject fails to recognize that its 'maxims' of universal recognition precipitate the emergence of atomism and acquisitiveness from the substrate of feudal bondage. Kantian morality, then, is presented by Hegel as participating in the origin and development of a distinctively modern form of social organization: the antagonism and self-interest of bourgeois property relations. As early as the essay on Natural Law, Hegel remarks of the 'ethical' relationship sustained by moral self-determination: 'This is the reflex which morality in the usual meaning would more or less fit – the formal positing, in mutual indifference, of the specific terms of the relation, i.e., the ethical life of the *bourgeois* or private individual for whom the difference of relations is fixed and who depends on them and is in them.'[33]

I am now beginning to move towards a more positive apprehension of why Hegel's critique of Kant is fundamental to my idea of a social science. First of all, if Hegel has succeeded in showing that the relationship between subjective representation and objective necessity cannot be contained within the (practical and cognitive) limits of Kant's critical philosophy, then 'reason' must be understood as an historical, rather than a transcendental, concept. For Hegel, the positive forms, in which self-consciousness has embodied its universality (concept), determine the substance of each particular epoch, and so it is through this finite/historical self-recognition that the contradictions inherent in the 'present' form of ethical life can become re-formative. The *Phenomenology of Mind*, therefore, is an exposition of the concrete forms through which self-consciousness has (mis)-recognized itself, and of the oppositions which always and necessarily afflict the substance of ethical life. Secondly, Hegel's account of the violence inherent in moral self-determination (i.e., its participation in the emergence of the acquisitive individual personality from the substance of feudal relations) discloses the necessity of acknowledging the power of the subjective forms through which social relations are re-presented. The idea of 'modernity', therefore, always requires acknowledgement of the separation, difference and mediation which has been released (and re-presented) within the substance of *Sittlichkeit*. Thus, Hegel's *Phenomenology* of 'moral' consciousness discloses: (1) the subjective conditions (rational self-certainty, cognitive re-presentation of the universal) through which modern differentiated relations emerge; and (2) the processes of abstraction through which these relations are (theoretically) reconstructed.

The background to the *Phenomenology*'s account of moral subjectivity, and its participation in the emergence of modern 'differentiated' relations, is Hegel's concept of Lordship and Bondage.[34] For Hegel, the constitution of 'Self-consciousness' is determined by the unreflective desires (sex and hunger, the categories of 'life') which pre-exist the formation of *Sittlichkeit*. In the 'state of nature', in other words, each atomistic consciousness confronts the other as a moment of pure desire, a desire which, given the scarcity of natural provision, threatens its very existence as a living thing. This condition of universal conflict and vulnerability – 'the war of all against all' – however, is not, as Hobbes claimed, resolvable through the reflective choice of 'natural' humanity to live under the rule of law (i.e., the social contract). Rather, the possibility of the social, or what Hegel calls ethical life, is opened by desire as an absolutely unreflective and non-rational form. The fact that the desires of 'life' embedded in each individual consciousness are momentary and unmediated means that death is essential to the (original) formation of ethical substance. The significance of struggle for existence, in other words, is not confined to the mere preservation of life in the sate of nature. Each individual is confronted by the other as a 'threat' only in so. far as there is a universal determination of (conscious) 'desire' as that which demands satisfaction at the expense of the other. Thus, the struggle for 'life' is implicitly a struggle for 'recognition': for the satisfaction of 'my' desire demands that it is recognized as 'mine', and, as such, is of universal importance. Hegel makes it clear that such a recognition is tremendously hard won – for it is only through the violence determined by 'my' desire to be recognized as 'human' (i.e., self-conscious, self-determining, purposive) that ethical substance can emerge.

For Hegel, the risking of death for the sake of recognition is an historical and metaphorical concept. His account of the dialectic of Lordship and Bondage in *Phenomenology* makes it clear that this relationship is produced through a violent (pre)history of conflicts in which one or both of the protagonists has died. It is only when the struggle for recognition is resolved through the capitulation of one of the combatants that Lordship and Bondage is instituted as a concrete historical relation. The Bondsman, who chose life over recognition, must now serve the Lord, who was prepared to sacrifice everything for the sake of his unrecognized humanity. The life of the Bondsman, in other words, belongs to the Lord, and he must serve him – and thereby avoid death – by preparing commodities which are reserved exclusively for his consumption. It is this relationship of pure domination, therefore, that underlies the premodern (feudal) constitution of ethical life. The Lord and Bondsman exist within an economy of desire and satisfaction which can admit no universal rights, laws or institutions; and so the development of self-consciousness through the transformative activity of the Bondsman ultimately assumes the perverse and degraded form of the 'Unhappy Consciousness'. The significance of Kant's moral subjectivity, then, must be understood in terms of its role in the dissolution of the originatory domination inscribed in feudal (premodern) social relations.

Under the conditions of feudal bondage, it is the absence of universal property rights which, for Hegel, determines self-consciousness's 'dissemblance' of its confinement within the limits of immediate consumption and desire.[35] Initially, self-consciousness determines 'pleasure' as its universal goal, and conceives the world simply as the object of its enjoyment. Such enjoyment, however, is always contingent. Each individual recognizes only its own pleasure (desire and consumption), and experiences the other as an alien 'necessity', or law, which thwarts its satisfaction. In the end, pleasure, taken as the exclusive principle of individuality, reproduces the 'life' of the individual as 'death', that is, as the constant and inevitable frustration of its enjoyment. This type of consciousness lacks any formal recognition of the other as participating in the substance of social/ethical existence. And so instead of trying to re-form the social relations in which it is situated, it attempts simply to assert its own contingent desires as a legitimate right against the alien necessity of the other. This 'law of the heart',[36] however, is universal in neither its form nor its content: each asserts its own absolute right, and, as such, contradicts the possibility of universal recognition. Self-consciousness, in attempting to legitimize the content of its own particular desires, creates a violent antagonism of each individual subject against the other. Finally, having recognized that the 'law of the heart' cannot be a law of common interest, each individual comes to experience himself and his activity as 'criminal and vicious'. Again, however, the reformative activity produced by the experience of acute antagonism is directed not at ethical life, but at consciousness itself as a criminally desirous form. Each individual establishes a relationship of denial between itself as a 'virtuous' subject,[37] and the work satisfaction and desire which it associates with corruption and criminality. Yet these 'virtuous' personalities must act in the world, and such action necessitates the exercise of the very enemy they wish to vanquish: their own 'corrupt' desire, pleasure and satisfaction.

For Hegel, it is these disturbed and antagonistic forms of self-consciousness which disclose the deep contradiction inherent in feudalism. The experience of pure pleasure, or the 'law of the heart', or the abstinence of 'virtue' is lived by consciousness as the exclusive principle of its existence; it is that which constitutes the 'substance' of the work, satisfaction and desire of the feudal order. These forms are all determined by consciousness's inability to overcome its preoccupation with the immediacy of consumption and desire, and to recognize the other as something more than a threat to its own particular satisfaction. Considered as a form of ethical life, therefore, feudalism is a coercive authority in which the Prince retains an absolute right of consumption, so long as he is strong enough to protect and appropriate wealth from his Bondsmen. The 'State', in other words, is experienced only as an accumulation of wealth and an object of desire; not as the 'objective' form of universal recognition and responsibility (the 'idea' of ethical life).

Kant's conception of 'Enlightenment', we have seen, is closely linked to the liberties enshrined in bourgeois property rights. The freedom of the individual to possess and dispose of property is, for Kant, an essential part of its moral self-determination, and of its universal recognition as an end in itself. Although it is acknowledged throughout his political writings that civil community can never 'embody' the realm of ends disclosed by practical reason, there does emerge a notion of 'progress' as the reduction of coercive/external influence (heteronomy) on the moral will. This 'reduction' takes the form of refining the institutions of civil life, such that it is positive law and 'public reason' which ordains the conduct of free individuals. The 'technical' co-operation which is brought about through the ownership of property is, for Kant, placed increasingly under the demand of ethical/legal recognition. Thus, it is rational autonomy that is the end for which civil community is constituted; or, as Kant puts it in the *Critique of Judgement*, 'Looked at from the point of view of his inner self, [man] is a contemptible object; and if creation is not to be altogether devoid of a final end, such a man . . . as a bad man dwelling in a world of moral laws, forfeits . . . his own subjective end, that is happiness, as the sole condition under which his real existence can consist with the final end.'[38]

The fundamental point of my exposition of Kant's philosophy was to establish how the legislative domains of the three *Critiques* inform the relationship of subjectivity and ethical life (civil community, sociality) embedded in his notion of 'Enlightenment'. I have argued that Kant's abstraction of the (morally) autonomous individual from its substantive forms of work, satisfaction and desire is the speculative condition of social scientific forms of explanation. The 'reflective' separation of subjectivity and objectivity, concept and intuition, law and substance, in other words, opens up the complexity of structural, systemic, functional and voluntarist explanations which characterize theoretical cognition of modernity. In order to re-cognize (speculatively) the Kantian (critical, reflective) necessities inscribed in this dispersal of perspectives, therefore, I must understand how Kant's moral self-consciousness participates in the constitution of 'modern' ethical life. I must then turn to Hegel's account of the role of (Kantian) morality in the emergence and determination of 'Spirit'.[39]

As we have seen, consciousness's development through the 'feudalistic' forms of particularity concluded with the antagonism of 'virtuous' personalities, none of which recognize the violence (exclusiveness) of their secular desire and activity. The state, under these conditions, is no more than a 'lawless', coercive authority, held together by the wealth and strength of the feudal Prince and his retainers. It is exactly these conditions which, for Hegel, precipitated the terror of the French Revolution. The revolutionary consciousness, in the absence of any formal legal recognition of the right to own and dispose of property, becomes opposed to every particular form and category of ethical life. As such, its 'reformative' intention – an intention which is 'spiritual' in the sense that it seeks to establish the state as a universal recognition of subjectivity – is constantly perverted by its own activity; for every realization (objectification) of truth and justice is destroyed by the constant movement of revolutionary transformation. This form of self-consciousness, therefore, is aware of itself as the 'object', or universal 'matter', of a freedom which is opposed to every finite determination of ethical life. The absence of formal property rights means that nothing outside consciousness's affirmation of itself as the infinite being of free will can remain in place as a substantive ethical form. The lawlessness of the feudal order, in other words, is made absolute by the 'stubborn atomic singleness of the infinitely free self'.[40]

For Hegel, French Enlightenment thought is characterized by a violent reductivism, in which every moral, ethical and spiritual form is reduced to its basic 'material' foundations. Each 'revolutionary' subject recognizes itself as the exclusive, elemental principle of social trasformation; and so the ethical life of a state governed solely by the 'law' of feudal appropriation is destroyed by the 'infinitely free self' as a lawless irrationality. Thus, the 'abstract materialism' of the Enlightenment passes over into a violent idealism, which treats any 'mediation' of individuality present in social relations as subject to the 'law' of its own unbounded freedom. The truth of the French Revolution, therefore, is an absolutely negative self-consciousness, which acknowledges nothing beyond the law of its own activity. The 'matter' which it constantly invokes as the substance of rational human association is completely indeterminate, and reproduces the individual as a form which is terrorized by its own activity. Speculatively conceived, then, the Jacobin uprising determined a complete dislocation of self-consciousness from the substance of ethical life, and the appearance of 'free will' as the agent of meaningless annihilation. The (feudal) lawlessness which self-consciousness sets out to reform was merely reinforced; and the constitution of *Sittlichkeit* more and more deeply disrupted by the lack of objective recognition.

Kant's moral subject appears within the structure of the *Phenomenology*, as the re-formation of consciousness's violent assertion of its independence and universality. The terror of the French Revolution, for Hegel, produces an acknowledgement on the part of 'free' self-consciousness that it is independent of the substance of ethical life, and that this independence cannot sustain itself simply as the 'vocation' to revolutionize every aspect of *Sittlichkeit*. Kantian morality, then, is the recognition of this abstract independence, not as a revolutionary 'vocation', but as the universal ground of practical self-determination. The moral law attempts not to re-form the 'lawlessness' of civil life, but to restrain the disorder of particular inclinations and desires. This restraint, we have seen, takes the form of the categorical imperative: the absolutely unconditional demand that self-conscious subjects pursue only those ends universally consistent with moral autonomy. For Kant, it is the suppression of inclination and desire which binds individuals to the community of absolute ends, and which is the ground of his concept of historical progress (or 'ethico-teleology').

The transformation from the lawlessness of feudal desire, through the terror of absolute freedom, to the inner-governance of the categorical imperative is crucial to the emergence of civil society as the realm in which 'concrete persons' develop their (abstract) particularity.[41] With the constitution of formal property law, each individual is given the right to pursue his/her productive activity in any direction he/she sees fit. We have seen that, for Kant, this legal recognition is essential to the exercise of a moral will whose concept is the negation of all external influence. 'Bourgeois' institutions are conceived by Kant as springing from the (historical/critical) exercise of free will as such, that is, as forms originally sensitive to their own heteronomy, and to the necessity of the moral law.[42] The critique of morality with which Hegel concludes the *Phenomenology*'s section on 'Spirit', however, attempts to show that Kant's concept of autonomy is implicated in the constitution of a distinctively 'modern' form of antagonism within ethical life. Specifically, Hegel claims that the formal universality of the categorical imperative cannot guarantee the unconditional nature of subjective maxims, and that consequently the moral law reinforces the exteriority and antagonism of the individuals who act within (bourgeois) civil society.

The conclusion of Hegel's account of spirit describes a condition in which self-consciousness, having recognized itself as an absolute moral end, attempts to withdraw from the secular world of work, satisfaction and desire. This withdrawal of humanity's 'beautiful soul'[43] from the 'corrupt' social relations in which it lives and acts, however, is a form of self-deception. We have seen that the Kantian subject is originally unable to guarantee the unconditional nature of its moral maxims, and that, as such, its motives remain 'conditioned' by the self-interest enshrined in bourgeois law and property relations. Work is generally recognized as the principle through which property and ownership are sanctioned; yet its 'ethical' significance (i.e., as the most basic presence of the state in the life of the individual citizen) remains obscured by the exclusiveness of particular interest. Self-consciousness's representation of itself through the apparent unconditional necessity of the moral law therefore produces what Hegel calls a 'spiritual animal kingdom':[44] a 'community' of individuals who, while recognizing themselves as moral beings, pursue their own interests to the exclusion of all others.

For Hegel, the violence that is determined by abstractly free individuality is reproduced through self-consciousness's misrecognition of its *actual* relations with the other. Speculatively conceived, the 'objective' opposition of nature and morality (heteronomy and autonomy) sustained in Kant's *Critique of Judgement* produces a kind of 'dissemblance',[45] in which the subject, unable to harmonize its actions with the heteronomy of civil life, has constant recourse to a transcendent idea of God as the guarantor of its duty. This postulated, or 'ideal', unity of particular moral actions with the concept of duty as such (i.e., the idea of God as a self-determining intellect) is deeply contradictory. God, as the idea, or 'thought', of this harmony, is non-actual; for His substance exists beyond self-consciousness's infinite task of moral self-determination. This transcendent idea of God (as both substantive and non-actual), therefore, is incapable of providing any 'objective' standards by which individuals could discriminate between moral and non-moral actions. Each simply does what he/she recognizes as his/her unconditional duty, and refuses to acknowledge the (heteronomous) happiness and satisfaction which actually determine its (antagonistic) relations with the other.

Self-consciousness's recognition of this deeply contradictory state of affairs does not, however, produce a transformation of its own hypocrisy, or of the antagonism of ethical life. Rather, each individual retreats into his/her self as a 'conscience',[46] which, having recognized the emptiness of the moral law, acts on the basis of pure conviction. As such, conscience is actively opposed to knowledge of, or conformity to, the relations and institutions of ethical life. This universal inability of the subject to 'realize' the demands of its moral conviction (in the 'objective' forms of work, satisfaction and desire) produces a violent opposition of undifferentiated 'egos', each of which conceives itself as the sole voice of the right and the good. It is these 'beautiful souls' who, while talking of their 'withdrawal' from the world of secular activity, continue to practise the violence of a universal self-interest which they are incapable of re-forming. In the end, this hypocritical self-consciousness is forced to admit that its judgement of the other as infinitely corruptible is not absolute ('divine'), and that, as such, it must ask forgiveness from 'others' whom it regards only as 'absolutely self-contained and exclusive individuality'. Such an 'exchange', however, remains merely at the level of subjectivity, and is powerless to re-form the conflict inherent in actual social relations.[47]

To conclude, then, Hegel's account of morality describes the phenomenological forms through which self-consciousness attempts to determine its independence from feudal domination. 'Conscience', 'Virtue', 'Duty' and the language of 'Christian Forgiveness' all presuppose the 'lawlessness' of the feudal economy (or rather of its anachronistic persistence alongside the recognition of rational subjectivity), and the absence of universal recognition in ethical life. These interiorizations of the moral law are originally 'spiritual' forms – for they all proceed from consciousness's determination to assert its essential selfhood, independence and purposiveness. Thus, even though moral consciousness is expounded through the antagonism it reproduces within *Sittlichkeit*, its formation and re-formation of the idea of autonomy must be recognized as constituting a true ethical demand. The account of Kant's ethics of individuality, sovereignty and legal recognition which is set out in *Philosophy of Right* makes it clear that although 'conscience' is implicated in the emergence of acquisitiveness, atomism and self-interest, the sphere of moral 'reflection' (civil society) remains essential to modern ethical life.[48] By positing the concept of freedom in opposition to 'necessity' and 'inclination', therefore, moral consciousness determines particularity, individuality and contingency as the principle of (modern) productive activity, political mediation and ethical recognition.

It is this idea of 'modernity' as the release of the 'particular', the 'contingent' and the 'individual' into the substance of ethical life which informs our account of social scientific explanation. Speculatively conceived, the liberation of reflective difference within *Sittlichkeit* is productive of contradictions which cannot be definitively 'totalized' through the idea of 'Spirit' or 'Absolute Knowledge'. Spirit, in other words, can only be known through the temporal forms in which it is deployed; that is, through the historical development of *Sittlichkeit*. As Hegel puts it in the Preface to *Phenomenology* 'if [spirit] must be presented to itself as an object, but at the same time straightaway annul and transcend this objective form, it must be its own object in which it finds itself reflected'.[49] I will suggest that the relationship of social scientific forms of explanation to the emergence and development of a differentiated type of ethical life is one of reconstruction and re-presentation. Each perspective 'objectifies' the concept of *Sittlichkeit* by abstractly prioritizing one particular element of the totality. Thus, the 'idea' of a social science emerges as a type of immanent critique, in which the (abstract) categories deployed in functional, systemic and voluntarist types of explanation must be re-cognized as both essential *and* non-comprehensive.

Speculative thought and modernity

Hegel's critique of Kant is fundamental to our idea of a speculative social science for three specific reasons. First, *Phenomenology of Mind* situates the relationship of practical reason to ethical substance within a concrete historical development (i.e., the postulation of a universal humanity in the demands of the moral law is expounded through its relationship to the 'rational' terror of the French Revolution). Secondly, the Kantian 'science' of the understanding (*Verstand*), with its formal oppositions of autonomy and heteronomy, subject and object, law and moral recognition, is shown to be essential to the emergence and constitution of modernity. The individual's recognition of itself as a 'rational will' which is independent of non-moral causes participates in the differentiation of ethical substance into a 'unity' of competing desires, satisfactions and interests (civil society). Moral consciousness, in other words, presupposes the contingency of 'my' actions within the sphere of difference and particularity, a sphere which, for Hegel, releases all the creative and destructive potential individuality into the substance of ethical life. And thirdly, it is self-consciousness's 'Kantian' reflections upon itself – its 'spontaneity' within the scheme of efficient causes, its 'critical' relationship to ethical life, its 'reflective' identification of morality, autonomy and self-consistency – which become (implicitly) inscribed in the 'paradigmatic' forms of social scientific explanation. I will argue that this inscription of the categories – and method – of Kant's philosophy (i.e., deduction of a priori necessity from contingent 'appearance', postulation of the 'universal' form of autonomy, reduction of dispersal and complexity through unifying synthetic principles) is essential to the theorization of modernity, and that it is only through this Kantian 'reflection' (on difference, autonomy and identity) that it is possible to re-formulate the concept of ethical substance.

The relationship between our 'speculative' conception of a social science and Hegel's critique of Kantian philosophy is now becoming more determinate. We have seen that, for Hegel, spirit should be understood as a 'rational' form which is determinable only in the finite relations which constitute ethical substance. And so the movement of spirit through its different historical 'epochs' 'includes the negative [factor], the element which would be named falsity if it could be considered one from which we had to abstract'.[50] What I must recognize, then, is that speculative thought does not simply posit an analytical doctrine of 'contradiction' and 'totalization' which opposes the categories of transcendental legitimacy. Rather, Hegel's Phenomenology of Kantian self-consciousness proceeds through an immanent critique of abstract understanding (*Verstand*). The exteriority of sense and reason, autonomy and heteronomy, moral law and ethical life are re-presented through the historical development which they have already produced – that is, the movement of self-consciousness through the absolute necessity of 'duty', the moral 'dissemblance' of inclination and self-interest, and the 'conscientious' abandonment of secular life (work, satisfaction and desire) as irretrievably evil.[51] The Hegelian notion of spirit, therefore, is a recognition of ethical substance as essentially contradictory, and that this recognition takes place through the positing of 'false' (i.e., abstract/a priori) categories of unity, mediation and identity among self-conscious individuals.

Speculatively conceived, self-consciousness does not wait upon the philosophical explicitude of its concept to 'engender'[52] the oppositions by which it develops: the necessity of 'mediation' (between law and autonomy, morality and justice, state and civil society) is reproduced through the contradictions which afflict particular forms of ethical life. The 'labour of the concept', in other words, is the constant re-cognition of the categories and relations of *Sittlichkeit*, a re-cognition which is originally – and necessarily – grounded in the abstraction (domination, exclusion, suppression of self-consciousness) inscribed in ethical substance. In order to understand the relationship of social scientific 'paradigms' to speculative Phenomenology, therefore, we must recognize that there is no determinate or definitive 'end' to the contradictions which afflict the social/ethical life of humanity. Each of the sociological traditions I will examine re-cognizes the concept of sociality through the (methodological and philosophical) prioritization of one particular element: economy/mode of production (Marx and Marxism); cohesion/interdependency/functionality (Durkheim, Parsons, Luhmann); and agency/meaning/cognition (Weber and Habermas). As such, I will argue that the explanatory paradigms, through which 'modernity' is re-cognized, presuppose the originally Kantian forms of opposition, identity and legitimacy set out in the preceding section.

My fundamental claim about the nature of social scientific explanations is that they formulate 'ethical' significance of modernity through abstract reconstructions of its substance. Speculatively conceived, this 'substance' is not a fixed or predetermined category: it develops (non-teleologically) through re-cognition of the contradictory relations into which the concept (universality) of self-consciousness is articulated. I have attempted to show that the 'science' of abstraction, which is developed in Kant's critical philosophy, is implicated in the constitution of modern social relations (i.e., in the differentiation of individual personalities), and that this implication is reflected in the 'modernist' sociologies which re-present the 'substance' of human sociality. The (Kantian) oppositions, estrangements and unities posited by Marx, Durkheim, Weber and Habermas, in other words, reproduce the idea of *Sittlichkeit* as a form which has constantly to be re-cognized. My speculative conception of a social science, therefore, demands re-cognition of 'heteronomy' (otherness, exteriority) as a form reproduced through the 'reconstruction' of ethical life: it is the 'thought' of reconciliation among elements (productive relations, social differentiation and interdependency, subjective meaning and cognition) represented, experienced and theorized as discrete independent and hierarchical.

I began my account of 'the rational and the social' by taking Hegel at his most abstract – that is, with his apparent assertion of the accomplished identity of being and reason: 'What is rational is actual and what is actual is rational'.[53] I have argued, however, that this apparent predetermination of universal identity as a realizable end belongs only to the body of prefatory remarks that Hegel offered as a guide to his logical, historical and phenomenological dialectics. As such, these remarks should not be regarded as definitive summations of a metaphysical system, in which social mediation and identity are logically fixed and uncontradictory manifestations of spirit. The categories of ethical, political and legal recognition set out in *Philosophy of Right* articulate no more than the conditions under which the 'reflective' differentiation of modernity might be acknowledged by a 'rational' authority. The political judgements of the modern state, in other words, are always concerned with spheres of contingency and abstract independence which it should not, in principle, attempt to dominate or suppress.[54] For Hegel, spirit is recognized through the oppositions inherent in its temporal embodiments; and so the 'substance' of ethical life is always reproduced through the 'idea' of unity inscribed in the state and its laws. Absolute knowledge, therefore, must always remain the 'restless activity of negation' – the re-formation of the abstract forms of individuality, autonomy and activity which are presupposed by a 'rational' political organization.[55]

My attempt to develop a speculative idea of social science is founded upon this 'activity' of spiritual negation. So far I have suggested that it is Kantian self-consciousness (with its abstract postulates of 'reflective' finality, transcendental ends, negative virtue and conscientious withdrawal from secular life) that opens the way into the separation and difference of 'modernity', and that this 'opening' should be understood as a constant, yet ultimately unrealizable, demand for mediation, identity and unity within ethical life. My account of the origins of social science developed the idea that sociological reconstructions of modernity articulate what are generically Kantian principles of separation, opposition and difference. Each type of explanation (I will call them 'paradigms', although not in a strictly Kuhnian sense)[56] attempts to describe the conditions under which the idea of 'autonomy' can be recognized as compatible with, and necessary to, the 'rational' (non-coercive) structures of social integration and identity. Such descriptions, I have argued, are characterized by their prioritization of one particular element or category, which is understood as constitutive of ethical content of modernity. What I am proposing is a speculative phenomenology of social scientific explanations, in which: (1) the (social/ethical) contradictions constituted in the development of modernity become explicit through the discourse of abstraction/separation; (2) the possibility of a rational recognition of the other is articulated in each paradigm as the negation of some negative necessity (capitalist production, bureaucratic organization, instrumental rationality/scientism); (3) this negation is recognized as taking some (immanently) positive form which ought to regulate the social totality (socialized production, organic solidarity, cognitive legitimacy, etc.); and (4), such a 'regulation' is conceived as reimposing the Kantian forms in which moral, legal and political 'legitimacy' are originally implicated in 'reflective' opposition and exclusion. Such a phenomenology, therefore, acknowledges *Sittlichkeit* as a form whose 'substance', or rational determination, is always afflicted with contradiction and opposition. We must, in other words, acknowledge the necessity of 'abstract' reconstructions of ethical life, while acknowledging their (original) inadequacy to its concept.

The general problem with the structural sociologies I will examine is their failure to recognize as a form which actively 're-presents' the structures, relations and institutions of ethical life. Marx, for example, understands individual subjects (under capitalism) simply as bearers of their economic function and class relation. Each individual is reduced to a moment of the structural conditions through which surplus value is created, and 'capitalism' reproduces itself. For Marx, this reproduction is expressed not simply in the categories through which capital circulates in the economy ('surplus' and 'exchange' value, 'fixed' and 'organic' capital, etc.), but also in the private appropriation/alienation of productive labour. Capitalism, in other words, is presented as a structural negativity, in which political, religious and legal institutions are determined by the necessity of maintaining the production of surplus value. In general, Marxist social analyses articulate a concept of negative economic necessity which, independently of all legal, ethical representations of autonomy, *determines* the alienation of humanity's 'natural' productive spontaneity. In the end, the emergence of a revolutionary proletarian class 'for itself' is determined by forms of estrangement which are exclusively 'capitalist' in origin. A communist form of social organization therefore represents the end of history in the sense that the structural/objective antagonisms of bourgeoisie and proletariat, use and exchange value, social production and private appropriation, have all been recognized and (violently) transcended. The socialization of production, for Marx, appears as the realization of sociality as (non-contradictory) ethical life.

The 'bourgeois' form of this structural/transcendental account of social necessity, is originally articulated in Emile Durkheim's account of social realism.[57] All of Durkheim's substantive works articulate a conception of individuality as ontologically dependent upon the life of the collective. The relations and institutions which bind society together, in other words, are conceived as objective 'facts' (*fait external*), whose necessity should be acknowledged as independent of all 'subjective' forms of recognition, reflection or representation. In *The Division of Labour in Society* (1964), Durkheim attempts to show that modern ethical life is characterized by a tension between morally deregulated ('egoistic') individualism and the increasing specialization and interdependency of social institutions. His claim is that the proliferation of highly specialized social, economic and political functions within the body of 'the collective' embodies the potential for an 'organic' (universally mediated) type of social organization. Unlike Marx, Durkheim conceived this potential as substantively present in the form of modern social differentiation: the contradictions with which modern industrial capitalism was afflicted could be resolved by recognizing and reconstructing modernity's 'normal' condition of economic integration. The explanatory power of Durkheim's social realism, therefore, is primarily concerned with the maintenance of ethical solidarity and the protection of the social body against 'anomic' (normless, amoral) human nature.

Both of these structural accounts of ethical life reproduce, in different ways, the Kantian separation of 'transcendental' necessity and 'empirical' contingency. So far I have claimed that the idea of a social science requires that the contradictions inherent in modern ethical life should be made explicit in the discourses of abstract separation and reconstruction. I have also maintained that, in general, social scientific perspectives articulate the possibility of rational recognition (of the other), as the negation of some negative necessity. It seems clear that Marxist and Durkheimian sociologies determine their ethical and political content in exactly this way. For Marx (and the Marxists), the 'superstructural' forms, through which 'bourgeois' and 'proletarian' subjects represent their (moral, legal and political) freedom, are determined by the economic relations whose inner negativity is described in *Capital* (1977d). For Durkheim (and those I will include in the 'social realist' tradition – specifically, Parsons and Luhmann), on the other hand, the development of a differentiated form of solidarity takes place through the individual's subsumption under the 'objective' progress of social specialization. As we will see, these accounts of ethical life – as a form 'realized' in the transition from an originally negative set of conditions (capitalism or anomic individualism) to a positive totality – tend to suppress the moral, political and cultural 're-presentations' through which self-consciousness acknowledges the 'objectivity' of ethical life.

This is not to say that neither Marx nor Durkheim contribute anything to our recognition of modernity. Rather – and this will become explicit in Chapter 4 – my claim is that both of these sociologies recognize the necessity of one particular element in the constitution (or 'substance') of modern ethical life. For Marx, this element is the relationship between creative spontaneity (freedom) and the organization of production, while for Durkheim, it is the moral significance of social differentiation. By subsuming the individual subject under the established necessities of 'capitalism', 'socialized production' or 'organic solidarity', however, Marxist and functionalist sociologies appropriate the concept of legitimacy as that which is determined by social structure. The 'objectivity' of ethical life is understood not as mediated through the re-cognition/re-presentation of self-conscious individuals, but as an independent form in which 'humanity' is either fully present/totalized (organic solidarity, socialized/communist production) or universally corrupted (capitalism, egoistic individualism). Structural conceptions of ethical life, therefore, should be recognized as formulating the totalitarian (i.e., exclusive and suppressive) potencies which always haunt the 'spirit' (universality) of ethical life. And as such, they remain essential to the idea of a speculative social science.

If, as I have claimed, the generic problem with structural sociologies is their failure to recognize self-consciousness as a form which 're-presents' the relations of ethical life, then it is the tendency to reduce or marginalize the power of social formation (of subjectivity), that is the defining problem with the linguistic–cognitive (Habermas) and *Verstehen* (Weber) sociologies I will examine. Thus my account of these two forms of social critique will concentrate first on developing their relations to Kant's idea of moral/practical necessity; secondly, on their respective conceptions of autonomy and legitimacy; and thirdly, on their reproduction of cognitive primacy within the mechanism/system of modern social relations. Again, my argument will not try to demonstrate that Habermas and Weber's respective deployments of Kantian ideals (cognitive independence, rational legitimacy, perfomative autonomy) are simply wrong, or that the attempt to distinguish moral–cognitive necessity within ethical life is, in general, outside the scope of social scientific explanation. Rather, my claim is that these reconstructions of rational volition demonstrate the necessity to conceive 'objectively' established forms of work, satisfaction and desire, not as external or causative powers, but as mediated through subjective re-presentations. Speculatively understood, it is the fate (and redemption) of self-consciousness to participate in the substance of even its most violent estrangements.[58]

The insights of Habermas and Weber into the history and development of modernity, therefore, are characterized by their separation of 'rational' subjectivity from the established conditions through which self-consciousness has been formed. For Weber, this takes the form of prioritizing the concept of 'meaning' over 'structural' forms of inter-dependence, antagonism and domination. The discipline of sociology, in other words, should be concerned with making explicit the meanings and motivations ('value rapports') through which individual subjects are attached to social groups and institutions. For Habermas, however, Weber's *Verstehen* sociology – which attempts only to develop an 'empathetic' understanding of social action – requires supplementation at the level of cognitive necessity. Habermas's concept of communicative reason, in other words, is an attempt to show that the possibility of 'the social' (i.e., of productive activity, moral regulation and cognitive development) is opened by the basic categories of language (the 'speech act'). This 'universal pragmatics' of communicative action, according to Habermas, is originally inscribed in the structures of the 'lifeworld' (the realm of everyday praxis and interaction), and so the presupposition of all forms of moral, instrumental, strategic and productive activity are the transcendental forms through which communication/intersubjectivity is opened and sustained. Thus, there emerges from Habermas's work an 'ethic' in which the clarification of subjective motives, the disclosure of 'systematically distorted' communication and the maintenance of performative/dialogical autonomy, are posited as universal ideals. My reading of Weber, therefore, will focus on his rejection of the moral necessity which Kant attributes to subjective 're-presentation', while my account of Habermas will expound his reproduction of the categories of critical ethics (autonomy, heteronomy, transcendental necessity, moral cognition).

I began this chapter by taking Hegel at his most abstract – that is, at the point where he seems to assert the immanent identity of being and reason as the 'true' object of social and historical thought. The claim that *'what is rational is actual and what is rational is actual'* seems to entail that speculative phenomenology is a form of (Platonic) 'logocentrism', in which each historical epoch is recognized exclusively in terms of its contribution to the 'substance' of absolute Knowledge. I have argued, however, that the 'actuality' to which Hegel refers in his Preface to *Philosophy of Right* should not be understood as the 'presence' (totalized totality) of the rational forms through which self-consciousness articulates its concept.[59] I have claimed that the historical nature of *Phenomenology of Mind* and *Philosophy of Right* show that Hegel's idealism is speculative rather than teleological; and that the temporal forms of ethical life in which self-consciousness embodies itself are always afflicted with violence and contradiction. Thus, Hegel's notion of 'the good' – or the totality of determinations through which the substance of ethical life is constituted – is always contradictory: even *Philosophy of Right* articulates no more than the conditions under which self-consciousness articulates its concept as the *demand* inscribed in the constitution of a rational state authority.[60]

The idea of a speculative social science, then, is best understood as an articulation of the contradictions determined within the 'substance' of (contemporary/modern) ethical life. This articulation is essentially bound up with the Kantian oppositions (concept and intuition, autonomy and heteronomy, noumena and phenomena) which, I have argued, are inscribed in the 'modernist' forms of social explanation. Marx, Weber and Durkheim establish discrete theoretical 'paradigms' in which the concept of the social is broken down into independent explanatory structures and powers. These reconstructions of modernity, I will argue, exist in a relationship of contemporaneous antagonism: each one abstracts a particular element from ethical life (productive activity, structural interdependence, instrumental rationality, etc.) and reproduces its priority in notions of justice, morality and universal recognition. A speculative understanding of contemporary social relations therefore demands acknowledgement of each of these sociological traditions, for it is only through the reconstruction of ethical 'substance' that it is possible to recognize the violence and exclusion it may produce. In the end, then, social scientific accounts of ethical life should be understood as contributing to an idea (of reconciliation) whose essence is historical; an idea whose modern formations always *remain to be* grasped in their 'true' significance.[61]

Put rather abstractly, then, the idea of a speculative social science is informed by four basic principles: (1) that Hegel's notion of 'spirit' is the recognition of the truth/finitude of its temporal forms; (2) that social scientific explanations recognize and abstract particular (and essential) forms from the totality of ethical life; (3) that this abstraction is acknowledged as the condition of social critique; and (4) that 'sociality' (ethical life) is recognized as formed through the differentiation (of the concept), not as the suppression of difference. The following chapters will attempt to develop the theoretical and methodological consequences of these four basic principles.

Notes

1. G.W.F. Hegel, *Philosophy of Right*, trans. T.M. Knox, Oxford University Press, 1967b, p. 10.

2. See K. Marx, *The German Ideology*, C.J. Arthur ed., Lawrence & Wishart, 1977c.

3. See E. Levinas, *Totality and Infinity: An Essay on Exteriority*, trans. A. Lingis, Duquesne University Press, 1994.

4. See especially J.-F. Lyotard, 'Hegel Notice', in Lyotard, *The Differend: Phrases in Dispute*, trans. G. Van Den Abbeele, Manchester University Press, 1988a, and J.

Derrida, 'From restricted to general economy: a Hegelianism without reserve', in *Writing and Difference*, trans. A. Bass, Routledge, 1990b.

5. This line of argument is has a long history and is pursued in different ways by Bertrand Russell, Isaiah Berlin, Karl Popper, Jean-François Lyotard and Jacques Derrida.

6. See I. Kant, 'What is Enlightenment?', in Kant, *Political Writings*, H. Reiss ed., trans. H.B. Nisbet, Cambridge University Press, 1991.

7. See I. Kant, 'An answer to the question: "What is Enlightenment?"', in Kant, *Political Writings*.

8. See T.S. Kuhn, *The Structure of Scientific Revolutions*, University of Chicago Press, 1970.

9. Kant regarded his transcendental arguments concerning the discursive structure of the understanding (*Verstand*), the 'categorical' demand of duty, and the 'reflective' reception of beauty, sublimity and purposiveness (in nature and history) as establishing 'analytical' truths about experience.

10. See D. Hume, *A Treatise of Human Nature*, Oxford University Press, 1975.

11. See E. Durkheim, *The Division of Labour in Society*, trans. G. Simpson, The Free Press, 1964.

12. See K. Marx, *The Economic and Philosophical Manuscripts of 1844*, Progress Publishers, 1977b.

13. For Kant, the concept of rational will (*Wille*) necessarily includes the moment of 'action', that is, the power to act in accordance with the demands of practical reason.

14. This is what Kant refers to in the second *Critique* as the 'typic' of the pure practical faculty of judgement.

15. See Kant's 'post-critical' exposition of the duties proper to rational humanity in the *Foundations of the Metaphysics of Morals*, trans. L. White Beck, Macmillan, 1985.

16. See M. Weber, *The Protestant Ethic and the Spirit of Capitalism*, trans. T. Parsons, George Allen & Unwin, 1978a.

17. See particularly Habermas's more recent elaborations of his theory of communicative action in *The Philosophical Discourse of Modernity* (1994), *Postmetaphysical Thinking* (1995a), and *Justification and Application* (1995b).

18. It is this reciprocal, yet unfulfilled, relationship of subjectivity and objectivity that Hegel calls 'actuality'. See especially Hegel's *Logic* and the Introduction to *Philosophy of Right*.

19. The notion of reflective judgement, which Kant expounds in the third *Critique*, refers not to 'presentations' which exemplify the determining conditions of cognition in general, but rather, to those feelings and sensations which refer to an Idea – the infinitely unpresentable unity of theoretical and practical reason – that must remain beyond the resources of cognition as such. Such feelings, according to Kant, are the origin of judgements of beauty, sublimity and purposiveness (in nature).

20. I. Kant, *The Critique of Judgment*, trans. James Creed Meredith, Oxford University Press, 1982b, p. 11.

21. Ibid., p. 15.

22. Ibid., p. 21.

23. Ibid., p. 27.

24. Ibid., p. 25.

25. Ibid., p. 29.

26. Ibid., p. 24.

27. See the notion of moral progress which is expounded in Kant's political writings, especially 'The contest of the faculties' and 'Idea for a universal history with a cosmopolitan purpose'.

28. See the third 'Notice' on Kant in J.-F. Lyotard, *The Differend*.

29. See J.-F. Lyotard, *The Postmodern Condition: A Report on Knowledge*, trans. G. Bennington and B. Massumi, Manchester University Press, 1991a.

30. See J.-F. Lyotard, 'Judiciousness in dispute, or Kant after Marx', in *The Lyotard Reader*, A. Benjamin ed., Blackwell, 1991b.

31. See Kant's 'Idea for a universal history with a cosmopolitan purpose', in *Political Writings*.

32. See Hegel's accounts of morality in the sections on 'Reason' and 'Spirit' in *Phenomenology of Mind*, trans. J.B. Baillie, Harper & Row, 1967a.

33. See G.W.F. Hegel, *Natural Law. The Scientific Ways of Treating Natural Law, Its Place in Moral Philosophy, and Its Relation to the Positive Sciences of Law*, trans. T.M. Knox, Pennsylvania University Press, 1975.

34. Hegel, *Phenomenology of Mind*, 'Independence and dependence of self-consciousness: lordship and bondage', pp. 228–40.

35. Ibid., 'Pleasure and necessity', pp. 383–9.

36. Ibid., 'The law of the heart and the frenzy of self-conceit', pp. 390–400.

37. Ibid., 'Virtue and the way of the world', pp. 401–12.

38. Kant, *Critique of Judgement*, p. 31.

39. See Hegel, *Phenomenology of Mind*, pp. 455–680.

40. Ibid., 'Absolute freedom and terror', pp. 599–610.

41. See the section on Civil Society in *Philosophy of Right*, pp. 122–55.

42. This is brought out particularly strongly in Kant's essay, 'An answer to the question: "What is Enlightenment?"'. See *Political Writings*, pp. 54–60.

43. See *Phenomenology of Mind*, 'Conscience: the "beautiful soul": evil and the forgiveness of it', pp. 642–79.

44. Ibid., 'Self-contained individuals associated as a community of animals and the deception thence arising: the real fact', pp. 417–38.

45. Ibid., 'Dissemblance', pp. 628–41.

46. Ibid., 'Conscience as the freedom of the self within itself. The reality of duty: conviction', pp. 644–63.

47. See Hegel's account of 'Revealed religion' in *Phenomenology of Mind*, pp. 750–85.

48. See Hegel's treatment of 'Morality' in *Philosophy of Right*, pp. 75–104.

49. Hegel, *Phenomenology of Mind*, p. 139.

50. Ibid., p. 105.

51. Ibid., 'Spirit certain of itself: morality', pp. 611–79.

52. See Lyotard's exposition of the 'Result' in *The Differend*.

53. Hegel, *Philosophy of Right*, p. 10.

54. See, for example, Hegel's account of the application of the law to particular cases in the 'Administration of Justice', *Philosophy of Right*, pp. 134–46.

55. Hegel, *Phenomenology of Mind*, p. 137.

56. See Kuhn, *The Structure of Scientific Revolutions*.

57. See E. Durkheim, *The Rules of Sociological Method*, trans. W.D. Halls, Macmillan, 1982.

58. See, for example, abstract 'culture' of subjectivity which Hegel describes in his account of the Jacobin Terror in *Phenomenology of Mind*, pp. 599–610.

59. See especially 'From restricted to general economy: a Hegelianism without reserve', in Derrida, *Writing and Difference*.

60. See 'The idea of the good', in G.W.F. Hegel, *The Science of Logic*, trans. A.V. Miller, George Allen & Unwin, 1969, pp. 818–23.

61. See Hegel's Preface to *Philosophy of Right*, p. 13.

2

The Structural Organization of Truth

My fundamental concern in this chapter will be to examine the 'powers' that Marxist and functionalist paradigms attribute to the concept of totality. I will argue that the possibility of these powers – such as the integrative force of 'moral density' (Durkheim), the pervasiveness of normative 'patterns' (Parsons), or the immanent necessity of 'socialized production' (Marx) – depends upon a certain idea of objectivity (and objectification) which can be traced back to Kant's first *Critique*. My account of the 'structurality' of structural sociology therefore will expound the history of this objectivity, a history which, I will claim, repeats (in the agonistic forms of Marxist and functionalist thought) Kant's original opposition of the understanding (*Verstand*) to substance and autonomy.

Kant's *Critique of Pure Reason* is divided into two sections: the Transcendental Analytic and the Transcendental Dialectic. Broadly speaking, we may say that the first of these sections is concerned with the a priori conditions which make experience of an external realm of objects possible, while the second is concerned with establishing the limits which these conditions impose upon the concept of cognitive subjectivity. Thus, it is the first *Critique* which establishes the system of faculties and legislative realms which Kant retains throughout his investigations of moral autonomy,[1] political and religious enlightenment,[2] and the possibility of aesthetic and teleological judgements.[3] Our first task, then, is to examine the transactions (between the discursive understanding and sensible affection) through which knowledge of an 'objective' reality is constituted.

In the second part of the section called 'The System of the Principles of Pure Understanding', Kant remarks that:

> Experience depends upon a priori principles of its form, that is, upon universal rules of unity in the synthesis of appearances. Their objective reality, as necessary conditions of experience . . . can always be shown in experience. Apart from this relation synthetic a priori principles are completely impossible. For they have no . . . object, in which the synthetic unity can exhibit the objective reality of its concepts.[4]

The relationship between the 'synthetic unity' of the understanding and the 'experience' (of objects) which is determined by this unity is extremely important to our exposition, and requires some unpacking. The first and most important thing to notice is that the relationship between the a priori concepts of the understanding and the 'modes' of sensible affection (space and time) is hierarchical. The possibility of experience, in other words, is made to depend upon the 'pure concepts of the understanding', whose discursive totality is expounded in the Transcendental Analytic. Kant's famous proposition that 'concepts without intuitions are empty; intuitions without concepts are blind' seems to postulate a certain mutuality among the determinations of affection and cognition. Knowledge seems to require both discursive synthesis *and* external affection. Yet it is the formal determinations of objectivity (the categories of quality, quantity, relation and modality) which control the subject's relation to the 'external' world: space and time, Kant's 'modes of intuition', are forms which channel (almost) every encounter with otherness into the unity of the understanding. It is this dominance of discursive intellect over the 'substance' of its intuitions which lies at the core of Hegel's critique of Kant. For by restricting the synthetic power of reason to the realm of 'appearances', Hegel claims that Kant fails to recognize the conflicts and mediations through which ethical substance (*Sittlichkeit*) is constituted. I will return to this later.

The fundamental problem which occupies the first *Critique* is how it is possible to distinguish between knowledge as such and the aporetic claims of rationalist thought. Kant's answer to this question, I will argue, is crucial to the concept of 'objectivity' which has developed within 'structural' sociologies; and so I need briefly to summarize his 'critique' of metaphysics. First, it is the mind which plays the active part in the constitution of experience: for it is the 'self-subsistent, self-sufficient' unity of the understanding which organizes the 'manifold' of sensible intuitions. Secondly, the possibility of knowledge as such, depends upon the regulative function of the intuitive 'modes': it is space and time which circumscribe the limits within which reason (the faculty of ideas) is able to make legitimate pronouncements about the nature of 'reality'. As Kant puts it in his *Prologomena to any Future Metaphysics*, 'it would be absurd to hope that we can know more of any object than belongs to the possible experience of it . . . since time, space and all the concepts of the understanding . . . can have no other use than to make experience possible'.[5] Thirdly, a 'critical' philosophy – in the Kantian sense – ought to concern itself with the transcendental conditions of experience; that is, with disclosing the 'synthetic a priori' propositions which make natural scientific and mathematical knowledge possible. Fourthly, this means that knowledge, as opposed to rationalistic conjectures about reason, totality and nature, is knowledge of appearances or 'phenomena'. For Kant, it is only by confining reason to the strictures of transcendental exposition (i.e., How is our experience possible? What are its universal conditions? What limits must be set upon the ideas of 'reality' and 'objectivity'?) that it is possible to avoid the aporias of traditional metaphysics. Finally, then, we must acknowledge that the realm of appearances is given through a categorial system in which 'efficient causality' is the dominant principle. The objectivity of phenomena, in other words, is dependent on a relation in which it is the exteriority of events, rather than their re-cognition or re-presentation, that is constitutive.

I am not claiming that the legislative unity of the understanding is a deterministic force which pervades every region of Kant's critical philosophy. The second and third *Critiques* expound independently legislative faculties – those of 'pure desire' and 'reflective judgement' – which maintain specific and irreducible relations to the faculties of knowledge. Indeed, the following chapter will look at the use to which the concept of an autonomous practical reason is put by Weber and Habermas, while Chapter 4 will examine the relationship between Kantian aesthetics and Lyotard's account of a 'postmodern' ethics and politics. My aim in abstracting the relationship of causality, objectivity and knowledge which is set out in the Transcendental Analytic therefore is not to deny the theoretical significance of the second and third *Critiques*. Rather, it is an attempt to highlight the constitution of 'objective' knowledge in the critical philosophy, and to show how this kind of transcendental argument might connect with certain 'structural' accounts of social relations.

The main concern of the present chapter, then, will be to suggest a Kantian homology between Marxist and functionalist sociologies. Again, it is important to note that I am not trying to show that Marxism and functionalism are ultimately the same; and that if I look closely enough, I can discover a common set of theoretical and methodological principles. The 'histories' I will construct in the following sections will try to preserve the difference between 'radical' and 'conservative' accounts of modernity and structural necessity. Yet within this difference, I will argue that there is a certain repetition, and that this repetition can be traced to an origin in Kant's critical epistemology. I need therefore to make some brief preparatory suggestions about the nature of this repetition.

The first *Critique*, we have seen, restricts the synthetic activity of mind/intellect to the constitution of a realm of appearances. The production of knowledge as such, presupposes the synthetic unity of the understanding which Kant deduces from nature of external experience. The structure of the understanding therefore stands as an organic whole, without which the 'manifold' of sensory affection would remain without objectivity, and the 'critical' science of reason without systematic relation of its parts (epistemology, morality and judgement). As Kant puts it in the 'Architectonic of Pure Reason':

> The unity of the end to which all the parts relate, and in the idea of which they all stand in relation to one another, makes it possible to determine from our knowledge of the other parts whether any part be missing, and to prevent any

arbitrary addition, or in respect of its completeness any indeterminateness that does not conform to the limits which are thus determined a priori. The whole is thus an organised unity (*articulatio*), and not an aggregate (*coacervatio*).[6]

Thus, if there is a generic 'structurality' to be found in the histories of Marxism and functionalism, I would suggest that its origin is postulated in the legislative powers which Kant attributes to the understanding in his first *Critique*. A few familiar comparisons between 'radical' and 'conservative' accounts of totality and modernity are brought to mind. First, there is the idea that it is only through the established unity of social structure that we can understand the 'causes' of individual actions, and the possibility of ethical responsibility. Secondly, that this established unity of social structure consists in an 'objectivity' which precedes and determines subjective forms of representation. Thirdly, that there is a tendency to attribute certain abstract powers to the concept of totality, powers which subordinate difference and individuality to the dynamics of structural necessity. I will argue that it is repetition of these 'objectifying' tendencies which constitutes the peculiar *telos* of structural sociologies, and that there is a certain violence which is always co-present with the repetitions of structure.

This reflection upon the nature of a structural–sociological violence returns us to the relationship of concepts and intuitions which is postulated in the *Critique of Pure Reason*. We have seen that the understanding (*Verstand*), as the unity of the synthetic a priori principles which govern the realm of appearances, occupies a privileged position in critical epistemology. For Kant, the 'substantive' categories (quality, quantity and relation), which are deduced from the nature of experience in general, control not only the constitution of the realm of phenomena but also what we, as rational subjects, must regard as logically consistent with the synthetic functions of our understanding. Thus, the categories of 'modality' (i.e., possibility, existence, necessity) which Kant includes among 'the list of all pure original concepts of synthesis',[7] express a certain extended and irreducible dominance of the understanding in the constitution of knowledge. If we are able to discriminate between what is possibly (problematically) the case and what is actually (assertorically) the case and between what is actually the case, and what must necessarily (apodeicticaly) be the case,[8] then this is because the understanding has already established the qualitative, quantitative and relational determinations which apply to experience in general. The categories through which Kant expounds the concept of experience, in other words, determine a realm of phenomenalistic causality, in which finitude, contingency and particularity have already been subsumed under the demands of 'the object'.

My speculative history of structure and its theorization, therefore will trace the persistence of this objectifying necessity within the 'modernist' traditions of Marxism and functionalism. As I have indicated, my particular concern will be to examine the causative powers which these paradigms have attributed to the concept of (social) totality, and to expound the violence which persists in the reification of systemic necessities. For Hegel, the structures, institutions and relations which constitute ethical life (*Sittlichkeit*) always refer to a formed, and potentially transformative subjectivity, which remains implicit even in the most external and coercive forms of necessity. The master's tyranny over the slave, for example, originates and sustains the ethical potential of the subject; for it is through the disciplined labour of the slave that self-consciousness becomes transformative of feudalistic domination.[9] I will argue that the language and ideas deployed in structural sociologies sustain a highly abstract relationship of subjectivity and objectivity, a relationship in which the 'true' determinations of structure constantly threaten to engulf (homogenize, utilize, pauperize, etc.) the substance and particularity of the subject. Thus, if there is an explanatory necessity sustained by the 'architectonics' of social structure, this must be recognized as an inescapable violence which demands the reflective and re-formative activity of the subject. I will examine this more fully in the concluding section.

Structures, functions and systems

Durkheim and social realism

This section will examine the development of functionalism as a distinctive type of sociological explanation. My exposition, which could have taken Comte or Saint Simone as its starting point, will begin with Emile Durkheim's account of the relationship between social structure, social solidarity and ethical recognition. The justification for taking Durkheim as my beginning can be made quite readily within the terms of my speculative approach to the idea of ethical life. For what makes Durkheim interesting is the tension between his faith in a statistical–postivist method and his assertions about the 'organic' composition of modern social relations. There is, in other words, a fundamental contradiction in Durkheim's sociology, a contradiction which coheres around the objectivizing methodology he sets out in *The Rules of Sociological Method*,[10] and the ethic of self-realization which is postulated in *The Division of Labour in Society*.[11] Thus, my exposition of Durkheim's work will concentrate on his attempts to make the idea of subjective autonomy consistent with the 'external and constraining' necessity of social structure. For it is through this irresolvable contradiction that the concept of 'functionality' begins to develop its modern, systemic powers.

In *The Rules of Sociological Method*, Durkheim attempts to circumscribe the province of sociology as those structures and functions of the whole which exist independently of contingent individual differences. Thus, he remarks that 'social facts' are:

[T]ypes of behaviour and thinking external to the individual . . . endued with a compelling and coercive power by virtue of which, whether he wishes it or not, they impose themselves upon him. Even if in the end they are overcome, they make their constraining power sufficiently felt in the resistance that they afford. There is no innovator whose ventures do not encounter resistance of this kind.[12]

The sociologist, in other words, should concern himself or herself with stripping away the show of contingent individual differences in order to disclose the 'objective' necessities constituted in different social forms. It is this attempt to determine the objective being of social collectives (i.e., the independence and coerciveness of their laws, institutions, customs, dispositions, etc.) which distinguishes Durkheim's social realism from what we might call rational anthropology. For Durkheim, individual subjects are always already absorbed within the forces, tendencies, trans-actions and dissolutions which animate the life of the collective. Thus, 'subjectivity' and 'individuality' are forms whose possibility is given through the evolution of the collective, an evolution which has no need to refer beyond itself either to the innately social disposition of human beings, or to the rational contractual foundation of the law. Yet this methodological commitment to the 'objective' life of the totality is difficult to square with Durkheim's remarks on the ethical significance of modernity. For the 'autonomous' individual, whose emergence occupies Durkheim throughout *The Division of Labour*, remains ethically dependent upon powers (of organization, integration and unity) which 'pathologize' contradiction, dispersal and reflection.

Durkheim's notion of an objective science of society, then, entails an original – or rather an 'ontological' – dependency of the individual upon the life of the collective. It is the nature of this dependency which informs his two major works on modern industrial societies: *The Division of Labour in Society* and *Suicide: A Study in Sociology*.[13] Both of these studies are concerned with three fundamental issues: (1) the breakdown of traditional structures of integration and regulation (church, family, occupational organizations); (2) the disintegrative isolation of individuals from the collective life of the totality; and (3) the kind of ethical–political action needed to restore the conscience collective within the structures of modern industrial differentiation. I will examine the ethical and political consequences of Durkheim's thought in a moment. My present concern is to examine the idea of community which is developed in *The Division of Labour* and *Suicide*, and to specify the relationship between the modern 'reflective' subject and the 'objective' elements of its activity (norms, values, institutions, structures, etc.).

Broadly speaking, both *The Division of Labour* and *Suicide* are attempts to conceptualize the ethical significance of increasingly specialized social and economic relations. The former offers an account of how modern individualism has emerged through certain 'morphological' changes in social structure. According to Durkheim, these changes are precipitated through forces of expansion, specialization, conflict and mediation that belong exclusively to the realm of 'objective' necessity. *The Division of Labour*, therefore, presents what Durkheim regards as the animating tension within modernity, that is, the tendency of its technical determinations (mechanization, capitalization, specialization) to outstrip traditional forms of solidarity (family, religion, occupational group), without being able to restrain the egoism which they liberate. Thus, the concept of 'organic solidarity' is posited as an ideal which is implicit in the increasing specialization of social relations; but one that requires reflection to move beyond the demands of immediate self-interest. The contribution which *Suicide* makes to Durkheim's social ethics, then, is its reaffirmation of the collective as an absolute, universal necessity. According to the explanatory hypothesis, it is the attenuation of social bonds which precipitates an increasing suicide rate: for those who can find no satisfaction in the elements of collective life are cut off from the 'object' which ought to govern individual appetites and desires.[14] This question of the relationship between the 'moral' law of the totality and the egoistic 'nature' which brings chaos to the sacred life of the collective is important, and I will return to it. For the present, however, we need to look at the relationship between suicide and ontological dependency.

My principal concern with Durkheim's work is his attempt to prosecute a modern social ethics; and so I will concentrate primarily on his account of 'egoistic' and 'anomic' suicide. (The 'altruistic' and 'fatalistic' types that are also specified in his typology refer to premodern, 'mechanical' forms of solidarity.) The first of these categories refers to the individual's lack of commitment to social purposes and ideals, whereas the second proposes a causal relation between suicide and lack of social restraint upon individual aspirations and desires. Durkheim's idea of egoistic suicide draws upon his conviction about the inherently sacred nature of the collective. For it is only through the regulative satisfactions afforded by religious society, family life, occupational structures, etc., that the individual can retain its psychological equilibrium and moral integrity. As Durkheim puts it, 'We cling to these forms of human activity only to the degree that we cling to society itself'.[15] Once released from the bonds which attach it to society, the individual becomes less able to give meaning to its life: it can no longer refer the questions of existence, purpose and morality to the transcendent ideals of the collective. Durkheim famously associates the rise of religious individualism (Protestantism), the scepticism of intellectual elites, the decline of extended family ties, and the recurrence of political crises with the relatively high rates of suicide afflicting the most industrialized of Western European societies.

This account of industrialization and social disenchantment seeks to establish a relationship between the technical dynamics of modernity (what we might call the functional requirement for efficiency, flexibility, mobility and productivity within the 'organic' body of the collective) and the decline of traditional forms of moral solidarity. Durkheim's 'egoistic' self must act within the context of progressively slackening social bonds, and the increasing power and dispersal of the economic productivity. It is this dynamic, in which the individual is ceaselessly encouraged to abandon the restraints of an already declining *conscience collective*, which determines the emergence of 'anomie' as the primary suicidal motivation.

Durkheim traces the influence of anomie (or the absence of normative restraint upon the desires he associates with a chaotic human 'nature') upon suicidal motivation to the decline of marriage and the increasing influence of the economy on social solidarity. In an analysis which echoes Rousseau's concerns about the libidinization of political society, he describes the pernicious effects of unfettering male sexual desire from the conjugal responsibilities of marriage.[16] The increasing laxity of sexual mores, and the decline of family life as a source of moral and sexual stability, in other words, express a dangerous encroachment of sensualism upon the objectivity of the moral law. It is the notion 'economic anomie', however, which marks the emergence of a general tendency to overreach the regulative satisfactions established in the collective. For Durkheim, the constant extension of needs and desires, which occurs through the development of the economy, leads to a condition in which the will of the individual becomes increasingly utilitarian. The 'insatiable and bottomless abyss'[17] of natural desire is released from the restraint imposed by traditional forms of equilibration and solidarity: each individual, to a greater or lesser degree, understands the satisfaction (and transformation) of its own desires as the ultimate goal of its activity. Both prosperity and slump, therefore, are catastrophic for individuals who have generally come to recognize themselves as the creators of their own desires and satisfaction:

> From top to bottom of the scale, greed is aroused unable to find a foothold. . . . Men thirst for novelties, unknown pleasures, nameless sensations, which lose all their savour once experienced. Henceforth, men have no power to withstand the least reverse . . . [while this] passion for the infinite is daily presented as a mark of moral distinction, whereas it can only appear within unregulated consciences which elevate to a rule the lack of rule from which they suffer.[18]

Thus, the slackening of social bonds which industrialized economies tend to produce is associated with a constant agitation of desire against the established forms of collective life. It is this volatile and contingent state of the 'sovereign' individual which Durkheim presents as the social condition (cause) of anomic suicide.

Durkheim's remarks on the 'external and constraining' nature of the social in *The Rules of Sociological Method*, and his account of the relationship between suicidal motivation and social dissolution in *Suicide*, raise some important theoretical and methodological questions. I have tried to show that the principle of social realism should be understood as an objectification of the moral law. The institutions, modes of behaviour and general dispositions established in a given society constitute an organized whole: they determine the 'objective being' within which individual motivations and desires find their 'true' significance. (Where this transcendent significance is lost, the life of the Durkheimian individual becomes dangerously contingent and prone to self-destruction.) In a sense, then, Durkheim's project can be seen as an attempt to reconcile the 'categorical' demands of Kant's moral imperative with the 'external' necessity determined in his account of phenomenal experience. Indeed, he makes it clear in *The Elementary Forms of the Religious Life* that the 'representations' through which individuals recognize themselves and their responsibilities towards the other are 'essentially collective . . . depend[ent] upon the way in which it [the group] is founded and organised, upon its morphology, upon its religious, moral and economic institutions'.[19] The fundamental problem Durkheim identifies in modern industrialized societies is their lack of a regulative principle of unity (what Kant's epistemology refers to as the 'architectonic' of the whole). Without such a principle, the 'representations' through which the group is recognized become disordered; individuals, made rapacious by the wealth of the economy, mistake their particular desires for the objective necessity of the collective.[20] I need, then, to return to *The Division of Labour* for it is here that Durkheim attempts to expound the 'ethic' of mutual dependency which is immanent in modern forms of specialization.

According to Durkheim, primitive societies have a 'segmental' structure: each element of the whole has the same simple internal constitution and is largely self-subsistent. This type of society is distinguished by what Durkheim has called its 'low moral density'; each of the segments has only limited and infrequent contact with the others that make up the group. Primitive social cohesion is therefore rooted in the simple, homogeneous structure of the segments; individuals are attached to their particular communities through concrete bonds which relate to their immediate experience. Thus, the 'mechanical' cohesion through which Durkheim presents the idea of primitive society in *The Division of Labour* presupposes an immediate identity of individual and community. The cohesion of the segments is based upon their simple resemblance, rather than the differentiation characteristic of 'organized' societies.

The segmental type of society in which the emergence of mechanical solidarity is grounded marks the transition from nature to civilization. For Durkheim, it is the struggle for existence – a struggle pursued from the beginning by primitive tribes of hunter-gatherers – that produces the undifferentiated cohesion of segmental societies. This principle of grounding the development of social forms in the 'natural' laws of evolution is continued in Durkheim's account of how the transition from segmental to organized society is brought about. The primary factor involved in the emergence of social specialization is the increase in the 'volume' of population. The homogeneous elements which comprise segmental society, in other words, are brought into increasingly regular contact by the increasing density and concentration of their populations. Progress in the division of labour therefore is in direct proportion to the interaction of the segments which make up primitive societies:

> The division of labour develops . . . as there are more individuals sufficiently in contact to be able to act and react upon one another. If we agree to call this relation . . . dynamic or moral density, we can say that the progress of the division of labour is in direct ratio to the dynamic or moral density of society.[21]

Thus the internal differentiation of the totality proceeds through a 'mitigated resolution' of the struggle for existence: specialization of functions within each segment produces 'coexistence' rather than natural selection.[22]

Durkheim's account of organic solidarity attempts to show that it is the structural interdependence established in 'organized' societies that is the necessary condition of both individual autonomy and social cohesion. According to the argument developed in *The Division of Labour*, solidarity within 'higher' forms of society is no longer determined by the identity of simple, homogeneous segments. Although each institution remains dependent upon the 'objective' being of the totality, its function is unique, and as such, performed autonomously. 'Society', Durkheim maintains, 'is more capable of collective movement, at the same time as each of its elements has more freedom of movement'.[23] We are now beginning to approach the fundamental difficulty with Durkheimian sociology – that of reification and the loss of subjectivity. The progress of social specialization, according to *The Division of Labour*, is the condition of individuation and difference: 'the activity of each is as much more personal as it is more specialised'.[24] It is the autonomous individual within the structure of functional interdependence, therefore, who becomes the object of moral responsibility. With the emergence of organic solidarity, the collective progressively relinquishes its sacred-repressive-punitive determination, and the body of law through which it sustains itself, becomes increasingly concerned with the restoration of 'normal' co-operative relations.[25] Thus, it is the progress of specialization and individuation that determines the possibility of a moral, or 'conscientious', reflection upon the life of the collective. A reflection in which each would recognize the fulfilment of his or her individual potential in the specialized functions of the whole, the dependency of each function upon all the others, and the necessity of universal co-ordination to preserve the 'normal' state of social integration.

I began my exposition of Durkheim's sociology by suggesting that there is a Kantian strand which runs throughout his theoretical and methodological precepts. I claimed that *The Rules of Sociological Method* articulates an idea of 'the social' which is analogous to Kant's concept of the understanding: a transcendent, self-determining totality in which the existence of the individual appears only as contingent and inessential. What is of fundamental importance in Durkheim's appropriation of this Kantian idea of totality is his attempt to reconcile the determinations of 'the real' (exteriority, constraint, temporal persistence, etc.) with the necessity of the moral law (reflection, subjectivity, judgement, etc.). For Kant, such a reconciliation is impossible: the categorical imperative commands through the formalization of a concept – the good will as such – which cannot be realized in the realm of phenomenal experience. The moral law, in other words, is sustained through a will which has determined itself independently of all 'heteronomous' (i.e., social) relations and dispositions. We only need glance at Kant's historical and political writings to recognize that what Durkheim presents as the embodiment of moral necessity (the weight, volume, extent and mechanics of the social) is, for Kant, a type of inertia which demands the constant attention of alert and critical minds.[26] This difference (between Durkheim's 'positivistic' notion of totality, and Kant's account of the irreducible tension between 'autonomy' and 'heteronomy') is crucial, for it points up a powerful 'reifying' tendency in Durkheim's work. The social is conceived not just as the condition of the moral law, but as its reality. And so if we, as rational beings, are to retain the freedoms which social evolution has made possible, we must concentrate on refining the established functions of the whole. As Durkheim puts it:

> There is no longer need to pursue desperately an end which recedes as we move forward [à la Kant]; we need only to work steadily and persistently to maintain the normal state, to reestablish it if it is disturbed, and to rediscover the conditions of normality if they happen to change.[27]

Kant's spontaneous 'daring to know', in other words, is categorized as a potentially suicidal pathology, and we are reduced to a passive and methodical reproduction of 'the normal'.

For Durkheim, the historical emergence of organic solidarity is causally determined by qualitative and quantitative changes that take place in the structure of 'segmental' societies. A sustained increase in the size, number and density of the segments which comprise the social whole constitutes the 'factual' conditions which produce an increasingly complex division of labour. The specialized institutions which emerge within the social body perform functions which maintain the solidarity and equilibrium of the whole, just as, on Durkheim's analogy, the organs of the physical body combine to sustain its biological existence. Thus, the transition from mechanical to organic solidarity presented in *The Division of Labour* discloses the priority of structural causation in Durkheim's sociology. For it is not until organic interdependency has begun to emerge as a 'social fact' that it is possible for the individual to become the object of moral responsibility. In a sense, then, the 'freedom' which is immanent in the specialization of social relations has already been placed in the service of the totality. The 'moral' demand which Durkheim places upon the individual to become functionally autonomous, in other words, is taken directly from the 'mechanics' of social reproduction. Indeed, if we look at the analysis of 'Abnormal Forms', with which Durkheim concludes *The Division of Labour*, it becomes clear that his primary concern is with achieving the regulated equilibrium he regards as immanent in social specialization. The persistence of class conflicts, the 'misallocation' of social roles, and the lack of administrative co-ordination, which Durkheim identified as retarding the formation of organic solidarity, are presented as deviations from the 'normal' equilibrated condition of organized society.

The fundamental problem with Durkheim's sociology, then, is that it fails to give a proper account of the processes through which society 'appears' as an external and constraining force. Throughout *The Division of Labour*, the dependency of the individual is conceived as an original condition, a condition which demands constant recourse to the 'objective' laws of social volume, density, displacement and differentia-tion, if subjective phenomena – like reflection, autonomy and judgement – are to be understood in their proper 'sociological' context. Thus, where the 'fact' of interdependency has yet to produce its 'true' moral outcome (i.e., a sense of integration and satisfaction among most individuals), the isolation, anxiety and egoism which pervade the social whole are presented as contingent and transitional 'pathologies' (pathologies which Durkheim encourages us to associate with the amoral desires of 'nature').

Zygmunt Bauman, in *Modernity and the Holocaust*, offers some caution-ary remarks about the civilizing power that Durkheim attributes to social relations:

> [For Durkheim] . . . what matters is that there must be a moral system in every society, and not the substance of the norms this or that society happens to enforce in order to maintain its unity . . . all moral systems are equal in the sole respect in which they can be legitimately measured and evaluated: their utility for the satisfaction of that need.[28]

For Bauman, the occurrence of the Nazi genocide demands a re-evaluation of this structural model of morality. Durkheim's radical distinction between 'evil' nature and 'good' society simply took it for granted that the establishment of a coherent set of interdependent rules and institutions would reproduce itself as the antithesis of 'natural' violence and destructiveness. Yet the fact that the Holocaust was carried out through social, political and bureaucratic institutions, which were already in place at the time of the Nazi's secession to power, is for Bauman highly significant. What it suggests is that the supposedly moralizing force of modern social relations must be recognized as estab-lishing the possibility – or perhaps even the inevitability – of the Nazi genocide. The very institutions which Durkheim conceived as opening the way to an ethical, meritocratic and integrated modernity (i.e., func-tional differentiation, technical specialization and the constitution of 'rational' state authority) are represented as 'countervailing social forces' which impede moral recognition and judgement of the other.[29] For Bauman, it was the functional pressure which had already been established in modern social relations, coupled with their technical and bureaucratic distancing of individuals, which allowed the Nazi's logistical accomplishment of the Holocaust.

What is particularly important in Bauman's treatment of Durkheim is his examination of the relations obtaining between morality and instrumental reason. According to Bauman's analysis, the fundamental flaw in Durkheim's account of 'organized' social relations is his faith in the moralizing power of functional specialization. The 'architectonic' of ethical life expounded in *The Division of Labour* springs from the mechanics of social reproduction: it is the result of pressures generated by the increasing densities, condensations and contacts of populations. Thus, the evolution of the group from mechanical solidity to organic equilibrium is, for Durkheim, the condition of moral recognition, that is, of respect for the work, satisfaction and desire of the other. Bauman's account of modernity, however, makes it clear that this identification of structure (unity, integration, etc.) as the purpose and condition of ethical life is highly problematic. The fact of the Holocaust demands that we look at the way in which the functional and bureaucratic necessities constituted in modernity have resulted in the breakdown of moral bonds. We need, in other words, to examine how the system of functionally and bureaucratically differentiated relations has come to appear to most individuals as the 'objective' (and exclusive) condition of moral action.

Bauman's presentation of the Holocaust as essentially related to bureaucratic and technical erosions of human proximity, should alert us to the danger of confusing moral with instrumental necessities. His account of the increasing 'distance' which chains of bureaucratic command and technical specialization introduce between actions and their consequences, is founded upon Emmanuel Levinas's ethics of care. Instead of starting from the 'sociological' assumption that it is only the enculturated individual, embedded in societal forms and institutions, who can be considered a moral being, Bauman, following Levinas, claims that moral responsibility originates in the 'uncontainable' demand of the human face.[30] According to Levinas, it is 'being with others' that is the original condition of humanity, a condition in which 'the Other', as the proximate, expressive and irreducible demand of the face, 'opens the primordial discourse whose first word is obligation'.[31] In order to understand the powers of the social totality, therefore, we must recognize that its categories (the species, the class, the genus, etc.) participate in a homogenizing necessity which Levinas calls 'the same'. The originally visual (i.e., infinitely open, expressive and transcendent) demand which the face makes upon humanity in general, is displaced into *'accomplished'* (i.e., objectified) relations which tend to exclude moral recognition of 'the Other'.[32] It is this exposition of the relationship between violence and totality which guides Bauman's attempt to formulate an ethical, 'post-Aushwitzian', sociology, a sociology which would, in his own words, 'reach over the socially erected obstacles of mediated action and the functional reduction of the human self'.[33]

I began my exposition of Durkheim's sociology, by suggesting that there is a profound and irreconcilable contradiction between the methodological precepts set out in *The Rules of Sociological Method*, and the 'idealist' ethic postulated in *The Division of Labour*. Durkheim's concept of organic solidarity, we have seen, attempts to reconcile the functional/instrumental demands of the totality (reproduction, solidarity, unity, order, etc.) with certain 'autonomous' powers of the subject. These powers, however, among which we might include the exercise of judgement, reflection, re-cognition or practical reasoning, are fundamentally incompatible with the 'objective' functionality of the whole. For if we proceed, as Durkheim clearly does, from the Hobbesian postulate of 'natural' chaos and 'social' restraint, then every exercise of reflection or judgement must ultimately refer to the established demands of unity and cohesion. Recognition of the other – its work, satisfactions and desires – as moral or immoral, therefore, is restricted from the beginning to the language of normality (integration/cohesion) and pathology (chaos/dysfunction).[34]

So, the question remains: if Durkheim's attempt to reconcile the structural demands of the whole with a certain 'moral' spontaneity of its individuals, ends up by subordinating every act of judgement and reflection to the logic of social reproduction, how should we theorize the relationship between subjectivity and the 'objective' determinations of the whole? We have seen that Kant's idea of practical reason postulates an absolute distinction between the 'good will' as such (rational autonomy) and the 'heteronomous' determinations of the subject's social existence. The categorical imperative commands a 'respect' for the other which supposedly transcends every 'utilitarian' consideration (even if the content of Kant's ethics suggests that 'pure desire' is rather unhealthily attached to the satisfactions of bourgeois civil society). For Levinas, on the other hand, the very condition of social ontology (i.e., the reduction of ethical proximity to the condition of Being) is its foundation in the relationship of obligation to the face of 'the Other'. The capacity to 'reason', in other words, springs from the resemblance of the human face to God, a resemblance which cannot be totalized, and which 'commands' beyond the violent closure of the (social) totality. Both Kant and Levinas, then, attempt to expound the difference between the 'exteriority' of the whole and the 'interiority' of the moral commandment: Kant by asserting the formal correspondence of free will, integrity and respect; Levinas (and Bauman) by claiming that we must understand the idea of totality through its disruptions of ethical proximity ('being with others'). Yet this kind of critical scepticism towards the 'materiality' (Being) of ethical life has its own difficulties, the most urgent of which concerns the opposition postulated between the moral subject and 'immediate existence' of the social. This needs to be examined a little more fully.

We have seen that Hegel's *Phenomenology of Mind* is ultimately concerned with the way in which the 'concept' of self-conscious subjectivity (i.e., rational free will) has laboured to determine itself within the 'objective' purposes, institutions and dispositions of ethical life. As Hegel puts in the Preface:

> The mind's immediate existence, conscious life, has two aspects – cognition and objectivity which is opposed to or negative of the subjective function of knowing. Since it is in the medium of consciousness that the mind develops and brings out its various moments, this opposition between the factors of conscious life is found at each stage of the evolution of mind, and all the various moments appear as modes or forms of consciousness.[35]

The development of self-consciousness through historical time, in other words, takes place through the formation of 'subjectivity' within ethical life, a formation which includes the participation of subjective wants, desires and representations in 'established' forms of dominance and subordination. (We might, for example, recall that the disciplined labour of the slave, and his 'enforced' asceticism, is what sustains, and ultimately transforms, the edifice of feudal relations.) Throughout the historical transitions expounded in the *Phenomenology of Mind*, it is the category of 'activity' – or 'the principle of negation, in the form of the activity of the Self' – which constantly transforms the 'inwardness' of the subject (intention, desire, reflection, etc.) into 'factual' elements within ethical life. Thus, the 'external' determinations of *Sittlichkeit* – what we might call its established content and organization – are 'necessary' (constraining, determinate) only in so far as they already include the 'inner' formation of subjectivity. Speculatively conceived, then, the structures, institutions and relations of the totality always refer to the 'formation' of self-consciousness; that is, to a 'subject' whose 'idea' is always active, but never historically realized.

The relationship I have attempted to expound between Kant's critical epistemology and Durkheim's social thought is important for two reasons. First, it has allowed me to specify a certain 'objectifying' force in Durkheim's account of sociality and the moral law: a force which repeats the Kantian dominance of 'unity and articulation' (the formal concept) over the particularity of 'affection' (the intuitions, inclinations, desires of the subject *formed historically within ethical life*). For Durkheim, in other words, the moral law is always identical with a positive, or 'postulated', integrity of the whole: 'social cohesion is maintained in the face of its perceived absence which is conceptualised as anomie or dysfunctions'.[36] Yet within Durkheimian sociology there remains the trace of an idealist ethic, which suggests that 'modernity' (once it has overcome its 'pathological' forms) will progressively reduce the deterministic constitution of the collective. For within 'organized' social forms, according to

The Division of Labour, 'the unity of the organism is as great as the individuation of its parts'.[37] In a sense, then, this returns us to the influence of Kant, for the primacy of practical reason which emerges from the critical philosophy (i.e., its dominance over the 'heteronomous' influences of the finite, the material, the embodied) turns upon a reworking of the idea of totality: in the second *Critique* it is no longer presented as the a priori condition phenomenal experience, but rather as the unity of the (good) will in willing itself as the universal 'end' of its actions. What is important here is that both Kant and Durkheim attempt to determine the 'organic' constitution of totality (i.e., the compatibility of a unified set of ends and relations with the moral freedom of the subject) through categories which have already excluded the possibility of ethical mediation. The individual, with its particular desires, satisfactions and recognitions, in other words, is always impossibly alien to the 'universal' (postulated, structural) conditions of rational autonomy. Thus, if Durkheim is a positivist, it is because he has taken the formality/ideality of Kant's moral imperative and reproduced it as the objective/determining necessity of 'civilization'.

Yet structural sociology does not end with Durkheim's heroic effort to integrate freedom, morality and functional necessity. Indeed, his 'ethical' struggle with the most basic problems of modernity – increasing industrialization, social disenchantment and moral deregulation – appears unreservedly idealistic in comparison with the more 'systemic' approaches his thought has inspired. So far we have seen that within Durkheim's work there is a tension between the demands of unity and order and those of subjective autonomy, a tension which tends to be resolved by maintaining the 'necessity' of social cohesion, even where that necessity has, as a matter of fact, become unrecognizable within the substance of ethical life. I will argue that the development of the structural paradigm in modern social thought is characterized by a progressive decline of ethical responsibility towards the subject, a decline which, while it has its historical roots in Durkheim's thought, has crucially shifted the debate away from the activity/spontaneity of the individual towards the 'administration' of the system. There is, in other words, a determination to treat the subject as a kind of 'micro-system' of the totality, rather than as a discrete form which demands recognition of its particularity. We need, then, to examine the consequences of postulating structure, function, integration and stability as necessities which determine the extent to which the individual can be recognized as an 'object' of ethical responsibility.

Structural functionalism and system theory

In one of his earliest works, *The Structure of Social Action* (1968), the American sociologist Talcott Parsons attempted to reformulate Durkheim's solution to the problem of social cohesion. Drawing on the voluntaristic elements of Weber's sociology, he attempted to show that the idea of organic interdependence, developed in *The Division of Labour*, involves a 'normative' aspect which is essential to the concept of social action. The norms and values which are established in any viable social form, in other words, do not determine the actions of individual subjects; rather, they provide the bases upon which voluntary choices are made and acted upon. Social action, as such, takes place within a context of normative presuppositions which it spontaneously reproduces. Thus, the apparent antagonism of autonomy and solidarity is overcome in *The Structure of Social Action*, by proposing that the conditions of voluntaristic activity are originally social, and that 'free' actions necessarily reproduce the value consensus which have made them possible. This early emphasis on the voluntaristic component of social action, however, is replaced in Parsons' later work by a concentration on the functional/ integrative necessity of normative patterns. It is this shift towards a general theory of social integration, therefore, which demands our attention.

In both *The Social System* (1951) and the *Working Papers in the Theory of Action* (1953), Parsons attempted to develop a universal hypothesis about the way in which social systems reproduce themselves. According to Parsons' hypothesis, any society which has sustained itself through time as a normative system must be considered as a unity of three analytically distinct systems: personality, sociality and culture. The first of these systems, personality, is conceived by Parsons as inclusive of all the psychological and physiological characteristics which affect social functioning. Thus, in order to develop his idea of society as an integrated whole, Parsons conceptualized the individual as a system of desires which it is possible to direct towards socially patterned goals. The social system, according to this model, functions to prioritize the cognitive over the 'cathectic' elements of action: it restrains the immediate psychological and physiological affections of the individual, and channels them into legitimate forms of satisfaction and production. Sexuality, for example, is integrated into the system through shared expectations about marriage, procreation and familial care. At the top of Parsons' hierarchy of systems is culture. This is the most organized and universal aspect of the totality, comprising the body of shared beliefs, standards and symbols which underpin every 'empirical' social form. It is through the cultural system, according to Parsons, that individuals are able to act purposively within a system of mutual expectations. For without this general agreement about what is ethically desirable, the social, economic, legal and political institutions through which society reproduces itself could not perform their universal/integrative functions.

For Parsons, social interaction is organized through roles whose significance is structured by particular institutions. These institutions, we have seen, can evolve as functional for society as a whole only on the presupposition of a fundamental value consensus, or system of cultural

legitimation. What Parsons' theory of social systems attempts to establish, in other words, is that the very possibility of social cohesion in
complex societies depends upon an original consensus, and that the
primary task of sociological research is to explain how social forms
institutionalize and perpetuate their core values. So, if it is given that a
particular society has been successful in deploying its values throughout
the institutional structure, and that it has ensured their intergenerational
transmission through the family and educational systems, how is social
change to be 'functionally' accounted for?

The Parsonian response to this question is that the theory of functional
integration should be regarded as an ideal (or analytical abstraction) to
which no society actually conforms. All empirical social types, according
to Parsons' hypothesis, must be able to meet three basic functional
requirements: (1) adaptation to, and control over, their environment;
(2) transmission of core values to succeeding generations; and (3) provision of opportunities for the achievement of socially valued goals. The
systems through which these necessities are met, are, on Parsons'
understanding, responsive to specific needs which change and evolve at
different rates. A particular society's potential to control its population
and environment, for example, may come into conflict with its basic core
values. Thus, each system is always changing and reproducing social
equilibrium as a state of dynamic action and reaction. Indeed, Parsons
and Bales, in their essay 'The Dimensions of Social Space', attempt to
express this general tendency of social forms to sustaining a dynamic
state of equilibrium, in four 'laws' of systemic interaction. Taken as a
whole, these state that all viable social forms are differentiated into
distinct systems which reciprocally influence each other's development,
and that the overall tendency articulated through systemic action and
reaction 'is the integrative balance of the system'.[38]

My exposition of Durkheim's sociology attempted to show that there
is a profound contradiction between, on the one hand, the positivistic
methodology prescribed in *The Rules of Sociological Method* and, on the
other, the ethic of mutual recognition postulated in *The Division of Labour*.
I suggested that this contradiction is important because it signifies an
acknowledgement of the individual as a form whose 'conscience' (self-
reflection, autonomy) demands recognition in (restitutive) law. Thus,
despite the obvious tendency in Durkheim's work to refer moral
questions to the established integrity of the whole, there is a tenuously
ethical acknowledgement of the individual, an acknowledgement which
remains troubling for the discourse of structural causality. Parsonian
functionalism can, in a sense, be understood as attempting to resolve this
tension between ethical and systemic regulation. For in treating society
purely as a systemic whole, Parsons' later work almost completely
subsumes the activity of the subject under the functional requirements of
integration and cohesion. Any attempt to describe subjectivity as a
reflective or critical element within the system is abandoned, and we are

left with an increasingly 'reified' conception of functional necessity. The logic of structural functionalism therefore determines a methodological approach in which: (1) the significance of social institutions is always assessed in terms of their contribution to the integrity of the whole; (2) antagonism, coercion and conflict are reduced to 'accidents', external to the 'Being' of the whole; and (3) consensus is simply assumed as the goal and foundation of every empirical social form.

So far, our account of functionalist rationality has concentrated on the progressive reduction of 'the subject' to a psychical/cathectic system, whose drives must be regulated by a coherent set of values, and whose abilities must be channelled into the achievement of socially sanctioned ends. By the time we arrive at Parsons' later work, therefore, the concept of social action has become intrinsically linked to the reproduction and gradualistic modification of established values and institutions. Yet Parsonian functionalism does maintain a certain generic relationship to Kant's critical idealism. For while there is an obvious movement away from the 'organic' conception of totality deployed in Durkheim's work, there is a sense in which Parsons' work still understands 'the social system' as a kind of articulated whole, whose universal reproduction is immanent in each particular relation and institution. The norms and values postulated as the condition of social functionality, in other words, presuppose an implicit identification of 'the whole' with the synthetic activity of 'the self' (i.e., Kant's 'transcendental unity of apperception'). In Niklas Luhmann's account of the social system, however, the referent of subjective idealism – the socially organizing concept of reflective con- sciousness – is finally, and explicitly, abandoned. We are left only with the punctual contacts of 'relations-to-self'.[39] This needs to be explained.

According to Luhmann, the 'hypercomplex' nature of modern insti- tutions and relations forbids the deployment of an idealist notion like 'value consensus' of 'organic solidarity' (both of these ideas presuppose that the social system is a unitary 'subject', which acts to preserve its socio-ethical integrity). Luhmann's individual is adaptive rather than reflective or critical (in the Kantian sense): it is a 'psychical system' that originates in 'vital bodily feeling',[40] and which 'learns' through the impingement of external stimuli. The subject/individual is cropped down to a punctual ego, whose 'consciousness' is rooted in the adaptive necessity determined by its immediate environment. It is this precon- scious, prelinguistic capacity to respond which Luhmann identifies with the origin of 'meaning': the set of internal, system-specific conditions which determine the potential for learning and action. It is this origina- tion of 'meaning' in the 'physical-chemical-organic' constitution of 'life'[41] (and its development through the 'private' functions of cognition/ consciousness) which therefore, determines the external and contingent nature of 'communication' in Luhmann's system theory.

Unlike Habermas, Luhmann does not elaborate his theory of com- munication through an originally intersubjective idea of consciousness.

Rather, the complex relationships which characterize modernity are presented as an outcome of the private/atomistic development of individual consciousness. The social system, in other words, emerges as a powerful modification of the environment of each meaning-possessing system: each consciousness ('psychical system') encounters 'the other' as an adaptive necessity to which it must continually respond. There is, for Luhmann, no transcendental or practico-linguistic unity to be discovered within the social system: there is only the aggregation of many 'system related environments', and their external and contingent relations:

> They [meaning processing systems] remain separate, they do not fuse, they do not understand one another better than they did before; they concentrate on what they can observe about the other as a system-in-an-environment, as input and output, and they learn self-referentially, each within its own observational perspective. They can try to influence what they observe through their own action, and they can learn once again from feedback. In this way, an emergent order can arise . . . we call this the social system.[42]

Rational thought, therefore, cannot 'productively' intervene in this systemic organization as long as it retains its attachment to 'metaphysical' ideas of totality, mediation and reflection. For Luhmann, any discourse which attempts to determine ends transcendent of the system specific meanings is 'metaphysical', for it has failed to recognize the ('politico-administrative') necessity of resolving localized disturbances in the 'emergent order' of the social system. It is worth noting here that this functional schematics is very close to Michel Foucault's exposition of the relationship between power and knowledge. For both Luhmann and Foucault, the categories of metaphysical thought (reflective synthesis, moral subjectivity, human essence, etc.) must be understood against the background of systemic integration. The issue, in other words, has become that of assessing the effects of holding something to be true (for example, that I am a moral consciousness whose autonomy springs from the legislative spontaneity of my reason), rather than attempting to stipulate the a priori conditions of moral, ethical or political truth. I will come back to Foucault's 'genealogical' account of instrumental reason in Chapter 4.

Luhmann's system theory works by originally embedding the concept of meaning in biological self-maintenance. As we have seen, his determination to theorize the emergence of consciousness as a continuation of organizational processes of adaptation sustains an irreducible distinction between the 'psychical system' of the individual and the communicative environment of the social system. Individual egos, in other words, only ever 'communicate' through external and contingent contacts, contacts which produce no more than discrete moments of self-referential learning. The fundamental difficulty here, as Habermas rightly points out,[43] is that the gap between the self-referential meanings attributed to consciousness and the social system always remains unbridged. The idea of 'sociality' is no more than an empty construction, with no history of moral, ethical or political formation of self-consciousness. There is simply the demand that the state should administer the system with the utmost regard for its untroubled ('noiseless') reproduction.

Habermas's own version of 'postmetaphysical' thinking, however, ultimately does little to reinstate the 'substance' of modern sociality. His critique of 'subject-centred' reason[44] attempts to show that subjectivity, in its very concept, involves reference to universal rules of communicative action. 'Consciousness', in other words, is originally grounded in practico-linguistic principles which refer to the 'intersubjective' (dialogical) conditions of experience. As we will see in the following chapter however, Habermas's idea of communicative reason retains a certain 'abstract' necessity: his postulation of the 'ideal speech situation' as a regulative idea strongly suggests the loss of the conditions of finitude through which mutual recognition is possible. Thus although Habermas is right to claim that Luhmann's cybernetic discourse is potentially a very powerful determinant of how the individual recognizes itself in modern society, he fails to acknowledge that the discourse of systemic reproduction has a history in which the reduction of contingency is the primary theoretical aim. It might be suggested, then, that there is a sense in which Habermas's communicative rationality substitutes an abstract conception of 'consensus' for the repetitions of Luhmann's system theory. Speculative thought, on the other hand, would be bound to investigate the conditions under which self-consciousness has come to abandon itself to this type of 'metamaterialism'. How has it been possible for 'individuality' to become so homogenized that it no longer recognizes itself as a 'subject' active within differentiated moral contexts? I will return to this question.

Historically, the (sociological) critique of functionalism has grown out of Marx's concern with the violence and distortion to which capitalism – or rather the capitalist mode of production – has subjected the whole of productive/creative humanity. Horkheimer and Adorno's attempt to 'focus understanding more clearly upon the nexus of rationality and social actuality',[45] for example, is an attempt to expound the way in which the logic of calculation and control has come to dominate the cultural and institutional life of modern capitalism. Anything which cannot be included in this 'positive' logic (critical reflection, individual difference, etc.) is determined as both 'meaningless' and 'unproductive'. This account of the relationship between capitalism/industrialism and the objectifying power of instrumental reason raises a number of fundamental questions about the relations sustained between modernity and rationality, and culture and subjectivity: (1) How does reason determine the limits and possibilities of emancipatory activity?; (2) What is the relationship between 'instrumental' reason and the exercise of power/force?; (3) How is it possible to understand ideas of judgement, reflection and autonomy within the edifice of social reproduction?; and (4) How can we recognize and understand the idea of difference – its

moral, social and political demands – within the determinations of
functional/instrumental necessity? These questions are, of course, the
staples of what Habermas has called the philosophical discourse of
modernity: they frame the possibility of modern social theoretical
discourse. As we will see in the following chapters however, the tendency in modern and, for want of a more precise term, 'postmodern'
social thought has been away from the Marxian categories which remain
essential to Horkheimer and Adorno's critique of 'rational' capitalism.
Indeed, the most urgent formulations of the relationship between
instrumental reason and social formation – those of Habermas and
Foucault – both attempt, in different ways, to specify the possibility of
'agency' (reflection, initiation, transgression, etc.) without adverting to
the categories of historical materialism (*homo faber*, alienation, productivism, etc.). I will return to these debates. For the moment, however, I
need to determine the relationship of Marx's critique of 'capitalism' to
my speculative account of ethical life.

Marx's critique of capital

In his preface to the first German edition of *Capital*, Marx famously
stipulates that the antagonisms determined within capitalist societies are
not a matter of localized conditions (nature), bad planning or differences
in the character of national populations: 'Intrinsically, it is not a question
of the higher or lower degree of the development of these social
antagonisms that result from the natural laws of capitalist production. It
is a question of these laws themselves, of these tendencies working with
iron necessity towards inevitable results.'[46] Capitalism, in other words,
has a single, unilinear 'history', the history of an increasingly sharp
antagonism between the exploiters and the exploited, the bourgeoisie
and the proletariat. For Marx, this distinctively 'modern' antagonism
represents the highest point in the evolution of exploitative relations. The
expropriation of surplus value from legally emancipated wage labour
allows the growth of a system of a moral, ethical and political institutions whose 'purpose' is to justify the continued existence of private
property and exploitation. Thus, the capitalist 'mode of production'
cannot reproduce stability and integration as a genuinely ethical
demand, for the very conditions of its possibility (extension of legal
freedoms, dissolution of feudalistic ties, decline of the rural economy)
mean that the institutions which have come to promote social solidarity
(law, family, church, education, etc.) are originally implicated in the
'demands' of capitalist accumulation. For Marxists, the discourse of
'functionalism' is essentially bourgeois, for it fails to acknowledge that
the history of capitalism – the demographic shifts, the concentration of
labour in manufactures, the introduction and development of productive technologies, etc. – is one of violence and coercion.

It is clear, even from this rather brutal introduction, that Marx's account of the 'iron necessity', through which capitalism determines its historical fate, involves a number of discrete elements that I will need to examine separately. The first of these is the notion of human essence which Marx develops in his 'early' writings – especially the *Economic and Philosophical Manuscripts of 1844* (1977b) and *The German Ideology* (1977c). Of particular importance here is the notion of *homo faber* – or man the free creator – which informs Marx's account of the 'history' of exploitative social relations. Secondly, I will need to look at Marx's claim that *Capital* (1977a) presents a 'scientific' critique of the capitalist economic relations. In particular, I need to evaluate his attempt to specify the 'law of the motion of modern society' (i.e., increasing polarization, exploitation, emiseration and alienation)[47] as something which operates universally and objectively in all capitalist economies. Thirdly, there is the question of the relationship between 'theory and praxis', or the way in which Marx's pronouncements on the – essentially negative – nature of capitalist reality can become a revolutionizing/emancipatory force. These questions will return us to many of the fundamental problems we have already encountered in structural thought, problems which, although differently formulated by Marx, repeat the Kantian oppositions of necessity and contingency, structure and agent, universal and particular.

In order to understand Marx's account of capitalist exploitation it is necessary to look in some detail at his early writings on the nature of self-consciousness, productive/transformative activity and human essence. The significance of these primary categories is most clearly set out in the *Economic and Philosophical Manuscripts of 1844*. Here Marx attempts to articulate the concept of human essence through the negativity of capitalist relations of production: private property, wage-labour, class antagonism and the division of labour are expounded in terms of what Marx calls 'the *actual* economic fact'[48] of productive activity performed in the service of capital. The structure of Marx's argument therefore attempts to establish labour (i.e., the spontaneous transformation of the 'inorganic body' of nature) as the activity through which humanity reproduces itself – both spiritually and materially. It also establishes the conditions of a 'materialist' critique, in which it is the antagonistic/contradictory organization of the forces of production that becomes the primary focus of social and historical analyses.[49]

The concept of 'estranged' labour which Marx develops in the *Economic and Philosophical Manuscripts* articulates the loss of a truly human existence, in which the transformation of nature is simultaneously the transformation of humanity (both individually and as a 'species'). It is only by objectifying itself in the natural environment, in other words, that humanity is able to recognize its essential freedom, that is, its capacity to create/produce independently of fixed, instinctual needs. As Marx puts it: 'An animal forms objects only in accordance with the need of the species. . . . Man also forms objects in accordance with the laws of beauty.'[50] Humanity's original recognition of itself as the universally creative species therefore presupposes an organic nature which has yet to be appropriated by 'objective' (antagonistic, historical) forces and relations of production. For while the commerce of human self-consciousness and 'nature' begins with the sentiments of 'natural religion' (awe, dependency, worship, etc.), Marx makes it clear that there is a moment when 'primitive' societies – with their spontaneously 'social' distribution of the means of subsistence – would have maintained a non-alienated, and essentially satisfying form of labour.[51] Yet this Rousseauist ideal of 'natural' subsistence and co-operation is doomed to be corrupted by the emergence of the division between 'material' (productive) and 'mental' (ideological) labour; a division which, according to Marx, is the precondition of the differential – and antagonistic – forms of 'enjoyment and labour, production and consumption'[52] which determine the history of class conflict.

Under the conditions of a capitalist economy (these conditions appear even in Marx's early writings as the finality of exploitation; the *telos* of the history of class conflict), the product of labour power – the commodity – is expropriated immediately it is produced. Thus, instead of transforming nature into a human realm – a realm in which the social, material and creative needs of humanity would be recognized and fulfilled – labour constantly recreates nature as capital. The commodities which are produced do not reflect the spontaneous creativity of the labourer; rather, they are established as a realm of objects which stand independent of, and opposed to, his/her humanity. As private property, in other words, nature has become estranged from the labourer both as the material condition of creativity (*praxis*) and as the 'means of life', for the propertyless class has no right to dispose of the product of its labour (either individually or collectively), and must subsist on wages fixed by capital. As Marx puts it, 'estranged labour tears from him [man] his *species life* . . . and transforms his advantage over animals into the disadvantage that his inorganic body, nature, is taken away from him'.[53] Considered on its 'subjective side', this relationship of the worker to the product of his labour power is one of constant self-estrangement. For the transformative activity which ought to express the universality ('species life') of human beings has become no more than the 'means to physical existence'. And it is only through the 'animal' pleasures of 'eating, drinking, procreating, etc.', that each individual recognizes – or rather misrecognizes – its 'humanity' (freedom, autonomy).

These early attempts to expound the relationship between capital and the 'species being' of humanity raise a number of important questions about Marx's work – including *Capital*'s 'scientific' account of the laws of capitalist production. The concept of 'estranged labour' which Marx sets out in the *Economic and Philosophical Manuscripts*, as we have seen, is determined through the idea of a 'natural' beginning. Human consciousness is originally submerged in a nature which is 'as yet hardly modified historically'.[54] Thus, there is little differentiation within tribes of hunter-gathers because their relationship to nature is one of almost complete, unmediated dependency. Yet, it is this origination of a 'conscious instinct' which presages Marx's notion of a 'natural' community of human beings. For the 'inorganic body' of nature, while it is still largely untransformed, supports a community in which the division of labour springs 'spontaneously' from the sexual characteristics of the species, and the distribution of the means of subsistence is uncorrupted by the demands of private property. This account of 'primitive communism' is important for a number of reasons. First, like Rousseau's conception of 'the state of nature', it establishes a kind of ideal against which the 'artificial', or rather, to use Marx's terminology, the 'abstract' relations of actual historical forms, can be judged. Secondly, it discloses a certain dialectical relationship between the 'perfectibility' (self-transformative power) of humankind and the 'corruption' it must suffer in order to regain its original humanity. And finally, it gestures towards a political ideal of 'socialized production', in which the natural unity of the 'beginning' will be reconciled with the productive forces which have developed through the history of class antagonisms.

The 'beginning' of Hegel's *Phenomenology of Mind* makes it clear that the movement of 'consciousness' (natural, immediate desire) into the determinations of 'self-consciousness' (i.e., the relations through which the other has become an object of 'ethical' concern for the living, desirous 'I') is the displacement of 'nature' as 'sensuous immediacy'. The struggle for recognition between immediately 'negative' individualities – a struggle in which each is fighting to preserve the 'consiousness' of an 'other' whom he must kill to preserve himself – eventually produces a moment of capitulation. One will break off from the struggle before the moment of its annihilation, and in so doing, will place himself in the service of the other. It is this moment of 'recognition' – the recognition of absolute dominance, the right of life and death – which founds the Hegelian conception of ethical life (*Sittlichkeit*). The slave, having sacrificed any right to universal recognition, must dedicate his life to labour and servitude: he must occupy the position of mediator between the brute exteriority of nature, and the violent, consuming consciousness of the master. What is important here is that Hegel's account of the transition from nature to civilization does not begin by idealizing the relationship between nature and humanity. Unlike Marx's account of the 'natural unity' that emerges from the instinctual/sensual life of human beings, Hegel's presentation of 'the state of nature' acknowledges that ethical life must emerge from the complete submersion of consciousness in the cycle of desire–consumption–satisfaction–desire. Such an acknowledgement means that the social being of humanity, once it has emerged from the repetitions of natural consciousness, must be conceived as the totality through which 'nature', 'work', 'satisfaction' and 'desire' are mediated. Speculatively understood, there are no 'abstract' social relations in Marx's sense: there is no single, homogeneous history in which each 'mode of production' (ancient slavery, feudalist agrarianism, etc.) determines a particular moment of 'estrangement' on the way to the universal alienation of capitalism. Thus, Hegel's proposition that 'What is rational is actual and what is actual is rational',[55] expresses the necessity we recognize as the infinitely re-formative relationship between 'objective spirit' (state, economy, polity, church, etc.) and self-consciousness. In order to understand the 'substance' of ethical life, in other words, we must recognize that there is no 'natural' (i.e., non-contradictory) unity immanent in its historical development. Such a recognition obviously demands a fundamental reassessment of Marx's social, historical and political thought. I will come to this in a moment.

Capital's analysis of commodity production presupposes the general conditions of expropriation and estrangement set out in the *Economic and Philosophical Manuscripts*. The wage labourer is presented as a legally (formally) free individual who is constrained to sell his labour power in order to acquire the means of subsistence. Capital, on the other hand, is organically and, as Marx would have it, fatally tied to labour power. For without it, the means of production (land, machinery, factories, raw materials, etc.) could not produce commodities for sale on the open market. Thus, it is labour (in its commodified form of labour power) which creates the exchange values through which capitalist economies revolutionize the forces of production. According to Marx, the products which constantly expand market economy take on an increasingly 'fetishistic' form. Their 'use value' is totally obscured by their 'exchange value', and the 'natural' bond between labour and communal need is utterly displaced from the sphere of transformative activity. As Marx expresses it:

> The character of having value, once impressed upon products, obtains fixity by reason of their acting and re-acting upon each other as quantities of value. These quantities vary continually, independently of the will, foresight and action of producers. To them, their own social action takes the form of objects, which ruled the producers instead of being ruled by them.[56]

In other words, the 'representation' of the commodity as 'exchange value' (i.e., as the general determination of 'objectivity' within civil society) has ceased to be purely 'subjective'; it has passed over into the realm of moral, ethical and political relations among self-conscious individuals. This is an unusually speculative piece of analysis given Marx's tendency to conceive capitalism as an 'objectively' negative totality. Indeed, its presentation of the relationship between 'subjectivity' and the 'objective' conditions of its action gestures towards a far more complex idea of social formation than appears in Marx's political writings.

In essence, *Capital* is an attempt to expound the 'iron necessity' with which capitalism determines its historical fate. The general tendencies he identifies as determining the way in which capitalist economies develop – equalization of the rate of profit, centralization and concentration of capital, the general tendency of the rate of profit to fall – are expressions of a fundamental antagonism between the 'social' nature of production and the private appropriation of surplus value. For Marx, the establishment of trade and the free market, together with a complex division of labour and the mechanization of production, constitute a 'socialized' activity which expands productive forces, increases the stock of social wealth, and develops human needs beyond mere subsistence. Under the conditions of private appropriation, however, this socialization can only serve to intensify the contradictions inherent in the mode of production. For as long as exchange value retains its 'fetishized' necessity for each individual producer, the expansion and intensification of productive activity will continue to be determined by the demands of profit, rather than social need. Production, in other words, is carried on in abstraction from the real needs of the community: commodities are produced only because they represent the best opportunity for profit at a given stage in the capitalization of productive forces. 'It cannot be otherwise in a mode of production in which labour exists to satisfy the self-expansion of existing values . . . instead of material wealth existing to satisfy the needs of development on the part of the labourer.'[57]

At the beginning of the section, I suggested that the difficulties involved in articulating distinctively 'Marxist' critiques of the social, ethical and political institutions of capitalist societies stem from Marx's account of the origin of human self-consciouness. The idea of a 'species being' which is articulated in the *Economic and Philosophical Manuscripts* and in the *German Ideology*'s 'Theses on Feuerbach' presents this self-consciousness as issuing from what Marx calls 'sensuous activity', that is, from the original unity of consciousness with its 'inorganic body' – the realm of nature. Thus, Marx's postulation of 'human-sensuous activity'[58] as a transformative commerce between nature and consciousness provides the foundation for a critique both of 'contemplative materialism' (in which nature remains a distinct, objective presence to be 'apprehended') and 'abstract idealism' (in which 'sensuous' activity awaits its integration into the higher categories of 'spirit').[59] What Marx is suggesting, in other words, is that the origin of 'humanity' must be understood as a 'practical' relation to nature; a relation in which productive activity remains the determining 'force' of social and historical change. As he puts it in the 'Theses': 'All social life is essentially *practical*. All mysteries which lead theory to mysticism find their rational solution in human practice and in the comprehension of this practice.'[60] What is important here, is that this supposedly *practical* account of consciousness's relationship to social life is grounded in a moment of non-speculative idealism: the concept of a 'natural' community of human beings. Marx's attempt to formulate a comprehensive critique of capitalism presupposes this unity, for it is only by postulating a naturally unified beginning that

he is able to expound the history of human social relations as the history
of estrangement, antagonism and conflict.

This essentially negative representation of 'superstructural' relations
('bourgeois' morality, legality, religion, politics, aesthetics, etc.) is fundamental to Marx's account of politics, revolution and social critique.
Throughout Marx's work, the 'practical' domination sustained by
capitalist relations of production is expounded as the absolute formative
moment of self-consciousness. In a 'class society', an individual's relationship to the institutions which constitute his or her social existence
(the law, the family, the education system, etc.), is always already determined by his or her relationship to the means of production. Marx's
'bourgeoisie' are therefore those whose collective interest is to maintain
the 'ideological' structures through which private appropriation is
legitimized, whereas the 'proletariat' are those whose class identity
is grounded in the universal estrangement of productive labour. Thus,
it is the identification and articulation of a proletarian identity that is the
essence of Marxism – both as a critical discourse and as a political
project. All those directly involved in creating wealth within the system
of capitalist relations – and by 'directly' Marx would understand the
'organic' contribution that only labour power can make to the production of commodities – are subject to the alienation, deskilling and
emiseration determined by the drive for profit. The relationship of the
working class to the social and economic relations of capitalism therefore
is universally negative, for it cannot recognize its humanity either in the
production of commodities, or in the moral, ethical and political institutions of bourgeois civil society. One of the major themes of Marx's
essay 'On the Jewish Question', for example, is the constitution of the
'Christian state' through political rights which reflect only the formal
freedom of the 'allegorical or moral person'.[61] It is this process of
theological re-presentation (man as equal in the sight of God, rather than
man as 'materially' equal) which serves to reinforce the 'objective'
necessity of capitalist economic relations.

Marxist 'science' has developed by constantly reconceptualizing the
relationship between the economic 'base' and the cultural/ideological
'superstructure' of capitalist societies. Thus, the evolution of capitalism
through forms which appear to displace the categories of historical
materialism (for example, the emergence of knowledge and information
as the new currency of exchange value) demands the continued production of a 'critique', which explains how bourgeois ideology has
managed to preempt revolutionary class consciousness. Ultimately, there
is no social form, institution or practice which can appear in the Marxist
equation without its already having been judged in terms of the (fixed,
posited) antagonism between capital and labour. It is precisely this
objectification of the relationship between transformative activity
(labour) and the universal estrangement of ethical life (capitalism)
that is central to our speculative understanding of the Marxist project.

Louis Althusser's attempt to expound the 'structural' truth contained in *Capital*, for example, maintains that although the legal, political and cultural antagonisms determined in capitalist societies cannot be reduced to the simple reproduction of surplus value, they must be referred to a 'structure in dominance', whose unity is 'fixed in the last instance by the level of the economy'.[62] Thus, even though this 'lonely hour of the "last instance"'[63] may never come, our search among the play of 'condensations' and 'displacements' of power in the mode of production has already determined the ground and possibility of this power, and of its exercise. The 'science' which Althusser attempts to extract from *Capital* therefore explicitly abandons the 'metaphysical' categories (dialectically transformative labour, perfectible human essence, ontological estrangement, etc.) through which Marx originally developed his account of bourgeois economic relations. The Marxist critique of modernity, in other words, must remain at the level of 'structural causes', for nothing of true social, political or historical significance can be attributed to individual subjects who are merely 'supports' of the 'places and functions determined by the mode of production'.[64]

Labour, for Althusser, has none of the excessive, transformative potential which Marx attributed to it in his early work. Modes of production are presented as structural/objective forms, in which labour, means of production and relations of use and appropriation must be understood as distinct from any idea of a self-creative human essence. Thus, the notion that it is transformative activity, in its non-estranged, non-commodified form, which lies at the foundation of a possible community of freely creative beings is completely absent from Althusser's reading of Marx. Revolutions are produced by the 'condensation' of structural contradictions; and men and women, even after the emergence of a 'classless society', would still remain 'supports' to the places and functions determined by the mode of production. Indeed, the persistence of this structural/organizational necessity within Althusser's idea of a communist mode of production makes it difficult to see how he can avoid the charge of reproducing the 'political-administrative' domination I identified as the core of Luhmann's system theory.

Althusser's determination to read *Capital* as the logical conclusion of the 'base-superstructure' relationship postulated in the 1859 Preface is instructive for a number of reasons. First, Marx's famous proposition that '[t]he mode of production of material life conditions the social, political and intellectual life processes in general',[65] is understood as marking the end of 'any anthropological [concept of] inter-subjectivity'.[66] The idea of a perfectible human essence, which is formed through progressive historical estrangement, in other words, is replaced by a transhistorical reduction of the subject to the 'bearer' of socio-economic functions. The continued deployment of terms like emiseration, alienation and estrangement can only serve to obscure the 'structural' dynamic of the mode of production, a dynamic in which social and political agency must always be referred to the current 'determination', or 'overdetermination', of superstructural contradictions. Secondly, this reduction of (human) subjectivity to the status of a 'support' to the present 'structure in dominance' is presented through an assimilation of Lacan's remarks on selfhood and egoity. For Althusser, the relationship of the individual ego to 'external' reality is conditioned by the symbolic designations of 'the object' which emerge with linguistic competence. Thus, 'the human subject is [originally] decentered, constituted by a structure which has no centre either, except in the imaginary misrecognitions of the "ego", i.e., in the ideological formations in which it "recognises" itself'.[67] The fact that 'we', as human beings, are 'always already subjects',[68] is founded upon this originary 'lack', for it is the timeless desire to be a subject among other subjects that is the exclusive condition of social formation (a condition which makes the ideology of the subject an integral part of *every* social form). Finally, then, the idea of 'socialized production' ceases to be aligned with a 'humanist' ethic of universal emancipation. The necessity of a communist organization of production is asserted purely on the grounds that it is the most rational way of integrating social need with the established forces of production (and not that it is the end of contradiction and ideology).

This attempt to expound Marx's critique of capital through the categories of structuralism, however, produces the worst possible determination of Marxist thought. I have tried to suggest that the fundamental difficulty with Marx's own account of capitalism is the want of a coherent conception of social formation. The 'human' subject, in other words, tends to be presented as the victim of historical forms of 'estrangement', forms which are ordered in terms of a progressive development of the contradiction between forces and relations of production. However, it is important to recognize that Marx's 'tendency' to present the estrangement of humanity through the laws of historical materialism does not present us with the (scientific/objective) 'truth' of his thought – i.e., the truth which Althusser professed to extract from *Capital*. Essentially, Althusserian Marxism is a refusal to acknowledge the (speculative) concept of actuality, which, as we have seen, constantly re-emerges in Marx's social and political thought. The 'subjects' who inhabit capitalism's 'structure in dominance' are simply the 'bearers' of particular economic functions; 'subjects', moreover, whose reproduction, not just of capital, but of 'community' in general, is determined through 'ideological' reproductions of the self. In the end, Althusser's critique of capitalism – as the form of absolute material inequality, antagonism, waste and injustice – leads no further than an acknowledgement that communist relations of production could not escape the dynamics of (ontological) dissatisfaction and dependency.

Thus, it is only if we allow that there is no clean 'epistemological break' between the ideals of creative essence, collective agency and freely associative labour expressed in Marx's early writings and his 'scientific' economics, that it is possible to understand the persistence of Marxism as a critical paradigm (and as a political ideology). Althusser's reading of Marx, in its determination to give a comprehensive account of capitalism's structural/systemic reproduction, excludes the traces of speculative recognition and judgement which give Marx's thought its historical potency. I have tried to show that the elements of Marx's ethical critique of capitalism sit rather uneasily with the the protostructuralism of the 1859 Preface. His remarks on the fetishism of commodities in *Capital* (*Volume One*), for example, gesture towards an idea of the ('objective') totality of social and economic relations as something which includes 'formation' of a reflective personality. The reproduction of capital, in other words, appears as 'mediated' through subjects who do not simply 'bear' their economic functions, but who 'act' (transform, reproduce, negate, re-cognize) through the concrete differentiation of *Sittlichkeit*.

The persistence of Marxism's power, I will argue, has depended upon a particular kind of theoretical labour: namely, the recognition/ reconstruction of his more 'speculative' remarks on the relationship between capital and subjectivity, economy and ethical life. It is the rigid determinism articulated in *Capital*'s account of the relationship between economy and community (i.e., the negative consequences of the division of labour, the introduction of technology, etc.), in other words, which lies at the foundation of a certain 'sociological' orthodoxy, in which the opposition between capital (external, coercive necessity) and labour (the negative/estranged principle of commodity production) is mechanically repeated as the universal 'cause' of social and political antagonism. The point is that by repeating the oppositions originally designated in Marx's thought, this kind of 'radical' critique – of culture, education, ethnicity, religion – failed to recognize fundamental changes in the nature of commodification, the organization of labour, the constitution of national and cultural identities. Clearly, it is to this repetitive orthodoxy that Foucault and Lyotard address their respective ideas about Marx's relationship to the 'metaphysics' of totality, and the violence inherent in his concept of proletarian justice. Yet there is a sense in which Lyotard and Foucault, while professing a debt to Marx (Foucault's 'genealogical' account of capitalism as an increasingly urgent demand for 'disciplinary' knowledges and techniques, for example), misrecognize the critical potential of his thought. For if we acknowledge that Marx's 'speculative' interrogations of the relationship between objective economic necessity and its subjective recognition have already begun to question the simple opposition of creative spontaneity and the negativity of capital, then we might perhaps have the foundation of a critical Marxism which no longer demands the violence of 'forced' historical transition.

Fredric Jameson's account of 'late capitalism', for example, maintains that while we can no longer uncritically accept Marx's account of the relationship between a 'natural' beginning (i.e., the original transparency and intelligibility of social relations) and the revolutionary transcendence of the commodity form of production, we should still be suspicious of 'postmodernist' claims that a new 'postcapitalist' culture has emerged to which the categories of historical materialism no longer apply. In a development of Adorno's account of the increasingly 'reified' nature of cultural production (i.e., the increasing tendency of popular culture – produced by 'the culture industry' – to conceal the processes of its own production, and thus to determine the sphere of social activity),[69] Jameson attempts to expound 'postmodernism' as a new form of subjectivity, which has developed through the hyperextension, hyperintesification and hyperflexibility of commodity production:

> The constitutive impurity of postmodernism theory . . . confirms the insight that must be insisted on over and over again, namely, that postmodernism is not the determinant of a wholly new social order, but only the reflex and concomitant of yet another systemic modification of capitalism itself.[70]

Now, although it could certainly be claimed that Jameson's depiction of 'postmodernism' (i.e., as a 'feeling' – of diversity, limitlessness, evanescence, fragmentation – whose theorization has increasingly dissociated collective experience from its socio-economic conditions) does not do justice to some of the more disquieting enquiries of recent French philosophy, his attempt to anchor the 'representation' of modernity within the 'structure and objective features'[71] of commodity production does articulate a certain critical judgement of Marxism's relation to ethical life. Indeed, his claim that we ought to understand postmodern ethics, politics and aesthetics as 'responses' to the hypercommodification and globalization of late capitalism refers explicitly to Max Weber's idea that the exercise of authority presupposes the emergence of shared socio-cultural 'meanings', by which individuals make sense of their social world. Thus, while we may have reservations about Jameson's attempt to ground postmodern and deconstructive theory in general (Derrida is particularly suspicious of attempts to present 'race' or 'gender' or 'nationality' as forms whose political significance has been decided within the legislation of 'the economic'), his work does at least acknowledge the kind of historical openness to subjective formation and representation which we have reconstructed from Marx's more 'speculative' reflections.

The powers of totality

I began this chapter by suggesting that there is a 'structural' homology between Marxist and functionalist paradigms, and that this can be traced to the presuppositions of Kant's first *Critique*. Marxism and functionalism both attribute a 'transcendental' necessity to the determinations of social structure; both tend towards a deterministic account of subjective formation; and both oppose the integrity/totality of the system to the contingency of individual action and recognition. Yet the point of my exposition has been to establish the difference between 'bourgeois' and 'radical' traditions in sociology, that is, to suggest that Marxism at least offers the potential for a kind of speculative recognition upon its relationship to ethical life – a reflection which is necessarily excluded from functionalist accounts of sociality. In conclusion, then, I will attempt to situate this difference in the context of Hegel's most urgent formulation of the relationship between reason and social transformation, that is, the account of the French Revolution presented in the *Phenomenology of Mind*.

Hegel's remarks on the French Revolution are essentially an exposition of the relationship between the 'irrationality' enshrined in feudalistic structures of authority and the capacity of self-consciouness to 'abstract' its activity from the substantive determinations of *Sittlichkeit*. The Revolution, in other words, presupposed what Hegel describes as a violent 'culture' of subjectivity, in which every structure, form and institution of ethical life is acknowledged only as an impediment to the exercise of 'my' essential and inalienable freedom. As Hegel puts it, 'the universal will goes into itself, is subjectivized and becomes individual will, to which the universal will and the universal work stand opposed'.[72] This universal failure of subjectivity to recognize the 'lawlessness' of the property form which has produced its 'abstraction' (i.e., the immediate power exercised by wealth in the absence of bourgeois property rights) deepens and reinforces that lawlessness. The self-consciousness produced by the French Enlightenment, therefore, is determined through an absolute opposition to *Sittlichkeit*: its 'reformative' intentions cannot realize themselves in 'objective' relations, for these are constantly subverted by its own transformative activity. It follows from this that revolutionary self-consciousness 'cannot arrive at a positive accomplishment of anything . . . in the way of reality, either in the form of laws and regulations of conscious freedom, or of deeds and works of active freedom'.[73] Thus, the concrete determinations of ethical life become subject to the 'stubborn and atomic singleness of absolutely free will'.[74] The absolute 'matter of human freedom' which the revolutionary consciousness attempts to realize (Hegel clearly has in mind Rousseau's conception of a pre-social and originally 'good' human nature), is speculatively recognized as a 'pure abstraction', or characterless object of faith and superstition.

The truth of the French Enlightenment's attempt to displace irrational faith in the established order, then, is an absolutely negative 'culture' of self-consciousness, which acknowledges nothing beyond the law of its own activity. The 'matter' which it constantly invokes as the substance of rational human association is completely without characteristics, and produces a self-consciousness which is absolutely threatened by its own transformations: 'The sole and only work and deed accomplished by [abstract] universal freedom is therefore death, a death which achieves nothing; for what is negated is the unfulfilled punctual entity of the absolutely free will'.[75] Speculatively understood, the French Revolution produces an utter dislocation of self-consciousness from ethical life, and the appearance of 'free will' as the agent of meaningless annihilation. The lawlessness which self-consciousness sets out to reform is merely reaffirmed, and the substance of ethical life is more and more deeply disrupted by subjectivity's want of objective recognition. This, for Hegel, is the 'Terror' of the Absolute Freedom.

In many respects, Hegel's presentation of the French Enlightenment and its relationship to the Revolution of 1789 defines the relationship of speculative thought to modernity. We can see from his insistence on the 'irrationality' of feudalist absolutism (the domination of the state by wealth in the absence of bourgeois property rights) that there is a sense in which, for Hegel, the Revolution expressed the inalienable right of rational subjectivity to transform the ('objective') conditions of its servitude. Yet this affirmation of the 'spirit' of the Revolution – the famous demand for liberty, equality and brotherhood – is tempered by an acknowledgement of the violence which becomes inevitable once 'the subject' has ceased to recognize itself in the institutions of Sittlichkeit. The 'materialism' of natural beginnings (a materialism that Hegel identified in Rousseau and which is repeated in Marx's early writings), in other words, encourages a kind of limitless agitation of subjectivity which threatens every established form of mediation, recognition and authority. For Hegel, then, the Terror of the Jacobin regime teaches us that if 'freedom' is conceived simply as a matter of individual conviction, then the exercise of 'authority', including the right of life and death, becomes a matter of sheer arbitrary force. We will see in the final chapter that such attempts to determine the 'original' (i.e., unmediated, pure) essence of humanity recur throughout the history of modernity. The centrality of Aryanism to the National Socialist movement in Weimar Germany, for example, determined racial violence as an illimitable political project (the Final Solution to the Jewish Question), which ultimately destroyed the 'rational' foundations of the nation state.

There is a sense, then, in which the tension between Hegel's approbation of the French Revolution and his admonitory remarks about the Jacobin Terror have a resonance with our account of 'radical' and 'bourgeois' traditions in sociology. I have claimed that there is a tendency in both Marxism and functionalism to postulate 'social structure' as an abstract, self-co-ordinating form which determines the activity of each individual subject. The crucial difference between these two explanatory forms, however, is that while functionalism continues a tradition in which established institutions are seen as embodying the originally 'social' purpose of human nature,[76] Marxism proceeds from a tradition in which socio-historical development is understood as deepening humanity's estrangement from its essence.[77]

What needs to be recognized here is that, for Hegel, radical transformations of 'the Good' (the 'actual' forms, institutions and relations of ethical life) are always prone to the temptations of subjective 'culture' – that is, to the violent idealism of a revolutionary *praxis* that disregards the history of the law. As finite (embodied) self-consciousness, human beings must acknowledge their formation within the substance of *Sittlichkeit*, a formation which includes the coercion, mediation, satisfaction and violence inscribed in the juridical expression of ethical life.[78] Yet the paradigm which puts the greatest emphasis on social conservatism – structural functionalism and its cohorts – fails to recognize that the 'rationalization' of society cannot be directly identified with the increasingly efficient performance and integration of discrete 'functions'. Within the substance of ethical life, work, satisfaction and desire inevitably determine conflicts which cannot be subsumed under the logic of integration: indeed, Marx's account of the contradictions inherent in capitalist relations of production makes it clear that the 'phenomena' of social stability (tradition, respect, continuity, etc.) presuppose a underlying economy of coercion and loss. The point, then, is that Marxist theory, once it has recognized its tendency to reproduce itself as a utopian/revolutionary culture, does allow us to frame speculative/historical judgements about the relationship of the 'mode of production' to moral, cultural, aesthetic and political representations of ethical life. Functionalism, on the other hand, progressively excludes such judgements, for the end (*telos*) of structural integration has been pursued to the point where culture, ethics and morality are reduced to mere 'modifications' of a complex system environment.

In the end, my speculative reading of Marx gestures towards the necessity of acknowledging the re-formative power that (rational, self-conscious) subjectivity exerts *within* the structures and institutions of *Sittlichkeit*. I will proceed, then, to an examination of the two most influential formulations of 'cognitivist' social thought: Max Weber's *Verstehen* sociology, and Jürgen Habermas's idea of communicative reason.

Notes

1. See Kant *Critique of Pure Reason* (1956) and the *Foundations of the Metaphysics of Morals* (1985).

2. See Kant's essays 'What is Enlightenment?', and 'Religion within the bounds of reason alone' in *Political Writings* (1991).

3. See Kant's *Critique of Judgement* (1982b).

4. I. Kant, *Critique of Pure Reason*, trans. N. Kemp-Smith, Macmillan, 1982a, p. 193.

5. I. Kant, *Prologomena to Any Future Metaphysics*, trans. P. Carus (revised by W. Ellington), Hackett, 1983, p. 91.

6. Kant, *Critique of Pure Reason*, p. 653.

7. Ibid., p. 113.

8. Ibid., p. 107.

9. G.W.F. Hegel, *Phenomenology of Mind*, trans. J.B. Baillie, Harper & Row, 1967a, pp. 228–40.

10. E. Durkheim, *The Rules of Sociological Method*, trans. W.D. Halls, Macmillan, 1982.

11. E. Durkheim, *The Division of Labour in Society*, trans. G. Simpson, The Free Press, 1964.

12. Durkheim, *Rules of Sociological Method*, pp. 51–2.

13. E. Durkheim, *Suicide: A Study in Sociology*, trans. G. Simpson and J.A. Spalding , Routledge, 1992.

14. S. Lukes, *Emile Durkheim. His Life and Work: A Historical and Critical Study*, Penguin, 1981, p. 51.

15. Durkheim, *Suicide*, p. 212.

16. Ibid., pp. 171–216.

17. Ibid., p. 247.

18. Quoted in Lukes, *Emile Durkheim*, p. 211.

19. Ibid., p. 436.

20. Durkheim's account of the descent of the universal into the chaos of particular desires, is similar in many respects to Hegel's account 'Pleasure and Necessity' in the *Phenomenology of Mind*. In both cases, the authority of the 'universal' appears as a hard and negative force, which is utterly opposed to subjective aims and purposes.

21. Durkheim, *Division of Labour*, p. 257.

22. Quoted in Lukes, *Emile Durkheim*, p. 171.

23. Durkheim, *Division of Labour*, p. 131.

24. Ibid.

25. Ibid., pp. 222–9.

26. See Kant's essay 'What is Enlightenment?', trans. H.B. Nisbet, in H. Reiss (ed.), *Kant's Political Writings*, Cambridge University Press, 1991, pp. 54–60.

27. Durkheim, *Rules of Sociological Method*, p. 104.

28. Z. Bauman, *Modernity and the Holocaust*, Polity Press, 1991, p. 172.

29. Ibid., p. 174.

30. E. Levinas, *Totality and Infinity: An Essay on Exteriority*, Duquesne University Press, 1994, p. 194.

31. Ibid., p. 201.

32. Ibid., p. 290.

33. Bauman, *Modernity and the Holocaust*, p. 221.

34. J.-F. Lyotard, *The Postmodern Condition: A Report on Knowledge*, trans. G. Bennington and B. Massumi, Manchester University Press, 1991a, pp. 11–14.

35. Hegel, *Phenomenology of Mind*, p. 96.

36. G. Rose, *Hegel Contra Sociology*, Athlone Press, 1981, p. 213.

37. Durkheim, *Division of Labour*, p. 131.

38. T. Parsons (with E. Bales and R. Shils), *Working Papers in the Theory of Action*, Collier-Macmillan, 1953, p. 103.

39. N. Luhmann, *Soziale Systeme*, quoted and translated in J. Habermas, *The Philosophical Discourse of Modernity*, trans. F. Lawrence, Polity Press, 1984, p. 370.

40. Ibid., p. 378ff.

41. Ibid.

42. Ibid., p. 381.

43. Ibid., p. 378.

44. Ibid., pp. 294–327.

45. M. Horkheimer and T.W. Adorno, *Dialectic of Enlightenment*, Continuum, 1986, p. xv.

46. K. Marx, *Capital: Volume One*, trans. S. Moore and E. Aveling, Lawrence & Wishart, 1977a, p. 19.

47. Ibid., p. 20.

48. K. Marx, *Economic and Philosophical Manuscripts of 1844*, Progress Publishers, 1977b, p. 67.

49. See K. Marx, Preface to *A Contribution to the Critique of Political Economy*, in *Karl Marx: Selected Writings*, D. McLellan ed., Oxford University Press, 1977d, pp. 388–91.

50. Marx, *Economic and Philosophical Manuscripts*, p. 74.

51. K. Marx, *The German Ideology*, C.J. Arthur ed., Lawrence & Wishart, 1977c, p. 51.

52. Ibid., p. 52.

53. Marx, *Economic and Philosophical Manuscripts*, p. 74.

54. Marx, *German Ideology*, p. 51.

55. G.W.F. Hegel, *Philosophy of Right*, trans. T.M. Knox, Oxford University Press, 1967b, p. 10.

56. Marx, *Capital: Volume One*, p. 79.

57. Ibid., p. 83.

58. K. Marx, 'Theses on Feuerbach', in *German Ideology*, p. 120.

59. Ibid.

60. Ibid., p. 122.

61. K. Marx, 'On the Jewish question', in *Karl Marx: Selected Writings*, p. 56.

62. L. Althusser, *Reading Capital*, Verso, 1983, p. 97.

63. L. Althusser, *For Marx*, trans. B. Brewster, Verso, 1986, p. 113.

64. Althusser, *Reading Capital*, p. 180.

65. Marx, *Karl Marx: Selected Writings*, p. 389.

66. Althusser, *Reading Capital*, p. 180.

67. L. Althusser, *Lenin and Philosophy, and Other Essays*, trans. B. Brewster, NLB, 1971, pp. 218–19.

68. Ibid., p. 172.

69. For an interesting discussion of Adorno's later remarks on the 'culture industry' and its relationship to social domination and control, see 'The Dispute over Modernism', in G. Rose, *The Melancholy Science: An Introduction to the Thought of Theodor W. Adorno*, Macmillan, 1978, pp. 109–37.

70. F. Jameson, *Postmodernism: Or the Cultural Logic of Late Capitalism*, Verso, 1995, p. xii.

71. Ibid., p. xv.

72. Hegel, *Phenomenology of Mind*, p. 602.

73. Ibid., p. 606.

74. Ibid., p. 605.

75. Ibid., p. 605.

76. See, for example, Edmund Burke's *Reflections on the Revolution in France* (1973), or Adam Smith's *The Theory of the Moral Sentiments* (1976).

77. See, for example, Jean-Jacques Rousseau's *Discourse on the Origin of Inequality* (1988).

78. See Hegel, 'Right as law' and 'Law determinately existent', in *Philosophy of Right*, pp. 134–40.

3

The Idealism of Autonomy

The preceding chapters have attempted two things. First, to establish the fundamental principles on which a speculative/Hegelian critique of social theory can be attempted. And secondly, to develop an historical account of the relationship between structure and reification: that is, to expound the paradigmatic diversity in which the idea of 'structure' has appeared as the determining *cause* of individual action. Taken at its simplest, our understanding of structural sociologies (specifically, Marxism, social realism, structural functionalism and systems theory) has attempted to elaborate the social theoretical significance of Hegel's concept of 'reflection'. The idea is that any form which is abstracted from the whole in which it has become 'determinate', takes on a priority which is reproduced in the explanation of concepts such as subjectivity, autonomy, justice and identity.[1] In general, structural explanations tend to prioritize the systemic, functional elements of societies: they take the idea of a 'productive'[2] interdependence among institutions as primary, and attempt to impose its explanatory power on the forms of recognition characteristic of the 'socialized' individual. We have seen that this idea of 'socialization' has developed historically along two distinct lines of critique: the 'bourgeois' sociologies of Durkheim and Parsons which maintain the moral dependency of the individual on the institutions of 'liberal capitalism', and the Marxist tradition, which maintains that the moral, ethical and political formation of the subject under the conditions of capitalist accumulation always reflects the domination of capital over wage labour.

The account of structural sociologies developed in Chapter 2, there-fore, should be conceived as an exposition of a particular form of 'reflective' understanding of sociality – an understanding which, in general, reifies the 'material' or 'systemic' or 'functional' necessities of ethical life, as causally independent of subjective recognition. The foundation of these systemic forms of social explanation, I have argued, must be sought in the doctrine categories, faculties and powers which inform the transcendental epistemology of Kant's first *Critique*. For Kant, knowledge is possible only if certain a priori conditions are assumed as constitutive of human understanding (*Verstand*), and that it is these conditions which organize our sense impressions into a realm of discrete bodies, causally interacting in space and time. Human experience of a world 'objectively' independent of the immediate apprehension of self-identity, or the formal consistency of abstract reasoning, is founded on a necessary relationship between the categories of the understanding (mind/intellect) and the sense impressions given through the modes of intuition (space and time). Without the limitation that sense data imposes on our deployment of categories such as causality or substance or reciprocity, we are led into the unresolvable 'antinomies' of traditional metaphysics and away from the 'science' of empirical causes.[3] Thus, although we cannot have knowledge of ultimate reality – 'things-as-they-are-in-themselves' – we can have a science of the universal laws which underlie the apparent contingency of our 'phenomenal' experience (i.e., 'things-as-they-appear-to-us'). This science of sensibly conditioned causes, however, presupposes Kant's account of human understanding as constituted through a set of a priori categories, whose discursive power *determines* the realm of appearances. The necessary spatio-temporal form of intuition which Kant describes in the Transcendental Aesthetic,[4] has no real independence from the categorial structure of the understanding; it is simply the dispersed and particularized reflection of the synthetic unity of the understanding. The experience of objects in space and time, as it is set in the first *Critique*, therefore reflects the domination of a formal synthetic necessity over the contingency of particular intuitions. It is this 'reflective' exteriority of a structural/synthetic universality and the 'contingent' content it controls/determines which, I have claimed, lies at the foundation of structural/systemic accounts of ethical life.

It should be clear from the preceding chapter, that I am not claiming that structural sociology, in its various paradigmatic forms, is simply wrong, or that it should be subsumed under a comprehensive account of the autonomous subject as the primary and determining category of human sociality. One of the fundamental claims which emerges from the *Phenomenology of Mind* (1967a), is that the autonomy of self-conscious individuals must be understood as formed by, mediated through, and ultimately excessive of the forms and institutions in which it is objectified/realized. Hegel's account of the dialectic of master and slave, for example, shows that although the victory of the master in the struggle for recognition is 'objectified' in the duties of service which the slave must discharge, the labour that he performs in the production of commodities 'forms' his self-consciousness as a demand for ethical recognition which exceeds the absolute authority of the master. It is the slave's largely implicit recognition of his universality which breaks down the objective relations of servitude, and precipitates self-consciousness into the moral, religious and political contradictions constituted in ethical life. The 'agency' of self-conscious individuals therefore is inextricably bound up with their historical formation. Yet for Hegel, this formation could not be definitively expressed either in terms of the dynamics of 'objective' necessities (categories such as functionality, moral density or alienation/class-consciousness) or, as we will see, by reference to the 'universal' form of subjective autonomy (specifically, Weber's concept of 'meaning' and Habermas's idea of 'communicative reason'). By abstracting generic notions such as 'dynamic moral density', 'functional prerequisite' and 'mode of production' from the substance of ethical life, structural sociologies contribute to our recognition of the totalizing potential inherent in modernity. For by explaining how the 'system necessities' of modern society might determine and homogenize self-recognition, structural sociologies allow us, as social scientists, to evaluate critically the relationship between 'autonomy' and 'totality'.

I began this chapter by suggesting that, in general, social scientific paradigms are characterized by their abstraction (and prioritization) of certain elements from the substance of ethical life, and that in the case of structural sociologies, this abstraction takes the form of positing a deterministic relationship between systemic necessities and the 'formation' of self-conscious individuals. I also suggested that this reduction of 'subjectivity' (i.e., the cultures of moral, religious and political recognition through which the 'objectivity' of ethical life is represented) to a contingent reflection of 'system necessity' has its conceptual foundation in Kant's account of phenomenal experience. The reflective domination of the Kantian understanding, in other words, can be traced not only in the history of 'functionalism' (i.e., from Durkheim to Luhmann), but also in Marx's exposition of the categories which determine antagonistic class relations in a capitalist economy.[5] Yet, as I have already mentioned, a speculative social science cannot simply turn to the moral spontaneity of the subject in order to apprehend the 'true' possibilities of liberty, autonomy and justice that are opened by modern society. Indeed, the present chapter will attempt to show that taken in abstraction from the objective/systemic necessities constituted within ethical life, the explanatory concept of 'subjectivity' has determined its own 'reflective' forms of domination, exclusion and misrecognition.

In order to understand fully the sociological significance of the concept of subjectivity, I must return, once again, to Kant's critical philosophy. We have seen that the doctrine of experience expounded in the first *Critique* institutes the domination of the synthetic activity of the understanding over the content of intuition. The science of efficient causes, therefore, is restricted to subsuming particular events in space and time under general, lawlike propositions about the substantiality of matter, the reciprocity of interactions, etc. Kant's second *Critique*, the *Critique of Practical Reason*, however, is concerned to distinguish this 'theoretical' function of reason from its ability to determine the 'categorical' ends in which humanity recognizes its freedom. The fundamental question which Kant is attempting to answer in the second *Critique*, therefore, is this: how is it possible for human subjects to act autonomously when the phenomenal world is determined exclusively by external causes? (This is what Kant means by 'practical' reason – reason's capacity to determine the human subject to moral action in the world.)

Kant's attempt to resolve the apparent contradiction between a deterministic account of the phenomenal world and the possibility of 'free' human action involves three different, but essentially related, elements. The first of these we might call the formal negativity of reason. Human subjects do not simply respond (behaviouristically/instinctively) to the appetites and inclinations which constitute their 'phenomenal' existence. According to Kant, the spontaneity of reason always inter-venes between the emergence of desire in the human subject and its actual fulfilment. This negativity in relation to the world of phenomenal causes is the 'fact' upon which Kant seeks to establish the practical/ethical power of reason. Thus, the second element which can be identi-fied in Kant's critical ethics, is the attempt to generate a positive content from the power of the rational self to intervene in the chain of phenom-enal causes. For Kant, the capacity of the human will to recognize its particular inclinations as non-rational (and thereby non-human) places it under an obligation to act only in accordance with the demands of practical reason. These demands take the form of 'categorical impera-tives', which command obedience under all possible circumstances and conditions. Kant famously offers the example of keeping a deposit entrusted by someone who has since died. Expediency demands that I increase my fortune by keeping the money. Practical reason, however, demands that I return it to its rightful beneficiaries; for if the practice of keeping deposits was universally adopted, the institution of private property (an institution which for Kant is originally consonant with the exercise of rational freedom) would cease to exist. Kant's position, therefore, is that one should always act as if the motivation (maxim) of one's action were a law for a community of autonomous individuals. Where this is shown to be impossible, that is, where one's motivation cannot be represented as compatible with the institution's universal autonomy, one's action belongs exclusively to the realm of (non-moral) inclination and self-interest. The final element of Kant's critical ethics is the idea that by adhering to the moral law, each individual determines his/herself as an absolute 'end' which ought to be universally respected. The community of transcendental ends, in other words, is governed by the laws of rational freedom as they are exemplified in the conduct of every morally autonomous being.

The argument I will pursue in this chapter is that it is Kant's original positing of the morally autonomous subject which underlies the two main sociological attempts to salvage the 'individual' from the reification of social structure: that is, Max Weber's idea of *Verstehen* sociology and Jürgen Habermas's account of communicative reason. My claim is that both of these sociologies, in different ways, reproduce Kant's reflective abstraction of the moral subject from the objective content of ethical life; and that both, again in different ways, posit a universal capacity of the individual to re-present social relations (and the contradictions they inevitably determine) as originally dependent on, and subject to, its rational spontaneity. Neither Weber nor Habermas, in other words, is able to determine an adequate idea of the social formation of the individual, as neither is able to acknowledge the independence, exteriority and factuality of the relations and institutions which are constituted in ethical life. As with my account of structural sociologies, however, I am not suggesting that the theoretical and methodological insights offered by Weber (and interpretive sociology in general) and Habermas are simply wrong, or that they totally misrepresent the constitution of subjectivity in modern 'rationalized' societies. What I am suggesting is that the ways in which Weber and Habermas respectively depict the autonomous activity of rational subjects reflects the self-recognition of discrete, 'legally' autonomous individuals, and that this reflection discloses the way in which rational autonomy – or rather its re-presentation – is related to the objective relations and structures of ethical life. The voluntaristic sociologies of Weber and Habermas, therefore, disclose the representation of rational autonomy (i.e., the categories and procedures through which it is recognized by the subject) as a formative power within the substance of ethical life. Speculatively conceived, however, this power must be acknowledged not as the ultimate explanatory category for a critical social science, but rather as something which is formed by, and re-formative of, the objectivity of social relations.

Briefly, I will begin my exposition of voluntaristic sociologies with an examination of Weber's attempt to institute the notion of 'meaning' as the primary and definitive category of sociological explanation. I will attempt to show that there is a fundamentally Kantian strand which runs throughout his methodological writings, and that, despite his claims to embrace a Nietzschean rejection of ultimate or substantive values, Weber's analyses of the modern 'bureaucratic' organization, political authority, economic activity and the institutional life of society in general disclose an implicit commitment to the values inscribed in Kant's critical ethics (i.e., independence of judgement, the valuation of the individual as an ultimate end and the postulation of social relations as a 'heteronomous' power which threatens the rational spontaneity of the individual). This commitment, I will argue, cannot be sustained by the idea of subjective meaning which Weber deploys throughout his substantive works. His rejection of the 'objective' historical necessity of practical reason, together with the claim that it is only the 'meaningful' representation of social relations which is of sociological significance, leads to a position in which he is forced to invoke the pre-social, re-fomative power of 'charisma' as the only way out of the 'iron cage' of bureaucracy.[6]

This supposed inability of the subject to receive and reproduce a plurality of meanings within the bureaucratized institutions of modern capitalist society (i.e., to sustain itself as an autonomous individual) is addressed in the idea of 'communicative reason' which Habermas has developed, articulated and defended over the last twenty-five years or so. I will argue that Habermas's idea of a 'universal pragamatics' of communicative action is essentially an attempt to reconstruct the primacy of practical reason posited in Kant's moral, historical and political writings, and that as such, the notion of the 'lifeworld', which has become primary in Habermas's later writing, is ultimately exclusive of the dispersal and particularity (of 'subjective' formation) which is sustained in ethical life. The 'autonomy' of the communicative subject – its ability to recognize the contingency sustained *within* the rules of universal discourse – returns us to the abstract exclusiveness inscribed in the ahistorical demands of the categorical imperative. First, however, we need to look at the instrumentality of Weber's conceptions of meaning and social action.

Max Weber and the concept of social action

At the conclusion of his most well-known work, *The Protestant Ethic and the Spirit of Capitalism* (1978a), Weber remarks:

> No one knows who will live in this [bureaucratic] cage in the future, or whether at the end of this tremendous development entirely new prophets will arise, or there will be a great rebirth of old ideas and ideals, or, if neither, mechanised petrification, embellished with a sort of convulsive self-importance. For the last stage of this cultural development, it might well be truly said: 'Specialists without spirit, sensualists without heart; this nullity imagines that it has attained a level of civilisation never before attained.'[7]

In one of his later methodological essays, 'The nature of social action', however, he makes the following assertion: 'It is a shocking misunder-standing to think that an "individualistic" methodology implies a certain valuation of "individualism" (in any possible sense of that word).'[8] Evidently there is a tension here: a tension between what Weber says sociologists *ought to do* in his methodological and theoretical texts (i.e., to concern themselves only with the *description* of particular 'value rapports') and what he himself does in his substantive works on politics, economics and culture; between his obvious concern about the 'moral' consequences produced by the homogenizing power of bureaucracy and his studious disavowal of value commitments in sociology; and, ultimately, between the Kantian values of independence and self-determination which pervade his critique of modernity and the Nietzschean idea of 'charisma' which he posits as the way out of bureaucratic stasis and stagnation. I will argue that the basic problem with Weber's *Verstehen* sociology is that it fails to acknowledge that the valuation of spontaneity over external necessity, or of individuation over (bureaucratic) homogenization, demands a commitment to just the type of ethical 'objectivism' which he is at pains to reject in his methodological writings. It is Weber's failure to make this commitment (a commitment that Habermas's sociology seeks to circumvent through the 'autonomy' reproduced within the 'norms of rational speech') which determines his account of modernity as a progressive erosion of culture, from which only the spontaneous interventions of charismatic authority could save us.

I have claimed that there is a basic, determining tension in Weber's sociology: the tension between his implicit valuation of the 'autonomous' individual (and its reproduction of encompassing meanings and ideals) and his methodological disavowal of value commitments in social science. In order to understand fully the significance of this tension for the concept of *Verstehen* sociology, we must examine in more detail some of the claims Weber advances in *The Methodology of the Social Sciences* (1949). In the essay 'Value judgements in social science', Weber remarks that, 'What is important from the methodological point of view is that the validity of a practical imperative as a norm, on the one hand, and the truth claims of a statement of empirical fact on the other, create problems at totally different levels, and that the specific value of each of them will be diminished if it is not recognised and an attempt is made to force it into the same category.'[9] Sociology, in other terms, ought not to concern itself with the question of whether a particular norm has an objective and necessary value for human beings as social creatures, but only with 'logical' description of the normative meanings ('value rapports') which orientate social action. The 'value-freedom' which Weber claims for sociology, then, consists in respecting this (Kantian) categorical distinction between statements of fact and statements of value: as sociologists, we should acknowledge that our subjective motivations for doing a particular type of research are limiting and perspectival, and confine ourselves to giving as clear a description as possible of meanings which generally inform the conduct of individuals at a given point in the history of a particular kind of society.

For Weber, the methodological devices of 'ideal typification' and 'empathetic understanding' are not only the *presupposition*, but also the *goal* of a generic sociological understanding.[10] In attempting to deduce subjective meanings from observable patterns of social action, and to formulate 'idealized' constructions of the most significant motivations within a given society or social group, the sociologist attempts to disclose how *existing* norms and values continue to sustain the patterns of reciprocal expectation and cohesion which they have produced. There should be no evaluative assessment of the ethical rightness of the values included in ideal typifications: sociological analysis as such is concerned only with bringing to light the patterns of motivation which underlie the external/observable forms of social cohesion. Such an enterprise excludes any idea of 'history' as a process either of cultural improvement or ethical decay; for in making the exclusion of questions of 'legitimacy' into a methodological precept, Weber is able to claim that his interpretive sociology merely clarifies the cultural, economic and political significance of actual motivational patterns, without imposing abstract conceptions of the right and the good on them. It is this attempt to distinguish social science from any involvement in the validation or substantiation of ethical demands which seems to link Weber's sociology to Nietzsche's rejection of absolute value.[11] I will argue that this linkage, although rather facile in the sense that Weber's relativistic idea of value does not sustain Nietzsche's 'genealogical' condemnation of moral life as culturally degenerative, has a profound significance for his substantive historical works.

In general, the precepts developed in Weber's methodological writings – the formation of 'empathetic understanding', the 'ideal typification' of motivations, the acknowledgement of values as contingent and perspectival – determine the sociological enterprise as disclosure of the subjective meanings which underlie, and cut across, the empirical/external forms of sociality (primarily, economic, religious and political institutions). This *Verstehen*, or 'interpretive', sociology maintains that the institutional forms in which social action takes place are no more than an 'outcome of relations between specific actions performed by individual human beings, who are. . . the intelligible performers of meaningful actions'.[12] For Weber, functional and systemic explanations of social phenomena, even though they are useful in identifying 'causal' regularities produced by individual actions, always carry with them the potential for 'reification' – the postulation of function, or system necessity, as a power independent of the meanings through which 'objective' relations are constituted. I can now begin to discern the Kantian influence in Weber's sociology. Like Kant, Weber conceives the individual subject, and its power to re-present the 'objective' institutions of ethical life, as primary to the understanding of social, political and economic relations. For Weber, however, this power of subjective re-presentation is not regulated by the demands of a universal procedural rationality: in studying the actual subjective meanings which precipitate social action, the sociologist is not charged with the 'idealist' goal of showing how these might contribute to the history of rational autonomy.[13] The primacy of meaning on which Weber bases his sociology, therefore, is studiously relativistic: the capacity of the individual to receive and reproduce the social, political and religious significations of his or her culture is given no 'value' beyond the methodological necessity of referring empirical social forms to general patterns of subjective motivation.

Weber's historiographical relativism, however, is not Nietzschean genealogy. The concept of meaning which is central to *Verstehen* sociology is articulated through ideas of individuality, subjectivity and cultural formation which, far from participating in Nietzsche's rejection of the logos of moral necessity, reflect an essentially Kantian valuation of socially sanctioned (legally reorganized) freedom. By making the re-presentation of social, economic and political institutions by 'intelligible performers' the object of sociological understanding, Weber commits himself to a recognizably 'moral' valuation of the individual as: (1) distinct from the 'external' necessity of system and function; (2) a category which is threatened by the homogenizing/self-perpetuating power which he calls bureaucracy; and (3) the producer/receiver of 'meanings' whose plurality and vivacity are the index of 'cultural', rather than 'bureaucratic', formation. I will argue, however, that the valuation of individuality, which is implicit in the concept of 'meaning', is suppressed within the (teleological) structure of his substantive works on religion, economics and political authority. The Nietzschean 'influence' on Weberian sociology is expressed in the denial that the meanings through which individual actors orientate themselves, could determine a categorical necessity which is prescriptive of (moral) freedom/autonomy in general. And so the histories of rationalization that Weber adduces in support of his critique of modernity disclose the 'spontaneity' of subjective meaning as a disempowered form, whose 're-presenations' (of the 'objective' tendencies present in contemporary culture and society) are unable to 're-form' the movement towards bureaucratic domination.

The basic theoretical problem with Weber's sociology, therefore, is that in attempting to weld a Nietzschean type of ethical relativism into an essentially Kantian account of social action, it loses the critical resources both of Nietzsche's 'genealogy' and of Kant's concept of practical reason. The form of methodological individualism that Weber develops in *Economy and Society* (1978c) and *The Methodology of the Social Sciences*, postulates subjective meaning as the primary concept in sociological explanation. The notions of 'empathetic understanding' and 'ideal typification' both aim at reconstruction of the motivational patterns which signify the 'social' engagement of the individual. Yet the individual spontaneity (in the production and reception of meanings) that Weber postulates as primary to the recognition of social action is unable to orientate itself to the culture in which it acts *either* as the 'reflective' citizen of a republic of transcendental ends (Kant), *or* in the destructive-creative excess of 'instinctual' life (Nietzsche). The analytical reconstruction of subjective meanings, in other words, produces a sociology in which individual freedom is restricted to its re-presentations of ethical life (work, satisfaction, desire): ultimately, there is nothing in Weber's typology of social action (value rational, rational purposive, affective and traditional behaviour) which determines a critical relation to the rationalizing/bureaucratizing trend of Western industrialized societies. I will argue that this methodological disempowerment of individuality is evident in Weber's historical works as a tension between his implicit valuation of subjective spontaneity and his 'Nietzschean' rejection of transcendental values and ideals. For in presupposing the individual as interpretive (re-presentative) rather than critical (re-formative) of social relations, Weberian historiography begins to look suspiciously like a reduction of ethical, religious and social meanings to the homogenizing/self-perpetuating power of bureaucratic rationality.

The significance of Weber's historiographic studies of Protestantism, Hinduism and Confucianism is related to his idea of progressive 'rationalization' as the defining characteristic of Western science, culture and economic activity. As I have noted, Weber's exposition of the relationship between Protestant asceticism – particularly Calvinism – and the transformation of productive activity into the rational, methodical accumulation of wealth emphasizes the role of theodicy in the constitution of work as a vocation, or 'calling'. The importance of Calvinism in the emergence of rationalized productive activity lies in the doctrine of predestination. Each individual confronts God as unable to alter the unfathomable purpose for which the universe was created, a purpose which has from the beginning predetermined the damnation or salvation of every created individual. Secular activity, therefore, is unable to influence divine judgement; my ultimate fate has already been decided, and God cannot be influenced by what I do on earth. For Weber, it is the austerity of this Calvinist doctrine which is of particular importance in the transition from a feudal, subsistence economy to the rationalized production of secular wealth characteristic of capitalism. Unlike Catholicism, with its ritualized forms of propitiation and redemption, Calvinism places the individual alone before God, without hope of influencing his or her ultimate fate through the intercession of the church. It is this state of religious isolation which, according to Weber, determines the Calvinist individual to concerted, methodical activity in the pursuit of wealth. While there can be no absolute assurance that one is saved, doubt about salvation is a 'sign' that one is not among God's elect. Thus, by working hard and constantly throughout one's life, by ploughing one's profits back into the business and avoiding the temptations of excess, and by using judiciously the rewards of one's labour, one can dispel any doubts about salvation. Protestantism, and particularly Calvinism, therefore, gives the accumulation of wealth a theological sanction: that which accrues to the individual in the pursuit of his or her vocation is conceived as a sign of salvation.

Weber's descriptions of the Hindu (Indian) and Confucian (Chinese) religions are related to his account of Protestantism through the concept of prophecy. As we have seen, the most significant – although unintended – consequence of Calvin's doctrine of predestination was to provide the motivational basis for the rationalized productive activity typical of capitalist economies. Calvinistic prophecy, in other words, organizes the universe into a particular system of relations between the secular and the divine, the sacred and the profane. God created the universe for a higher purpose which is unknowable by humankind; and it is the unknowability of one's predestined end (salvation or damnation) which determines the Calvinist to his or her life of hard work and restraint. For Weber, it is most significant that neither Hinduism nor Confucianism give such significance to the role of ascetic activity in their doctrines of divinity and the higher purposes ordained

for humankind. Hinduism, for example, could not originate the entre-
preneurial striving necessary for the emergence of capitalism because of
the limitation imposed on secular activity by the doctrine of Karma.
According to Hindu prophecy, the social caste to which one belongs in
this life has been determined by one's conduct in one's *past* earthly
existence. Thus, if one is a member of the lowest caste of Untouchables,
the only way to redemption is to endure the hardships of one's fate, and
to hope for a higher caste status in one's next incarnation. Such a
prophecy, according to Weber, places a fundamental restraint upon
secular activity. For if, as is the case with Hinduism, the only way to
improve one's spiritual condition is through acceptance of one's present
existence, and if the highest form of earthly life – the Brahmin caste – is
conceived only as a means to the spiritual perfection required to achieve
Nirvana (ultimate transcendence of all material restraints), then secular
productive activity will remain tied to the feudal subsistence economy
which supports the caste system. In the case of Confucian prophecy,
Weber emphasizes the doctrine of accommodation and adjustment to
one's lot, which is essential to Confucius's teaching. His claim is that
given the traditional clan structure of ancient Chinese society, and the
static bureaucratic control of specific social necessities (irrigation,
agriculture), the rational theodicy of Confucianism could not become a
radicalizing force within ethical life. Such powerful legitimation of the
traditional social order, in other words, prevented the emergence of the
dynamizing asceticism which is presupposed by capitalist economic
relations.

These ideal typifications of Protstantism (Calvinism), Hinduism and
Confucianism are deployed by Weber as an attempt to specify the
changes in subjective meanings, motivations and dispositions that are
necessary for the emergence of 'rational' capitalist enterprise. His general
point is that in the absence of the worldly asceticism demanded by the
Protestant religion, the dynamical forms which are characteristic of
Western economic development – the legal freedom of the work force,
the absence of restrictions on exchange, the increasing use of technology
and the appropriation of surplus value – could not have emerged as the
basis of the historical trend towards rationalization and bureaucratization. Unlike Marx, whose account of moral, religious and political
forms maintains that they are the 'ideological' spheres through which
technology determines the history of exploitation, Weber argues that it is
not until the asceticism of the vocation is recognized in the 'bureaucratic'
state that it is possible for technical innovation to become a powerful
(apparently independent) determinant of social relations.[14] 'Capitalism',
in other words, is understood by Weber as a form of rationalization
which: (1) originates in the worldly asceticism of Protestantism and its
sects; (2) is crucial to the replacement of traditional structures of authority by the bureaucratic administration of universal rights and duties;
and 3) becomes pervasive not just of 'productive' forces and relations,

but of the whole cultural, ethical and political fabric of sociality. As Weber puts it in *Economy and Society*:

> The fully developed bureaucratic apparatus compares with other organisations exactly as does the machine with non-mechanical modes of production. Precision, speed, unambiguity, . . . continuity, discretion, unity, strict sub-ordination, reduction of friction and of material and personal costs – these are raised to the optimum point in the strictly bureaucratic organisation.[15]

The process of rationalization/modernization, therefore, is incremental and self-perpetuating; under the sway of bureaucratic authority, technical efficiency and the predominance of rational purposive behaviour, the world becomes increasingly 'disenchanted', and the experience of social engagement increasingly homogenized and undifferentiated. Even the democratization that accompanies the establishment of a rational state authority is compromised, for the bureaucratic measures required to enforce formal equality simply extend the process of disenchantment.

I began my discussion of Max Weber's social theory by arguing that both his methodological and historiographic writings articulate a Kantian valuation of the 'autonomous' individual. I have claimed that the idea of meaning, which Weber conceives as central to sociological explanation, is a reconstruction of some of the fundamental principles of critical ethics: an original independence of the subject from causative or mechanistic accounts of sociality; the priority of subjective cognition/re-presentation over external (heteronomous) necessity; and, most importantly, the proposition of individual spontaneity/autonomy as primary in historical explanation. It is Weber's denial of 'practical reason' as an independently legislative power of the individual, however, that is crucial to our speculative understanding of interpretive sociology. Weber's abandonment of the resources of Kantian practical reason (i.e., the legislative power and critical judgement of the individual subject) does not, as is suggested by a number of commentators,[16] constitute a 'Nietzschean' rejection of absolute value. By claiming that sociology should content itself simply with formulating, rather than evaluating, the value rapports which motivate social action, Weber attempts to set the discipline exclusively in the (Kantian) realm of theoretical/instrumental reason, not to subvert genealogically the whole metaphysical basis of Western culture. As sociologists, we should not make *any* evaluative judgements – regardless of whether these might be Nietzschean/genealogical or Kantian/transcendental – on cultural values and ideals, but confine our analyses to clarifying the utility and realizability of those ideals for given types of social organization.[17] There are two major difficulties with this attempt to place the production and re-cognition of cultural meanings within the generic demands of an 'instrumental' sociology. First, the autonomy of the individual is reduced to its simple re-presentation of ethical life. In the absence of the critical resources provided by Kant's practical reason, the social actor is limited to receiving and conducting meanings that simply engage him or her with general patterns of social behaviour. And secondly, this utilitarian account of meaning generates an historiography in which the individual, as an 'intelligible actor', is increasingly subsumed under the social, economic and cultural consequences of his/her actions. Weber's account of the self-determining power of bureaucratic organization, in other words, derives its force from his *rejection*, on the one hand, of Kant's moral law, and his acceptance, on the other, of the value of individuation, spontaneity and subjective re-cognition.

Weber's attempt to write the history of Western society as the history of bureaucratization is instructive in the sense that, by denying morally legislative insight to the individual subject, he determines the modern condition as an 'iron cage' from which the 'universality of men' is progressively excluded.[18] What is particularly significant here is that, having excluded the resources of critical morality from the domain of social science, Weber's political writings have constant recourse to the quasi-Nietzschean idea of 'charismatic authority'. In his account of 'The three pure types of legitimate authority', Weber identifies charisma as a kind of primal, socially creative force, which originally binds individuals together through the sheer power and spectacle of its exercise: 'It [charisma] arises from the excitement felt by all members of a human group in an extraordinary situation and from devotion to heroic qualities of whatever kind.'[19] Thus, in a very significant sense, the progressive 'disenchantment' that Weber describes in *The Protestant Ethic* is the loss of charisma as a revitalizing force for those who live within the confines of bureaucratic organization. The power of Protestant asceticism in revolutionizing the traditional structures of Patriarchal and Patrimonial authority, in other words, cannot sustain itself as a spontaneously integrative force. For the tendency that Weber identifies in the rational/bureaucratic structures which proliferate from the core of Protestant self-denial is towards efficiency, uniformity and repetition. As such, it is these structures which constantly threaten the socialized individual with the loss of a spontaneously recognized and dynamically constituted identity.

What Weber seems to be gesturing towards in his account of charisma is the possibility of mobilizing politically the creative force through which social relations are originally constituted. The homogenizing power of bureaucratic organization is presented by Weber as self-perpetuating: once it is established, it tends to determine the limits of all individual wants, satisfactions and desires, and to contain them within the bounds of efficiency and productivity. Yet the description of the iron cage offered in *The Protestant Ethic*, it must be remembered, is an ideal typification; the 'legal' authority which binds the individual to the 'free' pursuit of rationally purposive ends does not, in reality, exclude the persistence of charismatic or traditional forms. Any existent state, that is, one which has sustained itself through time, must embody a mixture of legal, charismatic and traditional authority. This is very important for Weber's concept of political participation within the modern bureaucratic state. For, in the absence of any (Kantian) practical-legislative power of the individual subject, it becomes crucial that rationalized social institutions should retain the possibility of receiving and conducting the dynamical force of charisma. Thus, the notion of 'plebiscitarian democracy' that Weber expounds in his essay 'Politics as a vocation' is essentially concerned with the spectacle of conflict among charismatic demagogues. Ideally, the electorate should be drawn into the rhetorical battle of political leaders who compete for the right to impose their particular 'vision' upon existing social, economic and political structures. It is through this experience of participation, Weber claims, that the individual is granted some remission from the utilitarian constraints of the iron cage: each is given access to a dynamizing force which transcends and re-forms the inertia inherent in bureaucratic organization.

This 'Nietzschean' attempt to avoid the historical closure that is sketched in the conclusion of *The Protestant Ethic* is highly problematic. In a letter to Robert Michels in 1908, Weber wrote: 'Such concepts as "will of the people", genuine will of the people, have long since ceased to exist for me; they are fictions. All ideas aimed at abolishing the dominance of men over men are utopian.'[20] Weber, in other words, refers the question of political legitimacy directly to the *de facto* existence of particular states: if a state has sustained itself through time, then it must have been recognized as legitimate by those who live within it. There is no such thing as purely coercive authority, for in the absence of political consent, there can be no sustainable constitution of power. The notion of plebiscitarian democracy, of course, fits well into this functionalist conception of authority. For as long as charisma is conceived as the power whose presence/activity is essential to social formation as such, questions about the legitimacy of particular forms of domination will always be secondary to analyses of the ways in which charisma is conducted through the iron cage of bureaucracy.

Thus, Weber's account of charisma as that which is *necessary* to restore the strength of social bonds and the diversity of human experience is the point at which his ethic of individuation and re-presentative spontaneity is conclusively subsumed under the history of bureaucratic domination. The power of charisma emerges from Weber's political writing as 'diametrically opposed to the bureaucratic in all respects'; it is that which sustains its legitimacy by remaining transcendent of the demands of efficiency, uniformity and repetition.[21] Speculatively understood, however, this transcendent legitimacy of the charismatic is originally conditioned by the entropetal tendency of bureaucratic organization. In the end, it is the necessity to dynamize the structures of social and cultural reproduction which is served by the power of charismatic authority, not the moral existence of the individual. By abandoning any commitment to a (Kantian) legislative practical reason, then, Weberian sociology is unable to make any ethical distinction between states whose authority respects the life of the individual and those which simply suppress the plurality and spontaneity of meanings. For Weber, as Habermas rightly points out, 'sociological' distinctions can be made only between the relative psychological effectiveness with which different states maintain the fiction (re-presentation) of 'legitimate' authority.[22]

Throughout my exposition of Weber's sociology, I have attempted to disclose the tension between his idea of subjective meaning and the history of bureaucratic domination. I have claimed that this tension is determined by the ethic of re-presentative spontaneity implicit in the concept of social action; and that the oppositions (of universality and bureaucracy, individuality and uniformity, spontaneity and repetition), which disclose the 'moral' content of interpretive sociology, are ultimately resolved by recourse to the non-rational concept of charisma. Weber's precept that sociologists should refrain from ethical judgement of the value rapports they study presupposes a basic functionality of social and cultural meanings: their true significance is not to be found in the 'moral' life of the individual (in his or her universality, individuality and spontaneity in the production and reception of meaning), but in their reproduction of certain general types of social behaviour. It is this rejection of ethical values as legislatively independent of system and bureaucracy that is crucial to our speculative account of *Verstehen* sociology. For by reducing the re-presentative power of the subject (which for Kant is regulated by the autonomy of the moral law) to the voluntaristic counterpart of bureaucratization, Weber's social theory loses the force of an ethical critique. For however much he may regret the dominance of bureaucracy in modern Western societies, the absence of any rational principle through which it would be possible to distinguish 'ethical' from 'non-ethical' forms of authority, means that Weber's thought remains at the level of describing the subjective forms through which instrumental reason achieves its purposes.

Such a recognition, I would suggest, is not without significance. For if the autonomy of the subject is formed through its re-presentation of the 'objective' elements of ethical life (institutionalized forms of work satisfaction and desire), then Weber's concept of meaning at least shows how the demands of instrumental reason may determine 'ethical' recognition of the other. In representing the dynamics of modern industrialism as the expansion of bureaucratic time and space, in other words, his interpretive sociology distinguishes the imperatives of efficiency and uniformity as immanent in the demands of Protestant asceticism. Thus, subjective meaning is invoked as historically prior to the systemic (functionalist) and materialist (Marxist) necessities articulated in structural sociology. The problem with Weber's approach, however, is that by excluding the rational resources of critical ethics from his sociology, he is unable to formulate a *critique* of modernity, or to show how the individual could become historically re-formative of ethical substance.

(Ultimately, Geoge Ritzer's 'McDonaldization' thesis concludes that, if we are left only with the inexorable infringement of instrumental reason on every aspect of social life, those individuals and institutions which successfully resist this trend, will, for this very reason, become part of its necessity.) Yet, if I am right in identifying the basic deficiency of Weber's social thought as his failure to recognize the legislative power of Kantian practical reason, and if I am also right in claiming that it is the reflective oppositions of Kant's philosophy which, in general, limit and differentiate sociological perspectives, then the logic of my exposition demands that any sociological transcription of Kant's practical reason could itself only determine a limited and partial account of ethical life. I will argue in the following section that Habermas's idea of communicative reason is exactly this: a rigorous and consistent transcription of the principles of critical morality, into a sociological critique of community, ethics and identity. And that this 'communicative' account of practical reason reproduces the legislative powers posited by Kant in his concept of free will: the opposition of rational autonomy to the 'heteronomous' forms of ethical life; the prescriptive authority of transcendental reason; and the dominance of moral ideality over concrete, historical differentiation. In treating Habermas's attempt to construct a 'communicative ethics', then, I am no longer concerned with the *absence* of the Kantian resource of practical reason (Weber), but with the *reproduction* of the 'reflective' aporias which are originally determined by Kant.

Habermas and the ethics of communication

Autonomy, lifeworld and discourse

The social and political significance which Kant himself attributes to the sovereignty of practical reason is made explicit in his essay 'What is enlightenment?'. Kant's fundamental argument is that by thinking rationally, individual subjects sustain a critical relation to the ethical and political forms which govern them; and that as such, the authority of these forms should always be open to, although not immediately dominated by, reason's capacity for autonomous self-enlightenment. The primacy of practical reason, in other words, is articulated in Kant's political writings as the original postulate of historical progress, that is, the reduction of external ('heteronomous') influences on the sovereignty of the individual.[23] The theoretical development of this Kantian relationship between critical autonomy and the 'instrumental' constitution of social relations is important here, as it provides the background to Habermas's account of subjectivity, autonomy and ethical life. In the previous chapter, I looked at the two contradictory strands in structural sociology: the idea that sociological explanation must re-articulate the integrative, productive and universalizing power already accomplished in social relations (Durkheim, Parsons, Luhmann); and the idea that the history of this 'accomplishment' must be explained as the progressive corruption of an original (natural) productive spontaneity (Marx and Marxism). I have argued that the ideas of instrumentality, functionality and totality deployed in both of these traditions are determined within a conceptual structure that privileges the organization of ethical life over its subjective re-cognition. Luhmann, for example, postulates the individual as a unit whose 'behaviour' is a manipulable function of system necessity;[24] while for Horkheimer and Adorno, the dominance of instrumental reason in social relations accomplishes the transformation of rational enlightenment into the ideology/technology of mass homogenization and control.[25] My exposition of Habermas's social thought, therefore, will concentrate on his attempt to transcribe the critical resources of Kant's practical reason into an account of the communicative necessity inscribed within the origin of sociality as such.

Habermas's fundamental objection to Kant's idea of rational agency is what he calls its 'subject centredness': the freedom of Kant's autonomous individual is alienated to a transcendent realm of ends divorced from the empirical reality of the social world. Practical reason, in other words, always opposes rational subjectivity to the social forms and institutions to which it is essentially related. Thus, Habermas's reconstruction of Kant's notion of rational agency attempts to show that practical reason is capable of constituting universal demands, and of assuming a critical relation to social institutions, without reference to a region transcendent of ethical life. Or, to put it another way, Habermas's idea of communicative reason is an attempt to show that the dominance of instrumental reason in 'organized capitalist' societies,[26] can never come to the state of completion that either Luhmann or Horkheimer and Adorno claim, and that the communicative activity of rational agents always exceeds the positive (social, economic and political) forms which presuppose it. How then does Habermas make good these claims?

Habermas's theory of language is, above all, an attempt to elucidate the general, unavoidable presuppositions of the 'speech act'. His claim is that the inter-subjective experience, through which sociality comes into being, presupposes an original relationship of need and satisfaction to the 'pragmatic' forms by which it is communicated. Language, in other words, is the universal medium through which individual subjects express/recognize their particular needs and satisfactions; and so the speech act is essentially transformative of those needs and satisfactions into the shared experience which constitutes 'social' recognition. For Habermas, language opens, and develops with, the possibilities of the social: it is a 'universal pragmatics' of communicative action, whose logical structures must be understood as transcendent of the isolation, implicitude and antagonism (pre-sociality) which they presuppose. This is why Chomsky's theory of language as a monodological production of the individual is rejected by Habermas: the essential thing about language as such is that it cannot be abstracted from the recognition, expression and communication of mental states that Chomsky understands as essentially private/subjective. The concept of rational transcendence that Habermas deploys throughout his critical theory therefore refers to the essential re-formative power of communicative action (the speech act): that is, to the reconstruction of isolated wants and desires; the constitution of a realm of intersubjective experience (sociality); and the re-cognition of factual and ethical 'truth'.

The 'developmental logic' by which Habermas expounds the idea of historical evolution proceeds directly from this concept of language as originally constitutive of sociality. As we have seen, the transcendence of language consists in its universalizing of subjective need, satisfaction and desire – that is, in its constitution of a realm of intersubjective action and experience. Habermas's account of the development of this realm, which he refers to generically as the 'lifeworld', takes the form of expounding the relationship between the deep structures of individual moral and cognitive development and the development of 'technique' (material production), 'as if' this relationship were informed by a 'criterion of higher value'.[27] The pragmatics of communicative action, in other words, is conceived both as that which is presupposed in the technical fulfilment of social needs and as that which demands that this technical/productive development is regulated by consensus on the ultimate value of such needs. Habermas's 'rational reconstruction' of social forms therefore assumes that historical development is led by the moral and cognitive development of linguistically competent individuals, and that, consequently, the technical/instrumental evolution of productive forces is always situated within normative/communicative structures which limit its 'colonization' of the lifeworld.

It is this theorization of language as a transcendental pragmatics of communicative action that situates Habermas's critical theory within an essentially Kantian universe. The notion of linguistic competence, through which Habermas understands the autonomy of individual subjects in the lifeworld, has as its necessary counterpart a postulated ideal of 'symmetrical' communication – the ideal speech situation. This ideal is grounded in Habermas's account of the speech act as a form whose original possibility can be reconstructed only through the universal (a priori) conditions of dialogue/intersubjectivity. The pragmatic universals which linguistically competent individuals must, as such, be able to deploy (i.e., constatives, regulatives, representatives and communicatives) form the basis of an ideal of communicative transparency that is implicit in every form of social action. Individuals within the lifeworld, therefore, are always potentially able to reconstruct the rational communicative power of ordinary language: the very possibility of the lifeworld as a realm of intersubjective praxis and experience entails that ethical conduct must always refer to an (ideal) situation in which each linguistically competent subject could have participated in the determination of the truth. As Habermas expresses it in *Postmetaphysical Thinking* (1995a):

A peculiarity exhibited by these pragmatic presuppositions of consensus formation is that they contain certain strong idealisations. For example, the supposition that all participants in dialogue use the same linguistic expressions with identical meanings is unavoidable but often counterfactual. The validity claims that a speaker raises for the content of his assertoric, normative or expressive sentences are also bound to similar idealisations: what the speaker, here and now in a given context, asserts as valid transcends, according to the sense of his claim, all context dependent, merely local standards of validity.[28]

The forms of strategic action which come increasingly to colonize the lifeworld in late modernity, in other words, must be understood as embedded in (scientific, technical, administrative) discourses which presuppose the universal pragmatics of the speech act. For the subjects who must orientate themselves within the lifeworld, the ideal speech situation functions as a regulative idea which is capable of guiding moral and ethical judgement. Habermas's claim is that, unlike Kant's notion of practical reason, the moral, ethical and political demands represented through the ideal of symmetrical communication are constituted through the actual practices which constitute the realm of intersubjective/social experience. Moral self-determination within the lifeworld, therefore, should not be understood as reproducing the antagonism of a 'hetero-nomous' secular/social existence to a transcendental realm of fully human ends. For Habermas, the realm of social experience is the inescapable formative condition of all normative evaluations. The moral and political problems raised by late modernity require us to acknowl-edge that the a priori synthetic power of (transcendental) reason is a metaphysical ideal; and that communicative action is increasingly dispersed into a plurality of differentiated and autonomous realms. Thus, the universal interest recognized through the ideal representation of symmetrical communication presupposes: (1) the originally dialogi-cal/communicative character of ordinary language; (2) that the resolu-tion of practical and normative questions – that is the disputes and conflicts among different spheres of action and interest – is grounded in the formal generality of rational communicative action; and (3) that such resolutions necessarily produce a practical consensus which is uni-versally valid for linguistically competent individuals as such.

Habermas's attempt to distinguish a 'modern' communicative ethics and politics from the precepts of Kantianism seems to stand or fall on his idea of validity. The recognition of universally valid interests is, for Habermas, possible only through the unconstrained (symmetrical) representation of the systemic, subjectivized, objectivating and normative knowledges, which (as 'factually' autonomous) distort the communica-tive transparency of the lifeworld. This normative re-presentation of the content of sociality, we have seen, is grounded in, and necessitated by, the pragmatics of communicative action: the 'ideality' of the ideal speech situation is constantly redetermined in the universal validity claims which are always at stake in the speech act. As Habermas puts it, '[the] ideal speech situation belongs to the structure of possible speech . . . that in the execution of possible speech acts (and actions) we contrafactually proceed as if the ideal speech situation were not really fictive but real – precisely what we call a presupposition'.[29] The concept of an ideal speech situation, then, relates to the sphere of communicative action and experience as a formal ideal of dialogue, or 'discourse'. Thus the 'truth' of normative propositions about the constitution of the lifeworld cannot be maintained on the basis of reason's elucidation of its own essential (apodeictic) structures, categories and ends. Rather, the 'transcendental' nature of ordinary language must be conceived as opening the possibility of rational/symmetrical dialogue among autonomous subjects, about the contemporary form of moral, ethical, and political validity.

According to Habermas's conception of a critical theory, the legislative power of reason can no longer be regarded as determined either by the discursive/representational/objectivating structure of subjectivity (Kant and the Kantians), or within the historical-dialectical sublations through which reason reclaims what has been 'external' to it (Hegel and Marx). The notion of modernity that Habermas seeks to present, certainly from *Legitimation Crisis* (1976) onwards, involves the postulation of a chronic antagonism between factually autonomous realms of action and the (transcendental/ideal) communicative necessity inscribed in the pragmatics of the speech act. Any attempt to impose 'totalizing' categories of unity, identity, difference or legitimacy on the factual differentiation of the lifeworld must always fail to grasp the actual diversity of modern social existence. The social differentiation made possible by the pragmatic, communicative structures of language, in other words, always already exceeds 'metaphysical' determinations of unity and difference. 'Today', Habermas claims, 'philosophy could establish its own distinct criteria of validity . . . only at the price of falling short of the level of justification that has already been reached, i.e., at the price of surrendering its own validity.'[30]

The notion of communicative rationality entails a radical limitation of the scope and legislative power of philosophy. Habermas's expositions of the pragmatics of the speech act, of the 'communicative' constitution of the lifeworld, and of the conditions through which normative and cognitive validity can be recognized, circumscribe the 'modern' philosophical enterprise as an 'interpretive', rather than a legislative project. The possibility of reconciling individual autonomy with the demands of social cohesion and universal interest, we have seen, depends on the conception of the lifeworld as 'the non-objective whole [of communicative action and intersubjective experience] which . . . now present as horizon and background, evades the grasp of theoretical objectification'.[31] It is only through the idealization of this communicative 'horizon' (in the ideal speech situation) that each linguistically competent subject can re-cognize and judge the validity of established norms, values and interests.

Critical philosophy, therefore, should be limited to mediating between the intersubjectivity constituted in the lifeworld and the 'expert knowledges' which seek to colonize the realm of everyday communicative action. Thus,

> what remains for philosophy is an illuminating furtherance of the lifeworld processes of achieving self-understanding, processes that are related to totality. For the lifeworld must be defended against extreme alienation at the hands of the objectivating, the moralising and the aestheticising interventions of expert cultures.[32]

This statement clearly needs unpacking. First, Habermas's notion of philosophical discourse and its interpretive relationship to the lifeworld presupposes his idea of language as a pragmatic of intersubjective experience. It is only if the social existence of humanity can be truly understood as presupposing and sustaining an original communicative necessity that such an interpretive function can be claimed for philosophy. Secondly, this postulation of critical thought as a discourse which should address the 'ideological' validity claims of non-universal moralities, self-regarding avant-garde aesthetics, and the instrumentalist of science seems to entail a privileging of formal/discursive rationality over the diversified contents of ethical life. Critical analysis of these contents – that is, the re-cognition of their communicative significance through the ideal speech situation – is conceived by Habermas as the necessary counterpart of the autonomy of linguistically competent subjects. His distinction between the communicative background of the lifeworld (culture, tradition, popular norms and beliefs) and the diversification of 'expert cultures' posits the 'ideality' of the language as that which always exceeds the discourses of moral, aesthetic and scientific specialism. The praxis of subjects within the lifeworld therefore constantly redeploys the communicative resources of ordinary language – a redeployment which, for Habermas, presupposes communicative socialization and 'performative' autonomy.

In accordance with the logic of my exposition, then, I have begun to determine the reflective formality of Habermas's idea of communicative reason. His notion of autonomy as the 'redeployment' of dialogical rules certainly looks like an attempt to situate 'free will' within the parameters of formal procedural rationality. Communicative reason is posited as a universal authority and explanatory power: all social forms, practices and institutions presuppose the 'norms of rational speech', and so must be regarded as subject to the 'ideal' dialogical totality inherent in their deployment. I will argue that, despite Habermas's attempt to expound communicative pragmatics as the origin of ethical life and individual autonomy, the Kantian foundation of his thought excludes recognition of 'difference' as that which may include the 'rationally' incommunicable. It is this inability to acknowledge the necessity of implicit, non-cognitive satisfactions to the concept of ethical life (love/family, faith/religious allegiance, patriotism/war) which is the crucial misrecognition in Habermas's critical theory.[33] For as long as cultural forms and traditions are conceived as implicitly restrictive of 'rational' solidarity, communicative reason can re-cognize and evaluate only those forms of action which can be called 'discursive'. Thus, Habermas's account of historical progress is ultimately the progress of linguistically competent subjects towards self-transparency, self-determination and universal legitimacy of action. However, even considered simply as a 'guiding thread' for the evaluation of social forms, this ideal of communicative action is problematic: social, ethical and political legitimacy is recognized only in terms of rational standards it has yet to attain; and the actual mediations and oppositions of ethical life are conceived as subject to the 'higher value' of communicative legitimacy. I will examine the social and political implications of this approach in more detail.

Autonomy, solidarity and legitimacy

Habermas's attempt to mediate the ethical, political and economic dimensions of 'organized capitalism' into a generalized crisis of legitimation is founded on the idea of language, or the speech act, as opening a historical development which is originally tied to the validation of (cognitive) 'truth' and (normative) 'correctness'. In general, therefore, the exchange between social systems and their environments involves: (1) the appropriation and homogenization of 'outer nature' through productive 'technique'; and (2) the appropriation of 'inner nature' (i.e., the realm of abstract subjectivity – wanting, pleasure, pain, etc.) through socialization. These two processes, according to Habermas, must be conceived as presupposing the linguistic/intersubjective categories through which both 'truth' (as the criterion through which instrumental necessities are recognized and extended) and 'correctness' (as the criterion through which moral necessity is acknowledged) can be discursively established. This 'discursive' validation of cognitive truth and moral rightness means that, within a continuing socio-cultural tradition, such validation claims cannot be forgotten or dispensed with – in both dimensions, 'development follows rationally reconstructible patterns.'[34] Social evolution should, in general, be regarded as a 'learning process' in which determinate forms of social organization both facilitate and impede the moral and cognitive development of individual subjects (i.e., their capacity to recognize and deploy universally 'valid' propositions).

This idea of a logically reconstructible process of social evolution returns us to the historical and political thematics of Kantian practical reason. For Habermas, the necessity of presupposing ethical life as a sphere of communicative/intersubjective experience entails a categorical distinction between the imperatives of production (the reduction of environmental/natural contingency) and the general increase in linguistic competence involved in socialization (the adaptation of 'inner nature' to collective 'identity giving' structures – norms, values). Conceived in this sense of an increasing ability to deploy and recognize the universal conditions through which truth and correctness are validated, it is socialization which is the ultimate ground of individuation and autonomy. For, as socio-historical forms develop, and the political administrative processes of system 'steering' become increasingly dominant, the normative structures inscribed in particular socio-historical traditions 'become effective as a kind of self-inhibiting mechanism *vis-à-vis* imperatives of [systemic] power expansion'. The communicative constitution of the lifeworld therefore, forms an 'inner environment that is paradoxical from the point of view of steering': it is that which, within the logic of socio-historical evolution, reproduces itself as a limiting condition on the technical, instrumental and political-administrative demands of production.[35]

For Kant, we have seen, historical progress – or 'ethico-teleology' – is entailed in the concept of practical reason as that which ought to govern desire and inclination. Given the 'fact' of reason's ability to determine ends transcendent of mere animality, social evolution is conceived in Kant's political and historical essays as progress towards a universal reduction of 'heteronomous' influences on rational will. Thus, although Habermas attempts to distinguish this isolating and 'repressive' morality from communicative ethics, it seems clear that his 'pragmatic' reconstruction of the speech act retains the force (or violence) of cognitive universality over the implicitude, dispersal and misrecognition which is sustained in ethical life. The historical account of crises, stagnations and developments which is given in *Legitimation Crisis* presupposes a 'discursive' ideal of social solidarity in which the spheres of practical and theoretical validation are rationally differentiated, and 'reflective' learning predominates over 'non-reflective' attachment to particular traditions and identities. And so the project of a critical social science, whose scope includes evaluation of the validity of the ethical, political and economic organization of the lifeworld, is concerned ultimately with what Habermas understands as the 'ideological' impediments to learning – i.e., impediments to a universal (reflective) recognition of the communicative necessity inscribed in all practical and technical questions. 'Not learning, but non-learning', he remarks, 'is the phenomenon which calls for explanation.'[36]

The fundamental thesis developed in *Legitimation Crisis* is that the socio-cultural forms which have supported 'bourgeois capitalism' have been, and continue to be, eroded by the tendencies inherent in modern 'organized capitalism' – i.e., the 'socialization' of production and the expansion of the state to service the non- (or indirectly) productive individuals increased by this socialization. For Habermas, bourgeois capitalism is characterized by: (1) the 'unpolitical' nature of class rule (wage labour and capital confront each other as socio-economically distributed groups); (2) the ideology of economic integration (economic rewards, moral responsibility and political legitimacy are recognized through the mediating/co-ordinating power of the market); and (3) its susceptibility to 'system crises' (or the transformation of bourgeois–proletarian class antagonism into political–administrative 'steering problems' which directly threaten identity). This shift from bourgeois to organized capitalism, according to Habermas, is precipitated by the cycles of depression and prosperity which afflict bourgeois capitalist economies. The organized form of capitalism emerges when the ideology of the market as a self-stabilizing mechanism begins to be displaced by a political–administrative management ('steering') of the system necessities of capital accumulation. For Habermas, then, the 'crisis cycle' that afflicts liberal capitalist economies is not determined through a causative relationship between the 'objective' necessity of system contradictions (tendency of the average rate of profit to fall, increase in the proportion of fixed to variable capital, etc.) and bourgeois-ideological forms of consciousness (moral individualism, universal legal and political freedoms). Rather, his account of the transition from bourgeois to organized capitalism attempts to show that the development of 'production' (its techniques and system contradictions) presupposes the lifeworld as a realm of shared experience which limits the causative power of the capitalist economy – both as the progenitor of ideological legitimation and revolutionary praxis.[37]

For Habermas, the organized capitalist state is founded upon a limited ceding of power by corporate organizations. There is, in other words, a general recognition that the 'system necessities' of advanced capitalism (primarily, the maintenance of mass loyalty and the continued reproduction of private capital) require political–administrative management. The modern state, then, is originally charged with a responsibility that it is unable to fulfil: it must service an ever expanding 'socialization' of production (housing, education, etc.) through taxation, while remaining withdrawn from the private realm of wealth creation and appropriation – a realm which it must acknowledge as sacrosanct. 'Rationality deficits', therefore, are inevitable because the state is never able to service the social elements of production so rationally that 'crisis ridden' disturbances of growth are avoided. Rather, these 'crises' are displaced into the political–administrative sphere – which begs the question of whether a state which is stuck between the necessities of social intervention and private appropriation can sustain both a capitalist system necessity and the mass loyalty of those more or less indirectly involved in the creation and appropriation of wealth.

It is the contradiction between the political–administrative rationality of the state and the socio-cultural forms which supported the bourgeois capitalist economy that Habermas identifies as the cause of the modern crises of legitimation and motivation. Within the terms of his logic of social evolution, a categorical distinction is made between the 'nature-like' interpretive structures which sustain collective identity and commitment and the political–administrative rationality through which the late modern state attempts to negotiate the cyclical crises of capitalist accumulation. The lifeworld, as the sphere in which cultural/interpretive structures emerge as crystallizations of intersubjectivity, is conceived as the original condition of political, administrative and social authority – what Habermas calls 'social and system integration'. It is this relationship between the (implicit) structures of cultural identity and the rationality of social organization and control ('steering') which defines Habermas's conception of 'legitimation crisis' and its significance for our under-standing of late modernity. For while it is the case that legitimacy is sustained by structures whose communicative origin and significance remains non-discursive, the crisis of late modernity must be conceived in terms of the antagonism between the (corporate economic) system necessity serviced by the state and the inertia of bourgeois cultural tradi-tions which have become exorbitant from the point of view of steering.

We have seen that the constitution of the state under the conditions of organized capitalism entails a certain rationality of fiscal appropriation, and a 'pattern of priorities' in the deployment of funds in the service of socialized production. Such a state must be able to legitimate its interventions in the lifeworld as and when they arise. For Habermas, however, the demand for legitimacy, which is constituted through the state's political–administrative mediation of economic crisis, cannot be met by its deployment of 'functional equivalents' to the deep identity structures constituted in the lifeworld. Meaning and significance, in other words, cannot be administratively produced by the state: they are sustained by the cultural traditions whose formation, organization and legitimation of social action is intuitive, rather than calculative or strategic. The administrative planning characteristic of organized capital-ism therefore tends to erode the cultural and ideological traditions which supported liberal capitalist society and constantly to increase the demand for 'functional' legitimation which it is originally unable to meet. Mean-ing, significance and legitimacy become increasingly scarce resources, and the strategic/calculative pursuit of 'external' rewards offered by the system becomes the dominant form of social action. A legitimation crisis, then, arises 'as soon as the demands for such rewards rise faster than the available quantity of value, or when expectations arise that cannot be satisfied with such rewards'.[38]

The crucial point about the political–administrative rationality of the modern state is that having eroded the 'privatistic' motivational patterns which supported bourgeois capitalism, it is unable to compensate for the legitimation and motivational 'deficits' it causes simply by manipu-lating instrumental motivations. For Habermas, the 'civic' and 'familial-vocational' privatism, which was essential to the functioning of bourgeois capitalism, should be understood as grounded in traditional 'world-views' which were absorbed into liberal ideologies of the market as a self-regulating, socially integrative mechanism. Thus, the 'core components' of bourgeois ideology, such as the work ethic, possessive individualism and achievement orientation, are formed within an implicit background of socio-cultural 'world-views' which regulate and legitimate social action. The infringement of political–administrative rationality on these collectivizing structures progressively undermines the cultural legitimacy of the work ethic, achievement orientation, possessive individualism and the generalized orientation of individuals to exchange value. Each of these explicitly 'bourgeois' forms, in other words, is no longer recognized as essential to participation in the ethical life of the collective, but is seen as a contingent form of action which may be adopted if – and only if – it is likely to secure value excessive of that which is generally allocated to socialized production. Increasingly, the 'techniques' (i.e., socialization) and contents of culture are experienced as essentially contingent.

The experience of moral, ethical and political contingency is central to Habermas's concept of legitimation crisis. His argument is that the erosion of bourgeois ideologies by the administrative interventions of the state produces a cultural vacuum in which 'normative structures appear that are unsuited to reproduce civil and familial-vocational privatism'.[39] Among these structures Habermas includes the radical 'scientism' which seeks to replace the 'irrationality' of cultural forms with the ('esoteric') authority of technical knowledge, and a 'Post-Auratic Art' which reinforces the divergence between socio-cultural values and the demands of the political and economic systems. The most important structure from the point of view of Habermas's developmental logic, however, is the universalistic morality through which bourgeois capitalism sought to legitimate the 'freedom' conferred by the market economy. Formal bourgeois law represents the freedom of the civic sphere of 'norm contents' from the particularism of tradition. And so it is the bourgeois capitalist state which first becomes freed from the traditionalistic mode of justification: the values it sought to impose supposedly reflected the (ideological) universalism of exchange value equivalents. We have seen that, according to Habermas's argument, 'the foundations of this bourgeois mode of legitimation crumbled, while at the same time increased demands for legitimacy arise'.[40] Yet this historical movement towards universality cannot simply be forgotten. If the socio-cognitive development of humanity is founded on the recognition of truth, as Habermas claims it is, then the discourses of moral and political universalism which emerge from bourgeois capitalism must be recognized as demanding an explicitly communicative validation. This necessity is compounded by the state's inability to compensate the loss of cultural legitimacy: the ideological structure which supported bourgeois capitalism remains as an 'enfeebled' form which places increasingly exorbitant demands on the economic-political system. Possessive individualism, achievement ideology and the orientation towards use value, in other words, all assume an instrumentalist form, stripped of their implicit communicative significance.

Habermas's concluding remarks 'On the logic of legitimation problems',[41] foreshadow the communicative ethics he expounds from the *Theory of Communicative Action* (1987) onwards. His claim is that the only way in which the legitimation deficits that have emerged in organized capitalism can be made good is by 'uncoupling' legitimation from its foundation in cultural world-views, and subjecting normative propositions to the rational–dialogic procedures inherent in communicative action. Legitimacy would be established as an autonomous and 'symmetrical' connection of speech acts – a process whose critical relation to 'truth' is entailed in the (ideal/transcendental) universality of communicative action. The possibility of resolving the structural oppositions (of interpretive world-views and system necessity, of technical knowledges and communicative action, of art and everyday collective norms), through which problems of legitimation become generalized into a condition of crisis, therefore returns to the Kantian idea of practical reason that Habermas articulates in his later writing:

> [Practical] [d]iscourse can be understood as that form of communication that is removed from the contexts of experience and action whose structure assures us: that the bracketed validity claims of assertions, recommendations, or warnings are the exclusive object of discussion; that participants, themes and contributions are not restricted except with reference to the goal of testing the validity claims in questions; that no force except that of the better argument is exercised; and that as a result, all motives except the co-operative search for truth are excluded. If under these conditions a consensus about the recommendation to accept a norm arises argumentatively, that is, on the basis of hypothetically proposed alternative justifications, then this consensus expresses a 'rational will'.[42]

Social theoretical 'discourse', as a form of rationality 'bracketed off' from the sphere of everyday communicative action, therefore ought to base its judgements of the normative texture of the lifeworld, on what Habermas calls 'the model of the suppression of generalizable interests'.[43] The 'communicative' critique of ideology, in other words, attempts to disclose the suppressive nature of institutionalized norms (i.e., the degree to which they merely 'stabilize relations of power'), by comparing them with the 'hypothetical state of a system of norms founded . . . discursively'.[44] Ultimately, the pragmatics of the speech act are invoked by Habermas as the ground of a purified discourse, in which the maximum communicative potential of a given social 'organizational principle' (at a given stage of its development) is disclosed. The conclusion of *Legitimation Crisis* therefore crystallizes the Kantian presuppositions of Habermas's project into a categorical distinction between the concrete empirical content of ethical life and the transcendental ideal (of 'symmetrical' communication) entailed in the possibility of communicative action. What remains for us, is to evaluate the significance of Habermas's reproduction of this universal-empirical opposition for the idea of a social science.

At the beginning of my exposition of Habermas's work, I claimed that the essential difference between Weber's interpretive sociology and Habermas's critical theory is that while the former rejects the ethical resource of Kant's practical reason, the latter is an attempt to reconstruct the ideas of autonomy, universality and identity articulated in the second *Critique*. Thus, the forms of normative recognition that Weber sought to confine to the realm of subjective meaning (i.e., to the instrumental necessity of engaging the individual in social action) are conceived by Habermas as elements within the historical development of communicative consensus. I also claimed that this attempt to translate the determinations of the moral will into a communicative account of ethical life posits an abstract priority of 'universal' cognition over the concrete forms of moral, ethical and political differentiation (*Sittlichkeit*). This priority of 'reflection' over 're-cognition' (of ethical substance) lies at the core of Habermas's social theory; for it is only by understanding history as an implicit cognitive development (of intersubjectivity) that the fundamental ethical and political problems of modernity are disclosed, as well as their possible 'communicative' resolution. In order to evaluate the theoretical significance of communicative reason, therefore, I need to specify the arguments through which it is distilled from the evolution of concrete historical forms.

I can briefly summarize the logic of Habermas's critique: (1) Speech acts have a deep 'pragmatic' grammar which is originally communicative; (2) historical development (of the lifeworld) must be understood as a learning process in which the pragmatics of communicative action become crystallized into normative and institutional forms; (3) these forms can be categorized in terms of their 'organizational principles' (i.e., the way in which the realm of communicative action and experience is related to the 'system necessities' of given forms of social and productive organization); (4) thus, the notion of 'learning' that informs Habermas's 'developmental logic' proceeds through the determination of 'crises' specific to particular levels of social and productive development (primitive, traditional, 'bourgeois' and 'organized' capitalist); (5) the evolutionary 'learning' necessitated by the transition from bourgeois to organized capitalism takes place through the constitution of a legitimation crisis: the impossibility of providing 'functional equivalents' for the 'world-views' in which bourgeois motivational patterns are sustained constitutes a demand for universal communicative legitimation of normative patterns; (6) 'communicative' norms should reflect the 'performative' autonomy of linguistically competent subjects in the formation of universal interests, constitute the lifeworld as 'interpretively' independent of technical and scientific colonization, while remaining responsive to the socio-productive evolution and the 'organizational principle' (system necessity); (7) the critique of ideology therefore does not demand reflection upon 'bourgeois' politics, aesthetics, philosophy and morality as a universal justification of 'capitalist' domination. Rather, it requires that we recognize the specific cases in which the communicative necessity of the lifeworld is threatened by non-communicative accretions of privilege, and the 'specialism' scientific knowledge.[45]

The guiding presupposition of Habermas's work, then, is the transcendental grammar of the speech act. For it is the 'idealized' conditions of communicative action that originally open the lifeworld (as the realm of intersubjective action and experience) and sustain the possibility of rational normative consensus. However, this relationship of the communicative origin (of the lifeworld) to the dialogical ideal of legitimation, that Habermas develops in his account of modernity, is the focus of a debate in which the ethical claims of speculative reason and deconstruction are brought directly into conflict. In *The Postmodern Condition* (1991a), Jean-François Lyotard claims that Habermas's assumption of a communicative origin of the lifeworld commits him to look for 'consensus' even where the heterogeneity of (moral, aesthetic political, economic, etc.) discourses is already exclusive of a universally regulative cognition. The attempt to reconstruct Kant's critical ethics, in other words, determines an ethico-teleology in which 'humanity as a collective (universal) subject seeks its common emancipation through the regularisation of "moves" permitted in all language games and that the legitimacy of any statement resides in its contributing to that emancipation'.[46] Jacques Derrida, in his essay 'Violence and metaphysics', articulates a similar, although subtly different, argument, which suggests that language, far from opening the possibility of universal normative consensus, determines an 'economy of violence'. Speech, in other words, always expresses the practical, technical and aesthetic determinations of reason (*logos*), not as categories which presuppose and ideally reformulate consensus, but as moments which can only express the idea of 'peace' as an undeterminable 'silence' unforeseen in the economy of presence/totality.[47]

For Lyotard and Derrida, Habermas's determination to abstract unity and consensus from the dispersal of (post)modern discourses reveals an idealist origin that demands the regulation of justice and freedom by rational totality. I have argued throughout my account of Habermas's work that this origin is specifically Kantian; and that his 'secondarization' of the non-rational (i.e., implicit, or particularized) elements of ethical life is essentially related to Kant's categorical distinction between rational will and the 'external' satisfactions of civil community. Lyotard and Derrida's respective pronouncements on Hegel attempt to show that the 'totalizing' intention, which was partially restrained in Kant's critical philosophy, becomes completely deterministic in speculative thought. The concrete historical forms, through which self-consciousness develops, are conceived either as categories whose positive 'sublation' has already been determined by the 'Result' (non-contradictory ethical life),[48] or as a discourse of mediation which is unable to acknowledge (and take account of) its own originary moment of possibility.[49] In both of these accounts of speculative reason, the argument is that Hegel institutes a discourse which demands, far more than Kant's critical philosophy, the totalization of every contingent or unforeseen possibility of 'rational' sociality. A speculative idea of 'justice', therefore, is violent in its very inception: it necessarily excludes the 'otherness' (death, the Jew, the woman) that its categories have determined (and which they have always already presupposed). My claim, however, is that both Lyotard and Derrida misrecognize Hegel's mediation of difference and universality in ethical life, and that the deconstructive rejection of the 'logos' as the (a priori) form of justice points to a rejection of Kantianism and its oppositions (Habermas), rather than speculative reason.

I am not suggesting – and this will become clearer in Chapter 5 – that the notions of justice and autonomy that emerge from the deconstructive approach can be incorporated into speculative thought in any simple way. Rather, what I am suggesting is that 'social' necessity must be recognized through the dispersal of forms (work, love, desire, satisfaction, self-interest, morality, autonomy) which always exist in contradiction within ethical life. This is the inescapable 'clash within the good' that Hegel refers to in *The Science of Logic* (1969): ethical life can never be a 'totalized' totality, and its categories cannot be properly understood as articulations of a formal/a priori necessity. Speculatively understood, the concept of sociality demands that we conceive the formation of self-consciousness neither as an abstract cognitive development (Habermas), nor as an original violence whose (diverse and externalized) determinations can be 'sublated' only through the reproduction of 'totality' (Lyotard, Derrida, Foucault). My claim is that the determinations, through which self-consciousness is formed, constitute ethical life through contradictions (of liberty, identity, autonomy, etc.) which are never historically totalized or resolved. The speculative nature of ethical life therefore lies in the fact that its categories are always finite: they demand sublation, and yet their historical 'overcoming' (*Aufhebung*) always falls short of absolute totality. It is precisely this substantive recognition of 'universality' by subjects embedded in the violence and satisfaction of ethical life that is excluded from Habermas's communicative conception of sociality. He fails to recognize that the idea of ethical life is necessarily inclusive of 'non-communicative' diversity (i.e., non-communicative from the perspective of moral-cognitive progress), and that the recognition and diversification of universal interests might always produce liberty, identity and autonomy as contradictory forms.

To conclude then, I will make some brief remarks about the contribution that Habermas's idea of communicative reason makes to our speculative conception of social science. Most importantly, his theorization of modernity (its crises and deficits) specifies the importance of subjective re-cognition to the 'substance' of ethical life. The main point to have emerged from the previous chapter was that the reification of ethical substance, in general, tends to reduce autonomy to an accident of structural causes. Marxism, structural functionalism and system theory all reproduce – in different ways – an external relationship of subjective representation to the objective necessity inscribed in social forms. For Habermas, however, the constitution of the 'mode of production' or 'system necessity' or 'functional prerequisites' presupposes an originally communicative opening of experience. It is this 'opening' which constitutes the demand to treat social relations as more or less imperfect articulations of intersubjective experience – critical thought, in other words, must recognize established social and economic forms as potential impediments to the 'evolution' of moral-cognitive legitimacy. What Habermas's concept of communicative reason does, therefore, is to show that subjective representation (of extant social necessity) is essential to the concept of ethical life. For without re-cognition of the institutional forms within which the individual lives and acts, ethical substance could not (ethically, morally and politically) 'form' the individual; it could only dominate and overwhelm it.

As we have seen, however, Habermas's idea of autonomous re-cognition as central to the concepts of ideology, crisis and transformation carries with it a Kantian commitment which is highly problematic. The 'legitimation crisis', through which he characterizes modernity, is understood in relation to the social, political and cultural 'deficits' which afflict 'organized capitalism'. Yet the solution to the contradictions which he identifies – between social production and achievement motivation, cultural 'world-views' and administrative organization – involves the abstraction of the 'rational' subject from the concrete diversity in which it has been formed. Critical theory, in other words, can identify systemic distortions of communicative action only from the perspective of a posited ideal, an ideal which is derived from the transcendental pragmatics of the speech act. My fundamental objection to Habermas's social theory, therefore, is that its moral, ethical and political claims include a priori the 'performative' freedom of individual subjects – a power which continually re-forms an ideal, communicative totality. And so while a speculative social science demands recognition of critical autonomy (as that which re-presents and re-forms the 'reified' forms of social necessity), this must be acknowledged as formed (and dispersed) within the oppositions of ethical life. The 'hermeneutic' element of speculative thought, in other words, demands that we acknowledge the non-reflective and implicit forms (of recognition) into which rational association is diversified and differentiated. For without such acknowledgement (of love, faith, belief, sacrifice) the higher forms of ethical and political recognition must remain abstract – and ultimately exclusive – ideals.

Notes

1. See 'The essentialities or determinations of reflection', in G.W.F. Hegel, *The Science of Logic*, trans. A.V. Miller, George Allen & Unwin, 1969, pp. 408–43.

2. See 'The nature of the social bond: a modern alternative', in J.-F. Lyotard, *The Postmodern Condition: A Report on Knowledge*, trans. G. Bennington and B. Massumi, University of Manchester Press, 1991a, pp. 11–14.

3. See 'How is pure natural science possible?', in I. Kant, *Prologomena to any Future Metaphysics*, trans. P. Carus (revised by W. Ellington), Hackett, 1983, p. 38–64.

4. I. Kant, *Critique of Pure Reason*, trans. N. Kemp-Smith, Macmillan, 1982a, pp. 65–82.

5. See K. Marx, 'Preface to the first German edition', *Capital, Volume One*, trans. S. Moore and E. Aveling, Lawrence & Wishart, 1977. The Kantianism of Marx's 'Kritik' of political economy is made clear in his intention to set out 'the social antagonisms that result from the natural laws of capitalist production' (p. 19).

6. W.J. Mommsen, *The Age of Bureaucracy: Perspectives on the Political Sociology of Max Weber*, Blackwell, 1974, pp. 75–80.

7. M. Weber, *The Protestant Ethic and the Spirit of Capitalism*, trans. T. Parsons, George Allen & Unwin, 1978a, p. 182.

8. M. Weber, 'The nature of social action', in Weber, *Weber Selections*, W.G. Runcimen ed., Cambridge University Press, 1978b, p. 21.

9. M. Weber, 'Value judgements in social science', ibid., p. 79.

10. M. Weber, 'The nature of social action', ibid., pp. 8–10.

11. See F.W. Nietzsche, '"Guilt", "Bad Conscience" and related matters', in Nietzsche, *The Genealogy of Morals: An Attack*, trans. Francis Golffing, Doubleday, 1990, pp. 189–230.

12. M. Weber, 'The nature of social action', in Weber, *Weber Selections*, p. 17.

13. See I. Kant, 'Idea for a universal history with a cosmopolitan purpose', in Kant's *Political Writings*, H. Reiss ed., Cambridge University Press, 1991.

14. For a good account of the contrast between Marxist and Weberian critiques of modern social relations, see Chapter 3 of Mommsen's *The Age of Bureaucracy*.

15. M. Weber, *Economy and Society*, Vol. 3, p. 973, quoted in A. Giddens, *Capitalism and Modern Social Theory: An Analysis of the Writings of Marx, Durkheim and Max Weber*, Cambridge University Press, 1980, p. 159.

16. See Mommsen, *The Age of Bureaucracy* and D. MacRae, *Weber*, Fontana, 1976.

17. See Weber, 'Value judgements in social science', in *Weber Selections*.

18. Weber, *The Protestant Ethic and the Spirit of Capitalism*, p. 182.

19. Weber, 'The nature of charismatic domination', in *Weber Selections*, p. 236.

20. Mommsen, *The Age of Bureaucracy*, p. 87.

21. Weber, 'The nature of charismatic domination', in *Weber Selections*, p. 228.

22. See J. Habermas, 'Max Weber's concept of legitimation', in Habermas, *Legitimation Crisis*, trans. T. McCarthy, Heinemann, 1976, pp. 97–102.

23. The relationship between the moral demands of practical reason and the the history of 'civil community' set out in Kant's political writings presuppose the mediation of morality and nature expounded in the third *Critique*. See particularly Kant's account of 'Ethico-teleology', in *Critique of Judgement*, trans. J. Creed-Meredith, Oxford University Press, 1982b, pp. 108–14.

24. N. Luhmann, *Soziale Systeme*, 1984.

25. M. Horkheimer and T.W. Adorno, *The Dialectic of Enlightenment*, trans. J. Cumming, Continuum, 1986.

26. See J. Habermas, 'Crisis tendencies in advanced capitalism', in *Legitimation Crisis*.

27. See J. Habermas, 'History and evolution', trans. D.J. Parent, in *Telos*, 39 (Spring 1979), pp. 127–43.

28. J. Habermas, *Postmetaphysical Thinking*, trans. W.M. Hohengarten, Polity press, 1995a, pp. 46–7.

29. J. Habermas and N. Luhmann, 'Vorbereitende Bemerkungen zu einer Theorie der kommunikativen Kompetenz', in *Theory der Gessellschaft oder Sozialtechnologie – Was leistet die Systemforschung?* (Frankfurt, Suhrkamp), p. 66. Quoted and translated in J.B. Thompson, 'Universal Pragmatics', in J.B. Thompson and D. Held (eds), *Habermas: Critical Debates*, Macmillan, 1986, p. 123.

30. Habermas, *Postmetaphysical Thinking*, p. 17.

31. Ibid., p. 50.

32. Ibid., pp. 17–18.

33. Even Hegel's most 'rationalistic' account of *Sittlichkeit* (in the *Philosophy of Right*) makes it clear that ethical substance includes a content which is not realized in, or subsumable under, formal law. The moment of war (international conflict), for example, makes an ethical demand on the individual which could not be expressed within an abstract/transcendental conception of humanity. See 'Sovereignty *vis-à-vis* foreign states', in Hegel, *Philosophy of Right*, trans. T.M. Knox, Oxford University Press, 1967b.

34. Habermas, *Legitimation Crisis*, p. 8.

35. Ibid., p. 14.

36. Ibid., p. 15.

37. For an interesting account of Habermas's relationship to Marxism, see Martin Jay, *Marxism and Totality: The Adventures of a Concept from Lukács to Habermas*, University of California Press, 1984.

38. Habermas, *Legitimation Crisis*, p. 73.

39. Ibid.

40. Ibid., p. 87.

41. Ibid., p. 95.

42. Ibid., pp. 107–8.

43. Ibid., p. 111.

44. Ibid., p. 113.

45. Habermas, *Postmetaphysical Thinking*, pp. 50–1.

46. Lyotard, *The Postmodern Condition*, p. 66.

47. J. Derrida, 'Violence and metaphysics', in Derrida, *Writing and Difference*, trans. Alan Bass, Routledge, 1960b, pp. 116–17.

48. See the 'Hegel Notice', in J.-F. Lyotard, *The Differend: Phrases in Dispute*, trans. G. Van Den Abeele, Manchester University Press, 1988a, pp. 91–7.

49. See J. Derrida, 'From restricted to general economy: a Hegelianism without reserve', in Derrida, *Writing and Difference*.

4
Poststructuralism and the Violence of Truth

The speculative conception of social science I have begun to outline in the preceding chapters involves six essential points. First, the idea of the social – or what I, borrowing from Hegel, have called ethical life (*Sittlichkeit*) – demands to be understood as a differentiated unity, within which there can be no absolute powers of mediation, integration, dissolution or legitimation. Secondly, this demand is established through the critique of 'abstract' thought which Hegel develops in *The Science of Logic* (1969) and *Phenomenology of Mind* (1967a). I argued that it is the distinctively Kantian oppositions of concept and intuition, autonomy and heteronomy, noumena and phenomena, which refer the concept of social explanation to the speculative idea of 'substance' (unity, totality, community). Thirdly, these Kantian forms are essential both to the formation and recognition of modernity. They participate in the differentiation of ethical life into 'autonomous' regions of action and responsibility (the state, civil society, rational religious conviction, etc.), and also inform social theoretical reconstructions of *Sittlichkeit*. Fourthly, the Kantian origin of the categories, through which the critique of modernity is articulated, determines a logic of abstraction and prioritization that is essential to the idea of a social science. Each explanatory form, in other words, reproduces an hierarchical account of ethical life which is organized through the primacy of one particular concept – functional interdependence, systemic integration, subjective meaning, productive activity, etc. Fifthly, none of these 'paradigmatic' forms is capable of giving a comprehensive account of ethical life, and that, as such, each must be conceived as reconstructing an essential, but non-deterministic, element of modern social relations. Finally, I have suggested that the fundamental concerns of social scientific analyses, questions of justice, inequality, inclusiveness and difference demand a critical acknowledgement of the concepts deployed within each explanatory paradigm. Thus, the concept of a speculative social science involves a constant re-cognition of ethical life, in which a certain 'substantive' temporality of contradiction and mediation is expressed. I will examine this temporality in the following chapter.

For the moment, however, my account of how the critique of abstract thinking developed in Hegel's philosophy is related to the concept of a social science still begs the question of why speculative thought should be regarded as essential to the recognition of injustice, inequality and exclusion in modern ethical life. I have claimed that the paradigmatic forms through which the concept of modernity is articulated are based upon Kantian oppositions of truth and appearance, freedom and necessity, structure and agency. It is these oppositions that I have attempted to identify with the Hegelian ideas of limitation and negativity. For each explanatory paradigm, by postulating *Sittlichkeit* as an hierarchical organization of categories and powers, determines the history of self-consciousness as the closure/fulfilment of its concept. A speculative social science, therefore, does not presuppose the ideas of human nature, community and identity inscribed in different perspectives, as forms which demand to be integrated into a comprehensive account of 'spiritual' mediation. Rather, I have argued that speculative thought should be understood as acknowledging the limitation and partiality of these ideas as they are inscribed in their particular perspectives. Thus, I have tried to articulate the relationship between (speculative) philosophy and social science as one in which the necessity of each explanatory form is conserved in a mediated, non-deterministic form.

Ultimately, it is my account of the relationship between Kant and Hegel (i.e., between 'speculative' and 'abstract' thinking) which is the foundation of my claims about the nature of social critique. I have tried to suggest that the activity of mediation/reconciliation, that is characteristic of speculative thought, should be understood as a critical recognition of the categories inscribed in different explanatory paradigms. Marx's concern with economy and productive activity, for example, demands to be re-cognized as disclosing certain homogenizing potencies within the substance of *Sittlichkeit*. The concepts of ideology, alienation and commodification, through which the negative unity of 'capital' is described, are determined by an originally Kantian opposition of human (productive) spontaneity and the 'natural laws of capitalist production'.[1] Thus, it is through its abstraction of a 'naturally' creative human essence from the development of socio-economic antagonism that Marxism's account of historical necessity ('class-consciousness', 'revolutionary praxis', 'proletarian justice', etc.) must be re-cognized. The work of Durkheim, Parsons and Luhmann, on the other hand, demands that we acknowledge the functional/integrative necessities of modern ethical life, through their respective oppositions of rational structure to the contingency of subjective re-presentation and re-cognition. The concept of ethical 'substance', therefore, is developed through a critique of the forms in which history (repeatedly) appears as teleology, or the subject as universally legislative, or the the idea of community as a prescriptive end to violence and contradiction. Acknowledgement of hierarchy, dominance and exclusiveness as essential to 'sociological' accounts of totality, in other words, is given through the relationship of speculative to abstract thinking: for it is the 'posited' oppositions of subject and object, structure and recognition, essence and contingency, which disclose the idea of community (*Sittlichkeit*) as brought out of reflection and difference.

The account of 'poststructuralism' I will develop is an attempt to show that the ideas which have been most influential on modern social science – Foucault's power/knowledge identity, Lyotard's 'postmodern' fragmentation of narratives, and Derrida's deconstruction of 'presence' – should not be understood as a generic discourse against which we must oppose the precepts of speculative thought. The possibility of formulating a speculative response to the claims made by Foucault, Lyotard and Derrida, in other words, depends upon our acknowledging the heterogeneity which obtains among them. For it is only by examining the different metaphors, tropes and devices by which each attempts to articulate an ethics of difference, that we may be able to recognize which is the most powerful and consistent challenge to our concept of social necessity. There are, however, certain general 'anti-Hegelian' principles through which we might provisionally understand the idea of Poststructuralism. The rejection of universal subjectivity (and of the 'legislations' that are determined through it), the reception of 'difference' as a demand exceeding rational or cognitive categories, and the writing of 'truth' as a concept in which domination is constantly reinscribed, all gesture towards an idea of 'community' as the substance, or prescription, or legislation through which 'ethical' thought and action is made possible. Such a possibility, as we will see in my expositions of Foucault, Lyotard and Derrida, is written as that which cannot (and ought not) to be included 'within' the prescriptive ideal of ethical substance. And so the transgressive experiences released by Foucault's 'carceral' knowledges, the 'agitation' produced by Lyotard's incommensurable 'genres of discourse', and the 'idea' of peace sustained within Derrida's 'economy' of violence, are moments whose stricture is the loss of 'true' necessity.

The transaction between abstract and speculative thinking by which I have characterized the idea of social critique is therefore, generally understood as reimposing the identity of 'spirit' upon an economy of difference which always exceeds that identity. Michel Foucault's account of 'global theories' – specifically Marxism and psychoanalysis – makes it clear they retain their critical force only in so far as their unity is 'put in abeyance, or at least curtailed, divided, overthrown, caricatured, [or] theatricalized'.[2] The 'totalizing' potential of Marx's historical dialectics and the various strands of psychoanalytic theory, in other words, can be restrained only through the unforeseen consequences that each produces as a strategy of power. And so speculative idealism, as that which seems to eschew all positive engagement with the exercise of power, appears as a discourse of pure, metaphysical totality. For where there can be no technics or pragmatics of domination, there can be no possibility of the

localized resistances through which Foucault develops his conceptions of
ethics and politics. Jean-François Lyotard re-articulates this idea of
speculative thought as 'metaphysics' through his notion of the 'result'.[3]
For Lyotard, the 'postmodern condition' is characterized by the fragmentation of knowledge and the proliferation of generic 'discourses' (i.e.,
the contemporaneity of abstract and primitive art, of commodity production and information technologies, of folk wisdom and scientific
specialism, etc.). Within the context of this proliferation, the possibility of
unifying the different rules of conduct, technique, method and presentation inscribed in each particular 'genre' moves increasingly beyond the
resources of cognitive/conceptual knowledge. Hegel's speculative
philosophy therefore represents the foundation of 'modernist' sociological thought, in the sense that 'spirit' originates the search for ethical
life (community, identity) within the heterogeneity of 'social' discourses.
The dialectics of modernity, whether these are expressed through
Marxist, functionalist or system theoretical narratives, all presuppose
a cognitive ideal of totality (the result) – an ideal which is always
reimposed upon the moments and events of difference.

Jacques Derrida's relationship to speculative thought, and the ideas of
'trace', 'economy', 'presence' and '*différance*' articulated through this
relationship, is far more difficult to situate within a generic 'anti-
Hegelianism'. Derrida's reading of Hegel does not simply oppose the
history of poststructural diversity – a 'history' expressed through the
spread of the power/knowledge economy (Foucault), or the proliferation
of heterogeneous genres of discourse (Lyotard) – to the exhausted, but
still dangerously totalitarian, idea of spirit. Rather, his deconstruction of
speculative thought attempts to show that the contradictions determined
within the 'restricted economy' dialectics, presuppose the play of an
excessive difference which cannot be included within that economy.[4] The
concept of unity deployed throughout Hegel's thought, in other words,
is founded upon an original (and originary) moment in which the
excessiveness of difference is subsumed under the re-cognizing activity
of spirit. This 'moment' of subsumption, conceived within the economy
of Derrida's writing has a quasi-transcendental quality; for it is disclosed
in all the marginal transactions through which the necessity of dialectics
is sustained. For example, the reading of Bataille presented in *Writing
and Difference*[5], attempts to show that his idea of sovereignty gestures
towards an excessive experience (i.e., self-consciousness' confrontation
with death in the struggle for recognition) which both permits and
exceeds spirit's regeneration as knowledge. Also, the brief moment of
comparison between Heidegger and Hegel in *Of Spirit* discloses the
category of *Dasein* as an originally temporalized form, whose experience
is always already situated within the question of Being.[6] Thus, Hegel's
idea of time as that into which spirit deploys its identity is conceived as
presupposing the original openness of *Dasein* ('Being-in the-world'),
which cannot be included within the history of self-consciouness (the

cogito). This play of presence and *différance*, which Derrida discerns in speculative thought, demands that we acknowledge the violence that is *generally* deployed in categories of unity, totality and identity. For Hegel's attempt to determine the legislative necessity of spirit belongs to a philosophical tradition, in which 'nature', 'humanity', 'law' and 'community' are always written as positive stricture.

Derrida's reading of Hegel, then, is part of a comprehensive deconstruction of Western philosophy, in which the play of presence, trace and *différance* is followed through the writings of, among others, Plato, Rousseau, Hegel, Heidegger and Levinas. The style of Derrida's exposition is consistent throughout his writing: he attempts to disclose the conceptual resources of any given text as 'supplementing' the presence of its 'object'.[7] Rousseau's attempt to describe the regulative force of human nature, for example, is written through the economy of social and cultural supplements, by which the original sentiment of pity is corrupted. This antagonism between the immanence of pity and the acquisitiveness produced by civil society is expounded as the ground of humanity's moral-historical development. All the 'synthetic' forms of culture – all the music, literature and painting which prompt the imagination beyond its natural satisfactions – appear as corrupting the essence of humanity. Each individual becomes increasingly estranged from the compassionate life of family, motherhood, paternity, cultivation of nature, etc., and is constantly agitated by new and unlimited desires. Yet the emergence and proliferation of 'artificial' desire is necessary to the improvement of humanity; without it, the cycle of mere instinctual life could not have been broken. Thus for Derrida, Rousseau's idea of culture functions both as an analogue by which nature can be re-presented to 'civilized' individuals ('natural' writing, art and music reproduce the moral presence of compassion in the social body), and as a supplement which perpetuates the threat of corruption (culture, as synthesis and representation, is always excessive of natural virtue). The law prescribed within Rousseau's text, in other words, is never fully 'present': it is always revealed as a trace within the transactions between nature and culture. In general, therefore, Derrida's deconstructions of textual resources take the form of subverting the deployment of categories into hierarchical organizations of necessity and contingency, truth and falsity, universal and particular, or outside and inside. It is an attempt to disclose the 'economic' nature of violence, that is, the impossibility of thinking the ethical without recourse to moments of exclusion unforeseen in every speaking of justice and legality.[8]

Derrida's quasi-transcendental ideas of trace, *différance* and supplementarity, then, gesture towards a non-prescriptive type of ethics and politics. His claim is that language, as such, must be understood as having always already deployed (uttered/spoken) the 'substantive' categories through which justice and legality are determined. This deployment returns us to the deconstructive notion of 'economy'. For the concepts of essence, totality and identity, which have opened the possibility of speech, always retain a spatio-temporal type of exclusiveness which cannot be mediated in any particular set of prescriptions. The ideas of ethical and political responsibility that emerge from Derrida's writing therefore involve what he calls the 'giving of language by language to language', for, as linguistic beings, we are always faced with the responsibility of thinking the violence that is unforeseen in the utterance of truth. Such a responsibility can never be discharged by determining a more comprehensive form of political organization or ethical sub-stance, for as we have seen, Derrida's deconstruction of the resources offered by Western thought gestures towards the 'illegality' of positive stricture. The play of trace, supplement and *différance* is 'transcendental', in the sense that it is always simultaneous with the legislations of presence (nature, spirit, etc.). Thus 'we' – a 'we' that cannot be named through the generic categories of 'humanity' or 'subjectivity' – are 'pledged' to address the events of exclusion and domination originally inscribed in language.[9]

So where does all this leave us with regard to the possibility of defending a speculative idea of social science? As I have said, my expo-sitions of Foucault, Lyotard and Derrida will try to respect the difference generated by their respective themes, emphases and techniques. However, the general structure of my argument will develop the idea that it is Derrida who poses the greatest challenge to the possibility of speculative thought, and so to the concept of social critique I have developed. For by deploying an idea of the transcendental as that which is both present and non-present in the 'substance' of philosophical discourse, he problematizes the relationship between totality and differ-ence without reproducing oppositions of subject and power (Foucault), or judgement and 'realized' heterogeneity (Lyotard). Indeed, I will try to show that the concepts of difference, transgression and judgement set out by Foucault and Lyotard maintain recognizably Kantian ideas of ethics and politics. These expositions, however, are not intended to disclose deconstruction as the definitive ethics of difference. Rather, I will try to show that Derrida's account of the relationship between *différance* and the Hegelian notions of spirit, idea and concept represents a power-ful reinforcement of the abstraction sustained in modern ethical life (*Sittlichkeit*). For by writing the play of *différance* as simultaneous with the categories of Hegel's 'system', Derrida articulates a concept of 'violence' which has yet to distinguish its own 'general economy' from the 'restriction' of dialectical thought. My argument, in other words, will suggest that the 'metacritical' conception of social science I have devel-oped can be seen as regulative of Derrida's intensification of violence through *différance*, that is, that the ideas of nature, identity, humanity and community, that are deployed in social scientific paradigms, articulate a temporality of violence, re-cognition and mediation which is the 'substance' acknowledged by speculative thought.

Foucault and the modern domains of power

In his essay on Kant's concept of Enlightenment, Michel Foucault attempts to transcribe the Kantian idea of critique as an 'attitude' or 'ethos' that is addressed permanently to the discourses through which subject/self is constituted.[10] Unlike Kant, Foucault's account of the relationship between knowledge, autonomy and political action does not presuppose the transcendental resources of practical reason. Each individual is conceived as the 'subject' of knowledges which constitute the limits and possibilities of the social body; and so for Foucault, the 'self' has always already been situated within strategies of control which are the presupposition of modern social, economic and political institutions. Thus, although the work of such a critical attitude is always 'in the position of beginning again',[11] the questions we must ask in order to go beyond the limits which contemporary discourses have placed upon us are always concerned with: (1) the way in which we are constituted as subjects of our own knowledge; (2) the way in which we exercise and submit to power relations; and (3) the way in which we are constituted as moral subjects of our own actions. This kind of critical ethos – what Foucault calls the 'attitude of self-reinvention' – demands that practical and theoretical activity is related to the conditions in which liberty, spontaneity, resistance and independence have their contemporary significations. The possibility of 'Enlightenment', then, becomes a question not of recourse to the a priori necessity inscribed in practical reason, but of assessing the extent to which the interventions of medicine, psychiatry, criminology, sexual hygienics, etc. are deployed as 'strategies' of domination. Such an assessment, according to Foucault, is enabled by the very conditions which make it necessary, for it is only through the strategies and interventions of contemporary power relations that the 'self' becomes a point of unforeseen resistance/ reinvention.

The body of Foucault's middle writings is concerned with the way in which modern discourses of madness and sanity, sickness and health, legality and punishment, and normality and perversion are bound up with the establishment of control with the exercise of power.[12] Foucault's account of these discourses takes the form of a 'genealogical' history,[13] in which knowledge is understood as evolving through the economy of control and resistance constituted by its strategic deployment. The emergence and development of modernity, in other words, must be conceived in terms of hierarchical organizations of knowledge, whose general principle is the intensification of control over increasingly diversified and heterogeneous populations. The Foucauldian histories of madness, sexuality, punishment and medicine all attempt to disclose an inescapable relationship between power and knowledge – a relationship in which 'truth' becomes something which is produced and reproduced within particular systems of domination:

truth isn't the reward of free spirits . . . nor the privilege of those who have succeeded in liberating themselves. Truth is a thing of this world: it is produced only by virtue of multiple forms of constraint. And it induces regular effects of power. Each society has its own regime of truth, its 'general politics' of truth: that is, the type of discourse which it accepts and makes function as true. . .[14]

Thus, the idea of genealogy deployed by Foucault develops a radical distinction between the demands of 'Enlightenment' conceptions of ethics, politics and liberation and the discourses through which hegemony, cohesion and control are exercised within the social body. Kant's practical reason, Marx's proletarian justice, and Habermas's communicative ethics, for example, all presuppose truth as a form that is independent of contemporary power relations, and which opens the way into a mediated and non-coercive totality. It is this promise of liberation through the philosophical disclosure of truth which, for Foucault, is implicated in the constitution of 'humanity' as an object of universal/ scientific knowledge. By abstracting the self from the unforeseen possibilities of 'reinvention' which are opened by modern domains of power, Marxism, psychoanalysis, liberalism, rights theory, etc., all participate in the process of knowledge/objectification/control by which domination is sustained. The more fully the 'universal' attributes of human beings are specified, and the more adequately these attributes are related to their 'true' realms of sovereignty (i.e., the classless society, the ideal speech situation, etc.), the more determinately 'we' belong to the programmatics, teleologies and strategies through which power is exercised.

This conception of humanism – that is, the totality of discourses in which 'true' sovereignty appears as something transcendent of power relations – is a theme which is reproduced throughout Foucault's genealogical histories. *Discipline and Punish* (1979), for example, attempts to explain how the transition from the corporeal punishments of medieval society, to the 'humane' penal and judicial systems of the modern era, presupposes the need for a more discrete, regularized and efficient type of discipline. Increased accumulations of wealth among the bourgeoisie, the peasantry's loss of feudal rights and privileges, and enforced labour in the service of capital, constituted a shift in power relations which, for Foucault, set the real political agenda of the industrial revolution. In order to produce the work force it required, modern capitalism needed to re-form the individual both morally/ subjectively and physically/genetically. For without such re-formation, the development of the industrial economy would have been impeded, or even arrested, by those individuals who would have preferred stealing, vagrancy or vagabondage to working in the manufactures. Thus, for Foucault, Marx's attempt to write the history of the capitalist mode of production describes the necessary inter-relatedness of technical development, division of labour *and* techniques of collective discipline: 'Each makes the other necessary; each provides the model for the other.'[15] The growth of the capitalist economy, in other words, necessitates new techniques of discipline which come to invest 'diverse political regimes, apparatuses and institutions'.[16]

Foucault's concept of 'generalized punishment' develops the idea that it was only because 'humanistic' reform answered the necessity of systematizing punishment that it was able to 'pass from the project stage to that of an institutional set of practices'.[17] The development of knowledges, maintaining that the penal system must always respect the dignity of the criminal, does not, for Foucault, signify the progress of humanity towards moral Enlightenment. Rather, the philosophical, psychological and criminological discourses through which the 'soul' becomes an object of knowledge are expounded as the condition of a certain regularized and pervasive form of discipline. Thus the legal and juridical prescriptions sanctioned by humanistic discourses (i.e., the precise codification of offences, the diminution in the arbitrariness of punishment and the formation of a consensus concerning who has the power to punish) are originally engaged in the transition from one general politics of truth to another. Under the conditions of feudal bondage, the establishment of guilt and the determination of punishment consisted simply in the identification of the perpetrator, and the subjection of his or her body to the mortifications demanded for the offence. Within the feudal 'economy of illegalities', in other words, the law was an exclusively retributive force, which protected the social body through the spectacle of its enforcement. The emergence of the commodifying power of capital, however, produced a fundamental change in the constitution of social space. The relationship of property owners (bourgeoisie) to the propertyless (proletarians) became intensively determined by the production of wealth; and so the traditional rights of access and subsistence which were maintained under feudalism were displaced by the demands of commodification, capitalization and profit. For Foucault, this transition from a subsistence economy to the industrialized production of commodities presupposes a new form of discipline which exerts itself as a continuous regulation of the subject. This disciplinary type is directly related to the philosophical discourses in which the self has emerged as an object of respect and moral obligation. For it is through the 'humanization' of punishment, and the proliferation of the 'signs' through which the punitive power of the law is represented (and postponed), that discipline becomes formative of mind and subjectivity:

> This real non-corporeal soul is not a substance; it is the element in which are articulated the effects of a certain type of knowledge, the machinery by which the power relations give rise to a possible corpus of knowledge, and knowledge extends and reinforces the effects of this power.[18]

Foucault's genealogy of modern institutional forms, then, is written as the history of a 'carceral society', in which the 'exceptional' punishments

of bodily torture are progressively displaced by regularized and pervasive techniques of control. The 'figure of political technology', through
which this disciplinary penetration of everyday life is represented by
Foucault, is Jeremy Bentham's Panopticon. The architecture of Bentham's
prison-building – a central tower around which cells are arranged as
isolated theatres of an unidentifiable gaze – induces in the prisoner 'a
state of conscious and permanent visibility that assures the automatic
functioning of power'.[19] The life of every inmate is brought within the
sphere of a penetrative vision, which exercises its correctional power by
investing the technologies that conceal and dissemble its absence (the
back-lighting of the cell, the masking of the observation tower, etc.). Each
individual subject/inmate, in other words, is 'caught up with a power
situation of which they themselves are the bearers'.[20] Historically, the
hospital, the factory, the school and the asylum have become increasingly similar to the architectural configuration of Bentham's panoptical
prison. All, according to Foucault, incorporate features designed to
facilitate observation, examination and correction of 'abnormalities' in
the subject, which would impede the achievement of certain 'global'
objectives (continuation of the commodity form of production,
maintenance of the genetic health of populations etc.). The Panopticon,
then, schematizes the power-knowledge economy of carceral society: it is
the organizing 'figure' of a diffuse body of discourses whose purpose is
the penetration of 'local' moments of resistance and transgression. The
genealogy developed in *Discipline and Punish*, therefore, is an attempt to
show how the techniques of discipline which traverse institutional
relations serve to 'amplify' the effects of power by investing the language
and aims of 'established' social necessities: 'to increase production, to
develop the economy, spread education, raise the level of public
morality; to increase and multiply'.[21]

Foucault's history of carceral society is primarily an account of the
epistemic conditions through which economic, political and demographic
necessities have emerged as limits which define the freedom/self-
recognition of the subject. Knowledge – particularly the modern discourses of rational economics, politics and jurisprudence – is originally
bound up with the techniques of control; it is never 'free' from the power
relations from which it springs, and which are constantly transformed by
it. *Discipline and Punish*, therefore, develops the relationship between the
discourses which situate the self within the 'global' necessities of production, cohesion and identity, and the strategies through which
individuals are controlled. For Foucault, categories such as productive
utility, political citizenship, legal right and moral obligation are not limits
externally imposed upon an original freedom; they are forms which
have always already constituted the self as the 'subject' of universal/
homogenizing demands. The legally, economically and politically
disciplined individuals who make up the social body are formed (and
re-formed) through conceptions of 'normality' which invest the entire

institutional fabric of their lives. This account of the edifice of carceral society, however, retains the trace of an 'objectivism' – something which might tempt us to read *Discipline and Punish* as simply reinforcing a Marxist conception of the primacy of productive forces – which Foucault seeks to displace in *The History of Sexuality* (1980). By expounding the way in which ideas of sexual health have conducted the effects of power into the deepest recesses and earliest formations of the self, Foucault has tried to establish the originality of the relationship between power, knowledge and identity. The subject, in other words, does not come innocent to the realm of carceral strategies; the possibility of its modern 'self-normalizing' form is given through the discourses of sexual health which have penetrated familial relations.

Foucault's account of the importance of sexuality for the strategies of power coheres around two central ideas: 'bio-power' and 'confessional technology'. According to *The History of Sexuality*, the seventeenth century was marked by the rise of a political rationale which had abandoned established philosophical and theological ideas of the 'good life'. Hobbes's materialism, for example, despite its appeals to a political good which is possible only through the rule of law, constitutes the state as an absolute power which has the right of life and death over its citizens. This secularized political thought establishes the power of the state as an end in itself; the tactics of political prudence are replaced by an increasingly rigorous surveillance and control of populations. The specification of demographic discourses (epidemiology, criminology, ethniology, etc.), therefore, is stimulated by the proliferation of 'undisciplined' social spaces which the state, as 'legitimate' power, seeks to penetrate and control. For Foucault, the techniques of categorization and measurement, which characterize positivist social science, are rooted in the political demands constituted by the health, longevity, mobility and productivity of populations. Thus, the principal concern of the modern state is not the rule of law, or the protection of legal rights; it is the control and utilization of populations – a concern which passes easily from the care of life to the necessity of annihilation:

> If genocide is indeed the dream of modern powers, this is not because of a recent return to the ancient right to kill: it is because power is situated and exercised at the level of life, the species, the race, and the large scale phenomena of population.[22]

It is the concept of bio-power which, for Foucault, lies at the root of the Nazi Holocaust, and which accounts for the persistence of genocide as a political strategy 'after Auschwitz'.

With the constitution of bio-power as the central concern of the modern state, sex became the focus of an explosion of discourses concerning the health of the body. According to Foucault, it was these discourses (organic physiology, gynaecology, neurology, psychology, etc.) which established 'life' as the focus of power: '[their] primary concern was the body, vigour, longevity, progeniture and descent of the classes that ruled'.[23] Sex therefore began to emerge as a central focus of political investment: differences in the frequency of sexual activity, sexual hygiene, and the variety and intensity of pleasures began to be organized into a hierarchy of repressions, displacements and restrictions which reinforced the difference between 'bourgeois' and 'proletarian'. Within Foucault's genealogy, it is the figure of the 'Victorian regime' which schematizes this construction of sex as the object of surveillance and control.[24] The *scientia sexualis*, which came to dominate the sexual and familial relations of the Western/Victorian bourgeoisie, is understood as the paradigm of a hygienics which has penetrated every level of the social hierarchy. Thus, the four 'great strategic unities' that Foucault identifies within the plurality of sexual discourse – the 'Hysterization of Women's Bodies', 'Pedagogization of Children's Sex', 'Socialization of Procreative Behaviour', and the 'Phychiatricization of Perverse Pleasures' – are techniques of intervention which, having originated in the bourgeoisie, have made the demands of sexual conformity into the dominant self-normalizing principle of modernity.[25] The subjection of women to the instabilities of their reproductive functions, the proscription of childhood masturbation, the biogenetic responsibilities of procreative sex and the treatment of 'perverse' sexualities contribute to the formation of a self whose identity is given through the demands of a pervasive and prescriptive normality.

For Foucault, the central component in the technologies through which sexuality is deployed as an object of intervention and control is the necessity of confession. The experience of the modern subject is always already penetrated by the evaluative concepts of *scientia sexualis*; and so each individual 'self' is originally placed under the obligation to articulate the possible perversity of its desires. This modern science of sexuality has its genealogical root in religious confession: it developed the theological idea of unburdening one's sinful soul, as a 'general technology' deployed within the medical, psychiatric and criminological discourses of bio-power. Every individual is placed within a network of power relations, in which those who have expert knowledge of the 'truth' of sexuality are able to demand a continuous self-examination and policing of desires. Within this 'scientific' construction of sex, then, pleasure has ceased to be an end in itself; it has become the subject of knowledges which displace and postpone the danger of sexual activity into the language of confession, disclosure and divulgence: 'We have at least invented a different kind of pleasure: pleasure in the truth of pleasure, the pleasure of knowing that truth, the fascination of seeing it and telling it, of captivating and capturing others by it . . . the specific pleasure of the true discourse on pleasure'.[26]

In the brief methodological remarks offered in volume one of *The History of Sexuality*, Foucault claims that 'the object is to analyse a certain form of knowledge regarding sex, not in terms of repression or law, but in terms of power'.[27] The term 'power' does not name the institutional hierarchy through which the state retains its 'legal' authority, but rather signifies an economy of domination-resistance into which knowledge has emerged as a strategic force. Foucault's genealogies of sexuality and punishment develop this distinction between the 'repetitious, inert and self-reproducing' appearance of hierarchical structures (the law, the state, the economy, etc.) and the 'mobility' of the power-knowledge relations through which hegemony is maintained.[28] The formation of disciplined and productive institutions therefore demands that the categories inscribed in the modernist canon – 'moral density', 'bureaucracy', 'capitalization', etc. – are conceived as presupposing a play of antagonisms, resistances and investments whose plurality they can only intensify. For example, Foucault's claim that the critical power of Marxism is sustained only by putting its unity 'into abeyance' is a demand for a recognition of the disciplinary extremes necessitated by the politics of 'socialized production'. The labour camps of the former Soviet Union did not exist as 'transitional' institutions; rather, they attested to the economy of domination-resistance produced by the administration of 'proletarian democracy'.[29] Power, then, must be understood 'nominalistically': it is that which has always already invested the knowledges and strategies presupposed by 'established' relations; and as such, it opens the unforeseen possibilities of domination, resistance and 'reinvention' that spring from the constitution of hegemony. As Foucault would have it, 'relations of power are not superstructural positions, with merely a role of prohibition or accompaniment; they have a directly productive role wherever they come into play'.[30]

It is this 'productivity' of power relations which returns us to the ethical and political implications of Foucault's work. As we have seen, his idea of Enlightenment attempts to set out the possibilities of self-formation which are opened by the genealogical writings. The legislative spontaneity of Kant's practical reason (and the conceptions of liberty, emancipation and progress which this informs) is supplanted by an 'ethos of reinvention' in which the subject has recognized the 'productive' role of power in the constitution of community and identity. Foucault's essay on Enlightenment therefore presents us with a conception of power which is always excessive of the knowledges, techniques and 'fabrications' expounded in histories of punishment and sexuality. The disciplined and sanitized relations which have come to dominate the modern subject are re-presented as the conditions through which power incites resistance to the strategies in which it is deployed. For Foucault, the identity of each individual 'subject', in its 'subjection' to the techniques of power, is not a wholly determined form: it is reproduced as a reflective potential which constantly re-emerges through incitement of force relations. And so the questioning of modernity by which the 'attitude' of Enlightenment is characterized – that is, the subject's concern with itself as an identity 'fabricated' through strategies of power

– presupposes the specific limitations, prescriptions and intensifications through which force is effective. For it is only *within* the contemporary determinations of sanity, legality, health and sexual conformity that we are able to experience (and enact) the possibilities of resistance and transgression.

The concept of 'subjectivity' – or the 'non-corporeal soul . . . in which are articulated the effects of a certain form of knowledge' – is central to Foucault's politics.[31] Truth, we have seen, is presented in the genealogical writings as the production of different forms of social, economic and political organization: each type of society has its own 'general politics' of truth, through which power is exercised, resisted and redeployed. The modern subject therefore exists within a highly specific organization of force relations, in which the social body has been utterly penetrated by the knowledges and techniques of political control. The contemporary pervasiveness of medical, disciplinary and psychiatric interventions, in other words, has situated the self within an economy of discourse that demands constant confession, discovery and deployment of truth:

> We are subjected to the production of truth through power and we cannot exercise power except through the production of truth. This is the case for every society, but I believe that in ours the relationship between power, right and truth is organised in a highly specific fashion . . . we are forced to produce the truth of power that our society demands . . . in order to function: we are constrained to confess or to discover the truth. . . . In the last analysis we must produce truth as we produce wealth . . .[32]

This 'economic' production of truth is politically important for two reasons. First, the 'modern' relationship between power and knowledge exemplifies the relativity of truth. Each regime produces an economy of domination and resistance within which 'liberty', 'freedom' and 'autonomy' are circumscribed by contemporary strategies of intervention. The genealogies of punishment and sexuality, in other words, do not present a negative unity (i.e., the self-co-ordination of bio-power, discipline and legality) in which we can discern the possibility of a truly 'human' state. Rather, the 'nominalism' of Foucault's histories, that is, their construction of 'discipline', 'sexuality', 'health', etc. through a plurality of discrete knowledges and techniques, demands that we recognize power as that which invests every micrological production of truth. There can, therefore, be no universally just authority, for every 'legitimate' exercise of the 'general will' presupposes multiple strategies of intervention and control. This brings us to the political role which Foucault assigns to the subject in *Power/Knowledge* (1986). As we have seen, the carceral-eugenic strategies through which Foucault characterizes modern political authority take the form of interventions into local-specific types of identity. Power is conducted into these 'undisciplined' social spaces through the constitution of a certain kind of knowledge: that is, 'scientific' elucidations of the truth of human physiology, sexuality, rationality and culpability. Thus, for Foucault, the proper focus of political activity is the nexus between the subject and the homogenizing strategies through which power is exercised. For if genealogy has denied us the emancipatory promise of truth/totality, it has at least distributed the possibility of 'resistance' throughout the economy of power/knowledge. Or has it?

The politics of genealogy therefore acts through the incitement and mobilization of local-specific knowledges. For although the subject can never liberate itself from the discourses of power, it can resist, oppose and occasionally displace particular strategies of control. It is the possibility of this resistance, and its relationship to the ideas of subjectivity and autonomy, that Foucault addresses in his essay 'What is an author?'.[33] The moral significance of writing, according to Foucault, is the reproduction of a 'fictive' excess, whose circulation transgresses established forms of subjectivity. A literature freed from the questions concerning the originality and authenticity of texts, in other words, would constantly multiply the 'meanings' through which the subject understands and deploys its identity. It would demand that each of us question the strategies through which 'we' have been disciplined, sanitized and utilized, by placing us within the realms of possible/ unforeseen 'subject functions'.[34] These remarks on the relationship between subjectivity and the production of discourse, then, gesture towards the ethical position which Foucault began to outline more fully in his later writing. In the 1983 interview published under the title 'On the genealogy of ethics', he remarked that:

> another side to the moral prescriptions, which most of the time is not isolated as such but is, I think, very important: the kind of relationship you ought to have with yourself, *rapport a soi*, which I call ethics, and which determines how the individual is supposed to constitute himself as a moral subject of his own action.[35]

The concepts of authorship, autonomy and selfhood are brought into close proximity by this idea of ethics. Each individual experiences the strategies of modern political domination, not as a passively 'fabricated' identity, but as the focus of the 'polymorphous' incitements to resistance which accompany the exercise of power. If there is an 'ethical' relationship of the subject to its own actions, therefore, this cannot be determined through established procedural rationalities. Such a relationship is produced through acts of self-legislation which, in a certain sense, exceed the cognitive/scientific discourses of control and normalization. Famously, Foucault claims that as the self is not 'given' as an essential form or substance, 'there is only one practical consequence: we have to create ourselves as a work of art'.[36] This demand for 'artistic' self-creativity – a demand that is dispersed throughout the 'transgressive' practices which Foucault calls local resistance – marks the return of a certain Kantianism. For after his genealogies, Foucault expounds an idea of the ethical as that which is recognized and expressed beyond the (carceral, biogenetic, psychiatric, etc.) determinations of 'knowledge'. We make the moral law through our 'transgression' of contemporary strategies and techniques of power.

To conclude, I will make some brief Derridean remarks on Foucault's conceptions power, ethics and politics. Primarily, my discussion will address the question of Foucault's Kantianism, and the possibility of prosecuting an ethics of difference based on the power/knowledge relationship developed in his genealogies. I will argue that the notion of textuality which emerges from Derrida's thought discloses a certain homogeneity between the carceral/disciplinary implications that Foucault attributes to modern knowledges and the 'transgressive' practices and identities through which he expounds the concept of autonomy. Indeed, I will suggest that this 'homogenizing' movement of genealogical texts encourages a type of sociological repetition in which knowledge can appear as little more than the instrument of an amoral social power/necessity.

Derrida's idea of deconstruction is concerned with the disclosure and subversion of hierarchical organizations. As we have already seen, this project involves treating the world – nature, society, culture, ethics, etc. – as that which is constituted through the infinite productivity of writing. Within this general productivity, each literary, philosophical or scientific 'text' distributes the necessity of a particular concept throughout its economy of syntheses and oppositions. Hegel's conception of 'spirit', as well as Rousseau's 'nature', are expounded as forms which attempt to complete the unification of 'humanity' with the legal, moral and political determinations of ethical life. Each attempts to sustain an originary 'presence' – the interiorizing movement of self-consciousness, or the moralizing potential of 'natural' compassion – whose identity remains unaltered throughout the play of 'supplements' in which it is written. For Derrida, however, the philosophical ideals of spirit and nature are originally 'economic': their necessity/identity/presence is disclosed only in the 'traces' they inscribe in their textual reproduction (and restriction) of otherness/exteriority. The moralizing power of natural virtue, for example, appears in Rousseau's writing only through the play of *différance* sustained between the 'synthetic' (and therefore corruptive) productions of civil society and the 'natural' (and therefore moral) equilibrium of nature. The ethical and political significance of deconstruction therefore lies in its disclosure of the complicities of philosophical reason. Both Hegelian and Rousseauist thought contribute to the idea of a universal humanism, through which states have been able to 'announce' their contingent legality as the realization of ethical life. Such a humanism, by its refusal to acknowledge the violence of its own production (i.e., the originary refusal of the 'excess' which is pre-supposed by, and excluded from, the economy of the system), tends to exclude the moments of *différance* that are always simultaneous with its legislations. It is the enunciation of 'this' (spiritual, virtuous, etc.) legality as present/complete, in other words, which is the 'worst possible' violence; for it cannot allow that its prescriptions could be other than necessary or ethical.

What, then, is the difference between Derrida's deconstruction and Foucault's genealogy; or rather, how can we distinguish between their respective attempts to prosecute an ethics and politics of difference/heterogeneity/otherness? Perhaps the best way of doing this is to look at the presuppositions of Foucault's power/knowledge identity. As we have seen, all of Foucault's genealogies – from *Madness and Civilization* to *The History of Sexuality* – presuppose a close proximity of power and knowledge. The history of the modern social body is expounded through the repetition of this proximity: new techniques and discourses emerge, in general, from the need to 'discipline' social spaces which have, 'until now', been marginal to the exercise of political authority. As we have seen in Foucault's account of the transition from feudalism to capitalism, it was not until surplus wealth and property began to accumulate in the hands of the mercantile class that the old rights of common subsistence become a cause for political-disciplinary intervention. Thus, there is a sense in which Foucault's writings – even his account of madness as the 'other' of modern Cartesian rationalism – articulate the conditions under which the 'functional' aims of modernity are most effectively achieved. The knowledges which organize and control the reproduction of a 'normal' subject constitute a disciplinary, biogenetic edifice which becomes increasingly deterministic in its relations with the individual. We might, then, be tempted to read Foucault's genealogies as descriptive presentations, in which the sexual, psychiatric and disciplinary discourses of modernity are homogenized within a general understanding of the present as normative entrapment. Indeed, some of Foucault's remarks on the necessity of resistance seem to suggest that the act of transgressing established normative demands is self-legitimizing.[37] Yet this advocacy of 'resistance without principle' which has been attributed to Foucault misrepresents his ethical position. The later writings – especially volume two of *The History of Sexuality*[38] – do attempt to give an account of what practical/normative autonomy might be. I will suggest, however, that Foucault's attempt to distinguish between autonomy (self-governance) and the determinism inscribed in the discourses of power/knowledge maintains a certain 'repressed' form of functionalism.

Foucault's writing, I have argued, maintains a sense of historical objectivism. The knowledge regimes whose development is set out in the genealogies represent different aspects of the 'modern' identity between power and knowledge. Each describes the way in which certain changes in the constitution of the social body have necessitated the deployment of new techniques of penetration, surveillance and control. Thus, the implementation of 'humanistic' regimes of discipline, and the deployment of a generalized sexual hygienics, refer to the same historical demand: the productive normalization of the subject (both in its relations with itself and to others). The second volume of Foucault's genealogy of sex – *The Care of the Self* – however, is an attempt to abrogate this incremental determinism of 'carceral' knowledges. According to Foucault's remarks on the constitution of ancient Greek society, the most important ethical and political principle within the *polis* was the idea of moderation. Every (male) citizen, as the active principle through which the good governance of women and slaves was maintained, was obligated to master the appetitive side of his (Aristotelian) soul. In order to be fit to exercise political authority, in other words, the citizen of the *polis* was required to subject the chaotic – although still human – desires of the body to his rational apperception of the good. The duties and obligations of citizenship demanded constant 'moderation' of one's appetites and desires, a 'moderation' which engaged the exercise of political power with a code of practical self-governance. The 'political figure' that Foucault attempts to reconstruct from his account of the Athenian city-state, therefore, is the diametrical opposite of the passive paranoiac who exists under the gaze of the social panopticon. Such a figure represents the possibility of ethical self-determination (autonomy) within the carceral knowledges of modernity. For if (as Foucault claims in volume one of *The History of Sexuality*) the 'Victorian regime' begins as a set of strictures that the bourgeoisie imposes upon itself, then the genealogy of 'modern' sexual norms should not be understood as following the demands of a simple productive utility. Indeed, it has been argued that Foucault's inclusion of this collective self-regulation within the realm of genealogy displaces the objectivism of his account of modern power relations. A certain 'Enlightenment' sensitivity to the other as a 'subject' of power, in other words, is conceived as co-present with the recognition of one's 'self' as a practical demand.[39]

This 'ethical' reconstruction of Foucault, I will argue, fails to recognize the deep homogenizing necessity that is inscribed in his genealogical writings. The claim that the modern regime of sexual hygienics should be understood as originating in an act of 'practical' self-regulation, for example, does not seem to square with the explanatory function that Foucault attributes to the concept of bio-power. As we have seen, volume one of *The History of Sexuality* attempts to show that the demands of sexual normalization were not externally imposed upon the industrial working class. Rather, the practical demands of *scientia sexualis* are presented as displacing the ideology of 'blood' as the genealogical foundation of authority. This 'origination', however, takes place within a narrative that is, from the beginning, dominated by the utilitarian necessity of healthy and productive populations. If, in other words, the techniques of sexual normalization did take root in the middle classes, then the logic of Foucault's genealogy demands that this is understood as the *condition* of a more generalized control of the desiring subject. It is difficult to see, then, how we could recognize the medico-scientific necessity, which Foucault posits in the concept of bio-power, as the ground of a collective act of self-determination, for the concept of bio-power is originally concerned with the penetration and control of social spaces. The lesson we might learn from the Victorian bourgeoisie, therefore, is not one of a political self-regulation which moderates the effects of power through self-restraint; it is rather that the objectivism of Foucault's genealogy remains incompatible with the practical/ethical principle he attempts to salvage from the *polis*.

Foucault's genealogical link between power and knowledge therefore always reinscribes a certain utilitarian necessity into the constitution of power relations. Indeed, it is through this inscription that we should understand his Kantianism; for it is in determining one's self independently of established (medical, psychiatric, disciplinary, etc.) knowledges that one's action can become ethically and politically significant. Yet if the idea of genealogy cannot, as I have argued, make room for a moment of autonomous (i.e., non-utilitarian) self-determination, then the possibility of a Foucauldian ethics of difference begins to look questionable. Such an ethics would involve establishing that the moral law, which my action seeks to exemplify, is a spontaneous acknowledgement of the other as that which is, like me, subject to strategies of power. Thus, my recognition of racial, sexual, national or cultural differences as foci political strategies would have to be something that is opened by my own subjection to techniques of control. It is, however, precisely this 'opening' of a generalized sensitivity to difference that is denied by Foucault's genealogies. *The History of Sexuality*, for example, expounds the practices of 'normal' sex as a kind of 'heteronomous' domain, whose constitution/description determines the necessity of specific 'transgressive' practices. The constant deployment of the term 'man' and the refusal to acknowledge patriarchy as a theme of sexual genealogy are significant because of the authorial ideals they produce, ideals which originate in the inclusion of *male* sexuality (pleasure, desire) within the realm of the normal, the productive and the utile. Foucault's notion of a gay 'community' therefore seems to be originally exclusive of the feminine; the autonomous/transgressive practices through which 'individually modulated relationships' are created are 'homosexual' in the sense that their authors are invariantly male.[40]

The problem with Foucauldian genealogy, then, is the tendency to *determine* what is 'other' than the knowledges and techniques of domination. *The History of Sexuality* sets out a domain in which male desire can become energized and performative, but where the feminine appears only through the control of 'nerves' and hysterias. The possibility of ethical self-invention, therefore, is originally limited by what is included in, and excluded from, the history of Western sexuality. It might of course be argued that Foucault could have written a genealogical account of sex and patriarchy; and that he did not do so because he wished to avoid imposing particular forms of transgression upon the 'otherness' femininity. Women, he would argue, should be the ones to express their own subjection and political identity. Yet the general theoretical problem would remain: the concept of genealogy always involves positing a certain functional completeness between power and knowledge; and once this completeness has been specified, it becomes the 'other' of self-invention (autonomy). Thus, *The History of Sexuality* makes the ethical recognition of women into a secondary possibility of male transgressive action. For its account of 'normal' sexual practices has already determined their utility as something which operates through the 'active', and excessive, principle of masculine desire. Women, it seems, are reduced to a kind of secondarized resistance to the exclusiveness of 'man's' autonomy.

The deconstructive question, then, would be this: how is it possible to think sexual difference – and the affirmation of the feminine – without determining the necessity of its inclusion within this type of oppositional-dialectical economy? To answer this question I must return to Derrida's critique of metaphysics; specifically, to his deconstruction of Levinas's idea of the face as signifying an otherness which is beyond reduction to totality ('the same').[41] For Levinas, it is the 'resemblance' of the face to God which is the founding moment of moral responsibility: the undeterminable proximity of the divine in the visage of the Other is the (pre-social, pre-ethical) origin of my acknowledgement of him or her as human. The concept of resemblance/alterity expounded in *Totality and Infinity* (1994), therefore, is radically opposed to the categories of 'the same'; it is conceived as *prior* to the 'ontological' determinations which include the subject within systematic organizations of ethical life. Thus, the 'gendering' of relations (and the 'dialectical' attempts to produce mediation from antagonistic sexual identities) is understood by Levinas as a *relative* alterity, which excludes the infinite, genderless signification of the face. If we would only acknowledge the universality of the moral commandment, in other words, we would know our responsibility to the Other 'as Other', regardless of its gender. This absolute exteriority of the 'Other' and 'the same' is, of course, wholly unacceptable to Derrida. As we have seen in the notion of 'writing' developed in *Of Grammatology* (1976), the hierarchical organization of philosophical concepts always determines an 'economic' distribution of trace, supplement and *différance*. The 'other', which is secondarized in the text, does not remain as a kind of inert residue; as we have seen in the readings of Hegel and Rousseau, it returns as an 'excess' which threatens the 'legality' of the system and its mediations. Levinas's thought (of infinite alterity) does not, according to Derrida, escape this fatal inclusion of otherness *within* its textual economy: 'the other cannot be absolutely exterior to the same without ceasing to be other; and . . . consequently, the same is not a totality closed in upon itself . . . having only the appearance of alterity in what Levinas calls economy, work and history'.[42] How, then, does the thought of the feminine relate to Derrida's pursuit of the 'other' encrypted in the Levinas's economy of 'the same'?

As I have indicated, Derrida's approach to sexual difference is concerned with extricating the general significance of 'femininity' from oppositional-dialectical economies of the kind we found in Foucault. Thus, Derrida's return to Levinas after 'Violence and metaphysics' is an attempt to specify how the genderless infinity of 'resemblance' inscribes the absolute alterity of the Other within *the realm of the totality*.[43] According to Derrida, Levinas's insistence that the 'neutrality' of the face *precedes and exceeds* every determination of the same is a legislative moment which has taken the *relative* alterity of sexual difference and represented it as the *absolute alterity* of the Other. The economy of 'the same', in other words, includes and conceals a moment of *oppositional* difference – the difference of gender – which is encrypted in the 'infinity' of Levinas's moral commandment.

This deconstruction of the alterity of resemblance is an attempt to encourage us to think the other, not as that which is absolutely outside the determinations of reason, but as that which is traced within its structures and categories. The dialectics of opposition, we have seen, presuppose a male ('homosexual') principle of legislation, within which the feminine can act only to 'erase' imperfectly its difference. The relationship of deconstructive thought to the idea of legislation, however, demands that we recognize the feminine as a possibility of dispersal, rather than as a determined principle of opposition. For Derrida, the notion of femininity signifies an infinite blurring of the distinctions through which 'phallogocentric' authority is exercised. Its structures of reproduction are deeply troubling for the domain of masculine authority; the double significance of penetration and virginity signified in the 'hymen', or the external interiority of the vagina, for example, disclose the impossibility of a legislative break between outside and inside, mastery and slavery, privilege and subjection. Femininity, in other words, inhabits the 'margins' of masculine authority; it discloses the 'folds' – the 'outside' which is not outside – where phallogocentrism has yet to penetrate. Such disclosures of what is unforeseen in the discourse of masculine legislation, however, can only be temporary 'remissions'. The 'fold' (i.e., that which opens some practice or knowledge which has yet to be colonized by the discourse of truth) is not an absolute alterity; it is situated within the legislative domain of the 'masculine'. The affirmation of femininity, therefore, is an affirmation of that which disturbs the dominant phallogocentric discourse, without claiming to displace or avoid its necessity. It is that which encourages strange and unforeseen investments in the realm of prescriptive reason. Yet Derrida makes it clear in *The Post Card* (1987), that the articulation of such remissions must expose them to the 'inseminating' necessity of reason: for whatever I (the man, the male, the agent) tell you (the woman, the female, the patient) about the margins of masculinity, or whatever you (women) tell each other, the necessity of speech will always 'betray' the remission, whose event/occurrence is a painful silence.[44] Thus, Derrida's idea of a non-essentialized feminine schematizes a more generalized concept of the relationship between reason and autonomy: it is only through the acknowledgement of writing, and its 'economic' production of necessity, that we are able to experience the moments of 'remission' which, inevitably, demand speech and the return of the *logos*.

Femininity is inscribed in the oppositions of masculine authority; it 'names' possibilities of remission which are unforeseen in the legislative power of phallogocentric reason. Male hegemony is always haunted by the feminine; it deploys a certain 'undecidability' in which the man/agent can never be sure that his power will be acknowledged by a patient and receptive woman. Derrida's idea of the feminine, therefore, should be understood as participating in the 'economic' violence expounded in *Writing and Difference*. The necessity of speech ('the phrase'), according to 'Violence and metaphysics', is determined by a possibility which must remain forever beyond articulation. This 'possibility' – the *idea* of peace – is that which commands us to speak, for if we do not participate in the economy of articulation, peace (i.e., the 'horizon' of speech) will be drawn into the 'presence' of exclusive/totalizing legislations. Femininity, then, is part of this ethical necessity (of speech) to protect the 'indefinite silence' of peace; for it enters the economy of (masculine) reason as something *not yet* determinately opposed or resistant to it.[45] Julia Kristeva's idea of 'aesthetic practices', which subvert the 'singularized' forms of male and female sexual identity, for example, are moments of reflection which disclose the 'symbolic' (i.e., metapsychological) conditions of a patriarchal history.[46] It is this disturbing undecidability of sexual difference that is excluded from *The History of Sexuality*. As we have seen, the principle of autonomy which is activated by *scientia sexualis* is essentially 'homosexual': it is only through the normalization of male desire that the possibility of transgressive action is opened. Foucault's genealogy of sex therefore maintains a certain complicity with the 'dialectics' of sexual difference; the relationship between normalization and masculinity establishes the latter as an active, dominant principle, within which femininity can act only to erase itself. Perhaps, then, the affirmation of feminine difference requires us to take seriously Derrida's point about the (necessary) undecidability of male power.

There is an important point to be made here about the general possibility of an ethics of difference, and its consequences for the idea of a social science. Foucault's genealogical writings develop an ambiguous and unstable relationship between the Kantian concepts of 'autonomy' (rational self-determination) and 'heteronomy' (external necessity). As we have seen in *The History of Sexuality* and *Discipline and Punish*, there is a close proximity between the 'functional' need to control undisciplined

social spaces and the development of modern (legal, psychiatric, medical, disciplinary, etc.) domains of knowledge. The concept of 'modernity'
deployed in Foucault's writing is haunted by a sense of entrapment, in
which the 'hypothetical' imperatives of biogenetic and disciplinary
knowledge come to 'fabricate' their docile, self-normalizing subjects.
Indeed, the type of analysis encouraged by Foucauldian genealogy is a
constant registration of the effects of new forms of discourse on 'local'
identities. The question of control is endlessly repeated. However, we
know from his later writings that Foucault was unwilling to accept such
an understanding of his genealogies: modern knowledges are presented
as the conditions under which transgressive political practices are made
possible, rather than inscribing technical/functional necessity into every
aspect of subjectivity.[47] Modern knowledges, in other words, open the
possibility of 'autonomy' by constituting – or rather 'energizing' –
unforeseen moments of association, identity and resistance.

Yet it is precisely this 'opening' of autonomy through the technical
principles of control which has concerned us throughout our exposition
of Foucault's genealogy. Our account of Derrida's idea of the feminine
attempted to show that an ethics of difference requires us to think 'the
other' as that which *belongs* to the legislative (phallogocentric) text, but
only in the sense that its possibility is a questioning of the oppositions
through which it has become 'other'. Ethical responsibility is conceived
in the silence of unforeseen 'remissions' which, having inevitably
betrayed themselves in speech, contribute to the 'economical' distribution of truth and violence in which the *idea* of peace (its 'indefinite
silence') is protected. Language, as that which is prior to every possible
question or experience, 'promises' us to the dispersal which is within the
logos; 'we', as human beings, are responsible to the event (the 'address'),
as that which we are pledged to think or meditate upon.[48] The relationship between knowledge and autonomy that has emerged from
Foucault's historical writings, however, discloses the impossibility of
prosecuting an ethics (of difference) on the basis of what is originally a
description of technical necessity. As we have seen in *The History of
Sexuality*, the prescriptive discourses which constitute *scientia sexualis*,
ultimately bear upon a 'masculine' principle of desire, which is reproduced – or 'reinvented' – in 'homosexual' (i.e., male) transgressions of
normality. Thus, while it would be true to say that neither Foucault nor
Derrida attempt to set out a universal procedural rationality (i.e., a
Kantian form which would be originally sensitive to the other 'as other'),
it is perhaps the case that Foucault's genealogical writings leave us
requiring such a rationality. For how are we to make normative distinctions among (transgressive) actions and identities which appear to be
determined – albeit unintentionally – by techniques of control. I would
suggest, then, that the moments of 'reflection', through which the
difference of the other becomes an ethical demand, cannot be determined
within the confines of Foucault's power/knowledge identities. An ethics

of difference requires a more intensive dispersal of the 'otherness' inscribed in reason; a dispersal whose possibility Derrida names through the (quasi-transcendental) ideas of trace, supplement and *différance*.

I will examine more fully the implications of a 'deconstructive' ethics for our concept of a social science in the final section. For the moment, however, my attempt to develop a Derridean reading of Foucault's genealogical texts has aimed at disclosing the technical/functional necessity which is reproduced through his descriptions of modernity. I have tried to show that the relationship between power and knowledge, which is developed through the histories bio-power and panoptical discipline, has always already excluded the possibility of an 'ethical' recognition of the other. For in attempting to show that the techniques by which the modern subject is 'fabricated' (i.e., disciplined, normalized, controlled) are also the 'conditions' through which self-invention is made possible (energized), Foucault determines an opposition in which it is the technical necessity inscribed in knowledge which controls the 'events' of autonomous action and reflection. Freedom, in other words, even in its 'difference' from the strategies of power, is produced, and therefore circumscribed, by the conceptions of agency, productivity and utility determined within those strategies. Thus, the possibility of a certain 'Enlightenment' sensitivity to the other as a subject of authority depends upon the possibility of articulating the difference between 'established' structures of reason and the reception/recognition of what is 'unforeseen' in their legislative forms. As I have tried to show in my account of Derrida's idea of sexual difference, it is the notion of 'writing' – and its dispersal of reason's legislative 'presence' through the ideas of trace, supplementarity and *différance* – which encourage us to think the other as that which 'haunts' the oppositions of reason, that is, that which is always *just* beyond its legislative self-recognition. The project of articulating the difference between established conditions of rationality and the 'event' of ethical judgement, however, is not exclusively Derridean. Indeed, it is Jean-François Lyotard's attempts to relate the ideas of 'performative freedom' and 'agitated judgement' to a certain 'postmodern' fragmentation of knowledge which seem to have been more influential on contemporary social thought. It remains then, to examine the implications of this (neo-Kantian) organization of difference for the idea of a social science.

Lyotard and the community of judgement

My fundamental objection to Foucault's genealogical writings is that their reproduction of particular technical/functional necessities (the 'care' of the reproductive act, the disciplining of labour, the regimentation of the school and the factory, etc.) excludes the possibility of an 'ethical' reception of difference, or 'otherness'. I argued that the power/

knowledge relation through which Foucault develops the notion of carceral modernity cannot simultaneously act as the *condition* of a politics of moral recognition. I attempted to show that the 'text' of Foucauldian genealogy is haunted by the technical imperatives of control, and that, as such, his later transcriptions of power as opening the possibility of ethical resistance fail to move beyond the opposition of freedom to the 'present' determinations of authority. The acts of transgression which are 'energized' by modern discourses of power, in other words, always remain determinately opposed to the structures and techniques which have produced them. So far I have attempted to think this opposition in deconstructive terms; I have tried to show that the 'polymorphous' effects of Foucauldian power, remain complicit with the metaphysical categories in which difference 'dialectically' erases itself. An ethics of difference, therefore, requires a concept of the 'other' which, while remaining *within* the realm of philosophical reason, is unforeseen in its particular legislative determinations. It is this general conception of an 'unpredetermined' difference which I might conceive as the 'guiding thread' in the diversity of Lyotard's work. For while Derrida's writing is characterized by a meticulous and sustained deployment of the quasi-transcendental ideas of trace, supplement and *différance*, Lyotard's thought pursues the idea of heterogeneity through a series of 'readings', from which Marx, Freud, Bataille and Kant (among others) emerge as prefiguring an ethical sensitivity to the unforeseen. I will examine the difference – it would perhaps be too strong to call it a 'differend' – between Derridean and Lyotardian conceptions of writing and dispersal at the end of the chapter.[49] For the moment, however, I need to examine the significance of Lyotard's thought for my idea of a social science.

Lyotard's work, as we have already remarked, is characterized by a number of shifts and disjunctions in which it is difficult to identify a unifying theme or principle. Yet the distance that separates his account of the relationship between theory and desire in *Libidinal Economy*[50] from the neo-Kantianism of *The Differend* (1988a), is not an unbridgeable gulf. Even though Lyotard has expressed dissatisfaction with 'following nothing but the intensities of affects',[51] this dissatisfaction is with the 'ontological' assumptions that seem impossible to discharge from the economics of investment and desire, rather than with the search for disquieting singularities and events. The language of libidinal affects, through which Lyotard originally expressed his break with the 'scientific' categories of Marxism,[52] has encouraged a particular reading of *Libidinal Economy*: the intensities of libido that are channelled, blocked and intensified within every 'economic' distribution are conceived as a kind of absolute, anti-conceptual power. This representation of libido, however, is certainly opposed to the intent of Lyotard's writing; for, as such, it could only be understood as a transcendent force – or even as a 'subject' – whose necessity determines every movement of pulsion or desire. Indeed, it is just this kind of theoretical abstraction that *Libidinal*

Economy attempts to expose and subvert. For Lyotard demands that we acknowledge the impossibility of separating a complete (arrested, static) system of productions from the intensities (*jouissance*) of the 'libidinal band', and that we recognize the 'representations' of theoretical knowledge as determined within an economy of heterogeneous forms of investment.[53] These themes – the irreducible heterogeneity of different 'genres' of knowledge, the incompatibility of 'cognition' with a 'moral' sensitivity to difference, and the 'agitation' produced by the proximity of the unforeseen – recur throughout Lyotard's work, although the development of his ideas through *The Postmodern Condition* (1991a) and into the sophisticated pragmatics of *The Differend*, is marked by the emergence of a certain Kantianism, which will be the focus of my exposition.

The reading of Kant presented in *The Differend* develops Giles Deleuze's idea that the 'faculties' of cognition deployed in the critical philosophy are powers of judgement and negotiation, rather than analytical unities which belong to the concept mind, or intelligence, a priori.[54] In a sense, then, the four 'Kant Notices' through which Lyotard sets out his relationship to transcendental idealism represent a thoroughgoing critique of the dominance of cognitive knowledge over the moral, ethical, political and aesthetic sensibilities of the 'subject' (or 'addressee'). His reading of the critical philosophy, in other words, attempts to show that forms of cognition, through which Kant expounds transcendental subjectivity, depend upon metaphysical ideas of reason to guarantee the unity ('congruence') of experience. The claim is that the practical and theoretical cognitions of the transcendental subject are originally sensitive to the 'exteriority' which they organize (i.e., the chaos of pre-intuitive affection and appetitive inclination), and that Kant, in 'negotiating' this exteriority, discloses thinking's immediate receptiveness to the 'unrepresentable' as such. It is the account of reflective judgement given in the third *Critique*, which, on Lyotard's reading, establishes this receptiveness as both the condition and negation of legitimacy. The absence of determinate concepts in the reception of aesthetic and teleological finalities is abstracted from the third *Critique*, and presented in *The Differend* as a spontaneous activity independent of the rule of generic discourses. Thus, the idea of judgement which is expounded in the third *Critique* is conceived by Lyotard as the point at which Kant's 'metaphysical' representation of the experience and autonomy of the subject is displaced by the 'critical activity' which pervades his account of transcendental faculties. For Lyotard, Kant's reflective judgement is not a faculty, but the condition of discrete transcendental functions: it is the condition which *The Differend* presents as opening the possibility of non-metaphysical (non-totalizing) philosophy, politics and ethics.

The Differend's account of transcendental idealism sets out to show that the spontaneous reception of 'otherness' (the non-cognitive, the indeterminable, the sublime), disclosed in Kant's idea of reflective judgement, is ultimately disruptive of the cognitive limits he attempts to impose upon the event of difference. Lyotard's reading of each of Kant's three *Critiques* (and of the political essays) is concerned with the possibility of *Darstellung*, that is, with the possibility of conjoining the immediacy and contingency of events with the cognitive conditions through which they are 'experienced'. The critical philosophy, according to this reading, discloses a tension between the 'unrepresentable' element which exists as other to the transcendental I, and the activity of that I in constituting the unity of itself and its representations. In his account of the first *Critique*, Lyotard attempts to show that this tension is disclosed in the relationship of the modes of intuition, space and time to the matter of sensible affection. The temporal syntheses, upon which Kant's idea of a unified cognitive experience depends, presupposes a heterogeneity (otherness) which the 'Transcendental Aesthetic' has not subsumed under the deictic rules of the cognitive genre. In the second *Critique*, the persistence of this 'unrepresentability' is negotiated through the 'type', by which duty is enabled to present itself within a realm of 'congruent' human ends. Lyotard's transcription of the third *Critique*, with its concentration on the tension between the faculties of reason and imagination expounded in the 'Analytic of the Sublime', presents the notion of reflective judgement as an immediate sensitivity to the otherness 'negotiated' by Kant in the first and second *Critiques*. The moments of conjoining, or *Darstellung*, which Lyotard focuses on in his transcriptions of practical and theoretical reason, are produced through a 'metaphysical' presupposition of 'reality' as prior to the immediate reception of difference.[55] What Lyotard understands as the metaphysical elements of the critical philosophy, therefore, are presented as originally sensitive to the heterogeneity which they attempt to homogenize. It is this sensitivity which *The Differend* presents as distinguishing the Kantian project from the totalizing system of Hegel's speculative philosophy:

> With the notion of the sublime (and on the condition that *Darstellung* be understood as we have here), Kant will always get the better of Hegel. The *Erhabene* [sublime] persists, not over and beyond, but right at the heart of the *Aufgehoben* [sublation, preservation].[56]

For Lyotard, the activity of Kant's transcendental I, both in the constitution of experience and in its practical self-determination, constantly discloses the heterogeneity (otherness) which springs from representational thought. *Darstellung*, or the moment of conjunction, necessitates unpredetermined judgement, for neither practical nor theoretical reason can 'fill in the abyss' between its object (the unity of experience of objects, or the unity of human ends) and the otherness which it receives.[57] Thus, for Lyotard, the faculties of the Kantian subject are not fixed, analytical unities, but critically related realms whose legitimacy is judged and rejudged, each by the other. Each realm – or 'regime' – of cognitive necessity, through which the Kantian subject judges the moral, theoretical, political or aesthetic significance of its 'experience', is related to the others through particular 'litigations': 'Was my action moral, or did I simply act according to a hypothetical imperative?'; 'How far should I follow the demands of my autonomous reason where it contradicts the authority of the state?'; 'Is this object sublime, or merely the occasion of desire?'. Yet for Lyotard, such 'conflicts' always involve the presentation of a false contingency; for the conditions under which such questions have been formed, and through which they may be resolved, have already been set by the necessity of a universal cognitive recognition. The account of aesthetic finality given in the third *Critique*, therefore, is of central importance to the idea of judgement set out in *The Differend*. For according to Lyotard's reading, it is founded upon a moment of 'agitation', or 'negative pleasure', which cannot be subsumed under the rules of cognitive recognition (unity, totality, mediation, etc.).

The 'negative pleasure' described in Kant's 'Analytic of the sublime' is produced through the simultaneous impossibility and necessity of representing ideas in imagination. This unrepresentability presupposes the transcendental separation of reason and imagination (*Vernunft* and *Vorstellung*), which Kant has attempted to validate in the first and second *Critiques*. In the account of 'knowledge' given in the first *Critique*, the imagination is conceived as a faculty of pure intuition; it is that which allows apprehension of a spatiality which cannot be directly schematized by the understanding. This representational faculty, according to Kant, is the foundation of mathematical truths; that is, of propositions about quantity, relation, proportion, etc., which remain true independently of phenomenal experience. The faculty of 'reason', whose necessity Kant expounds in the second *Critique*, on the other hand, is concerned with the 'idea' of freedom; that is, with the concept of autonomy as pure, unrestricted self-determination. As such, Kant's moral will is bound to the self-consistency of the categorical imperative; it must respect the idea of 'humanity' which is inscribed in each particular obligation. In the 'Analytic of the sublime' this transcendental separation of reason and imagination produces a feeling of 'pleasure-displeasure' (i.e., a simultaneous 'pleasure' in possessing the faculty of ideas, and 'displeasure' at not being able to represent them), which is the result of the imagination's inability to find an analogue for the idea of totality:

In a literal sense and according to their logical import, ideas cannot be represented. But if we enlarge our empirical faculty of representation . . . with a view to the intuition of nature, reason inevitably steps forward, as the faculty concerned with the independence of absolute totality, and calls for the effort of mind, unavailing though it might be, to make the representation of sense adequate to this totality. This effort, and the feeling of the unattainability of the idea by means of imagination, is itself a presentation of the subjective finality of our mind in the employment of the imagination in the mind's supersensible province, and compels us subjectively to think nature itself in its totality as a presentation of something supersensible, without or being able to effectuate the presentation objectively.[58]

For Lyotard, this notion of the sublimity – 'the elevation of nature beyond our reach as equivalent to a presentation of ideas' – is crucially disturbing for Kant's account of a unifying cognition.[59] According to *The Differend*, the 'negative pleasure' of the sublime cannot contribute to an interiorization of nature, in which the contingency/otherness encountered in the moments of *Darstellung* would be reduced to appearances of conceptual identity. The feeling of 'agitation' through which the Kantian subject encounters the sublime, in other words, does not simply register a 'litigation' between two cognitive faculties. For Lyotard, it signifies the impossibility of reducing the difference (heterogeneity) between two regimes of discourse, regimes which, given their discrete rules of judgement and formation, cannot be subsumed under a 'unifying' set of rules.

In a sense, then, Lyotard's reading of the sublime returns us to the 'critique' of epistemological hierarchy set out in *Libidinal Economy*.[60] As we have seen, the metaphorical figure of the libidinal band is intended to refer us to the impossibility of determining a neutral 'space' from which it would be possible to criticize 'perverse' distributions of libido and desire. Every form of knowledge presupposes and reproduces libidinal investment. And so what distinguishes theoretical, scientific and philosophical knowledges is not their 'neutrality', but rather the desire to objectify 'true' forms of production, satisfaction and investment. For Lyotard, however, one cannot become 'theoretically' disengaged from the *jouissance* (the simultaneity of pleasure and suffering) which invests libidinal distributions; even the extended labour of writing the perversity of 'capital' involves a kind of pleasure in the struggle for completion.[61] What marks the continuity between the *jouissance* of *Libidinal Economy* and the sublime affection expounded in *The Differend*, therefore, is a certain 'affection' produced at the limits of cognitive thought. Lyotard has acknowledged that, within the terms of the former, our encounter with these limits could only reproduce a 'primary process' (the libidinal band) which invests every 'representational' form of knowledge. Our registration of the dispersal inherent in the categories of scientific and philosophical (metaphysical) thought would always be destined to return to the 'ontology' of pulsions and affects. The 'agitation' experienced by the Kantian subject in the presence of the sublime, however, points to an alterity which cannot be presented in any particular 'genre' of discourse. The a priori faculties of reason and imagination have to 'suspend' their legislative functions, and demand a judgement which is 'subjective' and without predetermined conditions. Thus, the reading of the 'Analytic of the sublime', presented in *The Differend*, is an attempt to disclose 'incommensurability' as that which is both the condition of 'knowledge' (I can only 'know' what is determined within a particular 'genre') and that which is 'unforeseen' within the established terms of discourse and 'litigation'. Lyotard's idea of philosophy, in other words, demands a critical sensitivity to the conditions under which difference (incommensurability) is communicated among heterogeneous forms of knowledge.

In his prefatory 'Reading dossier', Lyotard specifies the notion of a differend as:

> a case of conflict, between (at least two) parties, that cannot be equitably resolved for lack of a rule applicable to both arguments. . . . However, applying a single rule to both in order to settle their differend as though it were a litigation would wrong (at least) one of them (and both if neither admits the rule). . . . A wrong results from the fact that the rules of the genre of discourse by which one judges are not those of a judged genre or genres of discourse.[62]

It is this 'case of conflict' which occupies the philosophical project of *The Differend*; and so I will attempt to specify the terms through which Lyotard has deployed its moral, ethical and political significance. Lyotard's reading of Kant, we have seen, concentrates on what he understands as the tension between the idea of transcendental legitimacy and the discriminatory power of thought articulated in the third *Critique*. The a priori 'faculties' which Kant determines in the critical philosophy are transcribed by Lyotard as 'generic' discourses, whose respective rules of formation are ultimately incommensurable. Thus, the 'conflict' of reason and imagination which Kant describes in the 'Analytic of the sublime' is presented within the context of a certain epistemological pragmatics. The agitation of the subject is no longer thought as signifying a 'final' unity in nature, but rather as registering the irreducible differences among the 'generic' forms of knowledge. I will return to this registration – or judgement – of difference in a moment.

So far I have given a fairly provisional account of what Lyotard understands by a 'genre'. The forms of discursive knowledge presented in *The Differend* – Marxism, Hegelian 'metaphysics', Kant's critical philosophy, etc. – exhibit certain practical characteristics which Lyotard began to specify in *The Postmodern Condition*. According to the latter, these 'narratives' are essentially historical dramatizations of the 'social bond'. They situate the 'human' subject within a universal story, whose telling and retelling resists the intrusion of difference (the unpresentable, incommensurability) on the established rules of (social) formation, legitimacy and progress. Thus, the operational principles of scientific explanation, which demand 'accumulation and progression' in the state of knowledge, are inscribed in every 'narrative' account of the relationship between (subjective) identity and (social) totality.[63] The genres of discourse described in *The Differend*, then, mark a continuation of this account of 'narrative' construction: each provides a set of rules by which success, development and the acceptability of difference (heterogeneity) can be formulated and judged. As Lyotard would have it, 'there exist genres of discourse which fix rules of linkage and it suffices to observe them to avoid differends'.[64] That which is at stake in this notion of the genre, therefore, is what Kant might recognize as the ordering of 'experience'. Each generic discourse attempts to place the immediate singularities – or 'events' – presented to the 'subject' within a totality of *exclusive* rules, principles and ends. As we have seen, Kant's 'negotiation' of this immediacy is played out in the relationship between the deictics of intuition and the chaotic data of sensory affection. For Lyotard, however, the heterogeneous singularities which 'affect' the subject cannot be reduced to the 'outside' of a transcendental unity. Rather, their persistence as a subjective 'spontaneity', which generic discourses must constantly seek to include within their rules of 'litigation', demands its own formal expression. And so we are brought to Lyotard's idea of the phrase.

The notion of 'phrasing' deployed in *The Differend* returns us to the domain of 'quasi-transcendental' ideas:

> But if phrases belonging to different regimes or genres . . . encounter each other to the point of giving rise to differends, then they must have certain properties in common, and their 'encounter' must take place in a single universe. . . . No, I am not saying that this universe is reality, only that it is the condition for the encounter, and therefore for the condition of differends. – The condition of the encounter is not the universe, but the phrase in which you present it.[65]

For Lyotard, the phrase expresses the singular, irreducible moment through which the subject 'links on' to the phrase or genre which has preceded it. Without the pragmatics of 'addressor' (agent/sender), 'addressee' (patient/receiver), 'sense' (meaning) and 'referent' (object), through which Lyotard specifies the necessity of the phrasing, the 'subject' would be denied every determination through which it could respond, declaim, enjoin, specify or refuse. It could not, in other words, be understood as a 'subject' in Lyotard's sense of the term, for it would have no 'regime' within which to orientate its actions. Thus, the phrase is 'transcendental' in the sense that it stipulates the most general conditions of communication: it specifies the rules through which heterogeneous 'regimes' of expression (stipulatives, descriptives, narratives, interrogatives, etc.) are able to 'link on to' each other. The only necessity which is determined by the Lyotardian phrase, therefore, is that 'linkage' should occur; the events of communication which happen among different regimens are always contingent. For example, I might link on to the injunction 'fuck off and die!' as a joke, or as an expression of contempt, or even as the concealment of love: the point is that none of these linkages are *entailed* in the initial moment of exclamation. Phrasing, therefore, necessarily gives rise to differends; for there is no formal or substantive necessity which can regulate the moments of linkage. (I might perhaps recall the criticisms of Habermas which are set out in *The Postmodern Condition*. For it is there that Lyotard begins to distance himself from a certain legislative Kantianism which attempts to articulate the practico-linguistic 'development' sustained in the diversity of communicative action.)

Differends, however, do not just occur *among* phrase regimen and genres of discourse; they also occur *between* them: 'For every phrase regimen, there corresponds a mode of presenting a universe. A genre of discourse inspires a mode of linking phrases together, and these phrases can be from different regimens.'[66] We have seen that the Lyotardian phrase is a moment of immediate attraction and conductivity: it picks up some unpredetermined thread in what has preceded it, and occasions 'linkages' which it can neither control nor prevent. Differends, therefore, occur among phrase regimens as the confrontation of unmediated incommensurability. If, for example, I received the injunction 'Fuck off and die!' as somehow returning my love, when the sender had simply expressed that she found me insufferable, then there would be a differend between us, for there is no possible 'rule' through which our positions could be translated into a litigation, and we are simply left with the 'agonism' of the unresolvable. In a sense, then, Lyotard's notion of the genre of discourse presupposes this 'universe' of contingent linkages. The generic forms of knowledge which appear in The *Differend* are presented as 'imprint [ing] a unique finality onto a multiplicity of heterogeneous phrases by linkings that aim to procure the success proper to that genre'.[67] Thus, the differends that might occur between Marx and Kant on the nature of 'bourgeois' society, or between 'technical' and 'tragic' conceptions of history, or between 'radical' and 'black' feminism, are conceived as resulting from the necessity inherent in each genre to appropriate every phrase for its particular ends. Genres of discourse, in other words, attempt to control the contingency of every phrase by situating it within predetermined rules of linkage, formation and success. But what if the linkage I make on to your command cannot be received into the genre that has licensed your authority? what if there is no language in which I can express the wrong that is done to me by your rules of justice? what if, for me, there is only the silent suffering of this incommensurability?

We are returned, then, to the question of the relationship between violence and metaphysics. The section of The *Differend* which Lyotard calls 'Result' attempts to dramatize the end of dialectical necessity through its confrontation with the Nazi Holocaust – or rather with the 'fact of Auschwitz'.[68] Speculative phenomenology (Hegel), or the 'genre' in which the discourse of mediation/identity communicates with the emergence of 'modern' institutions (civil society, moral individualism, functional and economic necessities, etc.), is presented as the 'history' of an absolutely mediated form – Hegel's 'Absolute Knowledge'. The dialectics of ethical life (*Sittlichkeit*), in other words, are controlled by the operation of a concept which is outside every transition it 'effectuates': absolute knowledge is the result/origin which ensures that every possible form of violence will contribute to a higher form of self-recognition. For Lyotard, then, the 'law' of speculative dialectics attempts to turn every differend into a litigation: it stipulates that nothing determined as 'legislative' within the substance of ethical life could prevent the retrieval of universal culture and community. Even the destructive force of the French Revolution, according to Hegel, is animated by an implicitly 'rational' desire for a community of 'man'; a desire which is ultimately reformulated in the restraint of Kant's moral law.[69]

Following Adorno's account of Auschwitz,[70] Lyotard attempts to show that the regimen of 'law' which determines the relation between the SS man and the Jewish deportee cannot be included within the dialectics of 'human' culture and community. The command of the SS man to the Jew, 'That you die; that is my law', demands nothing more of the latter than his or her annihilation – not even the chastened productivity of the Hegelian slave.[71] There is no 'community' of victims at Auschwitz, and no possibility of a 'beautiful death' redeemed in the eternal movement of spirit towards its realization in time.[72] Each deportee is torn from the substance of his or her civil and religious life, and made completely subject to the law of the 'Aryan' mythology. The legislative 'terror' perpetrated in the death camps, therefore, is 'new' in the sense that it cannot reproduce the dialectics of a universal 'we' (of humanity). The 'law' of the Aryan is from the beginning determined as a law of exclusion and annihilation (of the Jew, the homosexual, the lunatic, etc.), an annihilation which aims to leave no trace of those elements 'excepted' from Aryan history and culture. The law of the SS, therefore, is non-speculative because its 'mythological' infinitude cannot pass over into the finite forms of work and conscience which the Hegelian concept of law requires; just as the deportees' obligation cannot pass over into the infinite: 'The infinity of the legislator would have to become for itself the finitude (of a good conscience, of the absence of risk, of force); the finitude of the obligated one would have to become for itself the infinity (that he knows and wants the ordering of his death)'.[73]

Two essentially related issues emerge from this account of Auschwitz. The first concerns the question of how Western metaphysical thought might be implicated in the event of the Holocaust. We have seen that, for Lyotard, the presentation of singular events, or phrasings, within generic systems of reason, always constitutes an otherness which haunts the 'inside' of constituted 'communities'. Thus, the systems in which Western thought has attempted to specify legitimate difference perpetuate a certain 'unconscious affect'; the feeling of an intolerable 'other' which lives *beyond and within* the ethical community. Auschwitz, then, becomes the emblem of this unthinkable 'otherness' which metaphysics attempts to forget, and which Nazism tries to annihilate in fact and in memory. As Lyotard expresses it in *Heidegger and 'the jews'*, 'the solution was to be final: the final answer to the "Jewish" question. It was necessary to carry out right up to its conclusion, to terminate the interminable. And thus to terminate the term itself.'[74] The second question that emerges from this writing of the event of Auschwitz, therefore, is the Adornian one of how it will be possible to think philosophically after the destruction of dialectical logic.[75] If, in other words, the law of the SS finally 'blocks' the reconstitutive power of ethical life (human culture and community), how then can philosophy approach the ethical and political questions that emerge 'after Auschwitz'?

For Lyotard, the event of Auschwitz necessitates acknowledgement that the 'moments, formations and entities',[76] through which 'Occidental' philosophy constitutes its 'memory' of the present community, are always subverted by the otherness that is reproduced at the very moment of sublation (*Aufhebung*). Following Adorno, Lyotard maintains that the Holocaust is the ruination of thinking's systematic pursuit of identity, and that the evil of the death camps can only be attested to by writing the untotalizable complaints and sufferings of those who survived the 'Final Solution'. The testimonies of survivors, as Primo Levi observed, can only be of limited significance; they can do no more than hint at the experience of the 'complete witnesses whose disposition would have general significance'.[77] In his 'Meditations on metaphysics',[78] Adorno remarks that 'after Auschwitz' it is only through such 'micrological' testimony that dialectics can sustain its claim to proceed through presuppositionless critique. 'Micrology', he remarks, 'is the place where metaphysics finds haven from totality. No absolute can be expressed otherwise than in topics and categories of immanence, although neither in its conditionality nor as its totality is immanence defined.'[79] For Lyotard, however, not even a negative dialectics can survive the racial heterogeneity of law and obligation which happens at Auschwitz. Adorno's project presupposes the same rule of immanent derivation that allows speculative dialectics to re-engender constantly the 'we' that 'results' in universal selfhood (the Hegelian *Selbst*). Negative dialectics, by always rejecting the immanence of identity, also, on Lyotard's reading, constitutes a teleology in which the 'critique' of representation becomes an end in itself. The other is never allowed to express – to 'phrase' – the particularity of the wrong that is done to it.

The demand which emerges from this destruction of metaphysics is for a non-prescriptive autonomy of thought in relation to the 'legislative' ideals of community (inclusive totality, universal identity, rational consensus, etc.). As we have seen, Lyotard's notion of a differend involves 'a case of conflict . . . that cannot be equitably resolved for lack of a rule applicable to both arguments'. Generic forms of knowledge, then, exist in a state of agonistic communication, for there is no philosophical discourse in which their differends could be reduced to the level of accidents, or 'litigations'. The point about litigation in Lyotard's sense is that it occurs within a set of pre-established rules; it will ultimately be resolved within the discourse which has produced it. A differend, on the other hand, is a moment of pure incommensurability. It is that which demands *not* to be taken into the language of established genres, but to be phrased in literary, artistic and practical 'idioms' which respond to the unpresentability of the other:

> In the differend something 'asks' to be put into phrases, and suffers from the wrong of not being able to be put into phrases right away. . . . They [human beings] are summoned by language . . . to recognise that what remains to be phrased exceeds what they can presently phrase, and that they must be allowed to institute idioms which do not yet exist.[80]

Thus, the feeling of 'agitation' produced by the occurrence of differends (i.e., by the dispersal of necessity, conflict and litigation among and between phrases and genres of discourse) is conceived by Lyotard as 'a region of resistance to institutions, where is inscribed and hidden what happens "before" we know what it is and before we want to make it into anything at all'.[81] A moral community of human beings, therefore, is 'only in principle communicable', for it is always dispersed through judgements whose origin is *prior* to the rules of generic knowledge.

If there is a 'we' of humanity, then it is not something that can be expressed in the determinations of concept. The very possibility of judging difference morally, depends upon a feeling, or *'sensus'*, which for Lyotard is 'suppressed without relief' in the history of metaphysical thought.[82] This feeling is universal only in the sense that it can, in principle, be felt by, and communicated to, any sentient being.[83] The occasion of this *sensus*, however, is always contingent, for it occurs as the agitation provoked by what is suppressed, or 'silenced', in particular differends. My obligation to the other, therefore, cannot be stipulated in the demands of a procedural rationality (Kant), or realized in the institutions of ethical life (Hegel). The rules which govern obligation in the transcendental and speculative genres of discourse, although heterogeneous, both determine cognition as the ground of ethical responsibility. I cannot act ethically until I have recognized that my action will conform to the concept of self-determination (Kant), or that it will not transgress the established forms of *Sittlichkeit* (Hegel). Indeed, Lyotard's reading of the second *Critique* attempts to show that Kant's postulation of a spontaneous 'free will' (the undeduced condition of moral obligation) is 'incompossible' with the recognition of a community of autonomous beings. If there is 'causality through freedom', in other words, it cannot *presuppose* the legislations (integrity, negativity, consistency of identity, etc.) through which the other is deemed universally worthy of respect. In the end, Kant's 'getting the better' of Hegel depends, for Lyotard, upon the account of feeling which is given in the *Critique of Aesthetic Judgement* (1982b). The agitation felt by the subject in the presence of the sublime is conceived as a purely spontaneous response (to the incommensurability of reason and imagination) whose conditions cannot be cognitively specified. In 'our' encounters with particular differends, therefore, 'we' should judge the conflict of the parties in the absence of 'preconditions'; we should seek to phrase the silence of the victim, and to register the violence of its 'passage' into established litigations.

The possibility of justice depends upon a 'critical' sensitivity to the violence inscribed in knowledge – or rather, in the heterogeneous genres through which knowledge is determined. Lyotard's reading of the third *Critique*, we have seen, attempts to show that such a sensitivity is acknowledged by Kant as the condition of reflective judgements in general. For it is only through the subjective affections which he attributes to the separation of the faculties ('pleasure' in the conformity of intuition and understanding in 'Analytic of the beautiful', 'agitation' at the distance between reason and imagination in the 'Analytic of the sublime') that we are able to apprehend the 'finality' of nature. However, there remains a certain violence in this Kantian idea of judgement. The 'passages' made between discrete faculties in the third *Critique* have been forced into the service of cognition, and so the feelings produced by the proximity of difference, respond to the demands of a transcendental subject ('addressor') – that is, to nature conceived as a rational totality. What is at stake in *The Differend*'s third 'Kant Notice', therefore, is the possibility of transcribing the Kantian *sensus* – or more specifically, the feeling of sublime agitation – as a general, presuppositionless response to the generic determination of knowledge and the multiplication of differends. For Lyotard, in other words, Kant's account of tension among the faculties of the transcendental subject,[84] demands to be 'intensified' by an analogue of communication and dispersal (the archipelago) rather than 'reduced' by one of synthetic necessity (a priori 'fields' of legislative autonomy).[85]

It is in his fourth Kant Notice – on the historical and political writings – that Lyotard specifies the differend between constitutive aims of transcendental idealism and the 'aesthetic' sensitivity of thinking to the incommensurable, the heterogeneous. In order to understand this differend, we must return to the tension between the faculties of reason and cognition which is posited in the 'Analytic of the sublime'. For Kant, the moral nature of humanity is disclosed in reason's 'practical' capacity to determine itself independently of immediate affections and desire. The historical development of this 'formal subjective capacity' for choosing its own ends independently of inclination is a development of humanity's 'culture': 'The production in a rational being of an aptitude for any ends whatever of his own choosing, and consequently of the aptitude of a being for his freedom is culture.'[86] Reason, as the faculty of ideas, is 'distressed' by the chaos of empirical history and the apparent lack of improvement in humanity's moral culture. Kant's solution to this antinomy (i.e., to the contradiction between our 'cognition' of a chaotic empirical history and reason's 'speculative' expectation of moral improvement) is to assume a purposive nature as the 'guiding thread' of historical enquiry. Thus, the historico-political judgement, whose concept Kant expounds in his political writings, is reflective rather than deductive: it evaluates particular events in the absence of determinate concepts, judging them 'as if' they disclosed an objective development of moral culture.

For Kant, the progress of humanity towards a truly moral culture (a republic of freely chosen ends) is signified in its affection of those who witness the chaos of revolution. It is those who observe from states not directly involved in the present upheavals of human improvement who register what is truly at stake in such conflicts. Thus, the event of this signification – what Kant refers to in 'The contest of the faculties' as the *Begebenheit* – does not take place within the 'formlessness' through which the history of moral culture is made. The actors who respond to the universal demands of 'Enlightenment' cannot disengage their interests from the particular interests from the states in which their conflict occurs. It is only in the 'enthusiasm' of those who have no material interest in the outcome of such civil conflicts (i.e., the feeling of sublime agitation produced by what is 'Ideal' in the violence of the struggle – the idea of freedom) that the postulate of moral improvement is validated. The judgement of historical approbation is a 'sign' both of accomplished improvement and of a necessary development towards a cosmopolitan (non-conflictual) republic of states.

What is important to Lyotard in this notion of the *Begebenheit* ('the sign of history') is the nature of its mediation between the faculties of reason and cognition. For Kant, the feeling of agitation produced by proximity to the violent momentum of reason signifies the accomplishment of a certain level of moral culture. Our sense of historical enthusiasm 'does not merely allow us to hope for human improvement; it is already a form of improvement in itself, in so far as its influence is already strong enough for the present'.[87] The fact that we are able not only to register the idea of freedom, but also to proceed 'as if' it were a law governing the occurrence of particular events means that, as rational beings, we participate in a history which is 'purposive', but which is unable to realize its purpose (the infinite, the idea of freedom). The 'as if' structure of Kant's exposition is crucial here. For it is that which allows a 'critical' orientation to particular historical events, while excluding the possibility of realizing the moral, ethical or political 'substance' of freedom. Ideas of reason, to put it in strictly Kantian terms, cannot be brought into the realm of cognitive (phenomenal) reality.

It is this transcendental prescription which is the focus of *The Differend*'s account of Kant's political essays. We have seen that, for Lyotard, it is through the notion of the sublime that the critical philosophy demands to be evaluated as distinct from the dialectics of the result. The incommensurability of reason and cognition, which lies at the core of Kant's aesthetics, is reproduced in his political writings as a contingent and unpredictable sense of reason's activity in history. Yet the production of this *sensus* as 'culture' is only ever 'strong enough for the present': it is a 'sign' of the idea of freedom, and as such, resists transcription into the rules of cognitive reality. Rational human beings, in other words, are always responsible to the infinite unknowability of their freedom; and so for Kant, the enthusiasm provoked by certain historical events is simply the condition of judgements which attest to the possibility of 'culture' as the counterpart of autonomy. The differend between revolutionary politics, specifically Marxism, and Kant's 'critical' account of the relationship between freedom and history, therefore, is marked by the violence to which feeling (*sensus*) is subjected in the logic of the result. For Lyotard, the constitution of a universal working-class identity cannot take place among the mutually 'opaque' traditions of different societies. The notion of 'the proletariat', as opposed to the heterogeneity of working-class cultures and traditions, is what Kant would recognize as an idea of reason: its 'activity' depends upon the 'aesthetic' enthusiasm of those (proletarians) who witness the particular forms in which the differend between capital and labour is violently exposed. The 'passage' from the idea of the proletariat (universal productive humanity) to the 'real political organization of the working class', which Marx expounds as an objective historical necessity, is for Lyotard a confusion of 'sign' and 'referent': the nationally dispersed enthusiasm for the revolutionary activity of the proletariat cannot guarantee its 'real' existence as a universal class.[88] Thus, an illusory passage is made between the regimes of aesthetic reaction (that which for Kant and Lyotard registers the difference between the infinity of freedom and the rules of cognition) and practical necessity; a passage which is subsequently compounded by 'the party's' attempts to enforce the universal demands of the proletariat on the empirical working class.[89]

For Kant, we are entitled to assume the agency of reason in human affairs, because of the feeling of 'distress' that the rational subject feels at the prospect of a purposeless history. The sign which licenses the moral significance of historical enthusiasm (i.e., the spontaneous 'distress' of the 'critical watchman'), therefore, is inscribed in the demand for a unity of reason, understanding and imagination in the 'noumenal' identity of nature. So, although the culture of judgement which Kant presents in his political writings cannot determine the idea of freedom as a cognitive reality, there remains inscribed in that culture a demand that 'we', as rational subjects, remain receptive to the signs (of unity, mediation, integrity and progress) given by nature as a transcendental subject. It is this Kantian logic of inscription, and the receipt of signs from a unknowable 'addressor', which marks the differend between Lyotard's concept of judgement and a certain 'generic' idea of 'the postmodern'. As long as postmodern philosophy and politics define themselves through their search for 'unconsciousnesses, lapses, limits, confines, goulags,

parataxes, non-senses, or paradoxes', they remain faithful to the 'signified' demands of the infinite – the unknowable/transcendental identity
of nature. As Lyotard puts it:

> Whatever acceptation is given to the Idea of nature, one's right of access to it is
> only through signs, but the right of access to signs is given by nature. Not even
> a denatured nature and signs of nothing, not even a postmodern non-
> teleology, cannot escape this *circulus*.[90]

The political culture that Lyotard is attempting to encourage in *The
Differend* is one in which reflective judgement is no longer obligated to
the demands of a transcendent identity – no matter how these may be
signified. The occurrence of differends, we have seen, demands that the
subject – or 'addressor' – acknowledge its responsibility to 'phrase' what
is 'silenced' in particular cases of conflict. Such a demand originates in
the feeling (*sensus*) that a particular wrong has occurred for which there
is no established language or expression. This feeling – 'a kind of
agitation in place, one with the impasse of incommensurability' – cannot
be subsumed under the rules of either critical (Kantian) or speculative
(Marxist and Hegelian) formation; for it is that which makes us immediately responsible to the 'otherness' determined by genres of discourse in
general.[91] The possibility of justice therefore depends upon a spontaneity
of linkage which Lyotard calls 'ethical time': for it is only in so far as the
wrong which is done in a particular conflict is phrased without recourse
to established rules of litigation that linkage on to the event (of 'this'
particular differend) is ethical.

Paradoxically, the 'performative' necessity of the ethical phrase presupposes a certain culture of reflection, in which time has been allowed
for the development of an 'unproductive' sensitivity to difference. *The
Differend*'s account of the increasing domination of the 'economic genre',
however, suggests that advanced capitalism is radically opposed to
expenditure of time on anything which does not presuppose immediate
acquittal in the terms of its particular genre (i.e., money, or goods, or
services which represent an equivalent expenditure of 'accountable
time').[92] Indeed, the 'Reading Dossier', which Lyotard supplies as a
preface to *The Differend*, makes the ironic suggestion that if the reader
wishes to 'gain time', then he or she will be able to 'talk about the book'
simply by skimming the introductory remarks.[93] Yet in the end we need
not resort to Marx's 'metaphysics' of productivism in order to challenge
this hegemony of the economic genre. The community of ethical
judgement springs not from the constitution of a universal (proletarian)
will, but from the 'heterogeneity of phrase regimens and of genres of
discourse'. We are responsible to the 'occurrence' of the unforeseen, the
unpresentable, the heterogeneous, simply because the possibility of
generic discourse is, in general, given through the infinite singularity of
the phrase. The temporal economy of capitalism, in other words, cannot
annul the conditions of its own possibility.[94]

Violence, rationality and community

I began my exposition of *The Differend* by suggesting that there is a sense in which the 'subjects' who move through the universe of differends and singularities, remain 'external' to the differences they encounter.[95] We also suggested that although it might be too strong to claim that there is a differend between Lyotard and Derrida, it is possible to register a certain difference – a difference which is specified in their respective notions of 'living in' the structures of reason. It is the proximity of *The Differend* to Kant's critical philosophy, particularly the aesthetics, which allows us, as speculative thinkers, to differentiate between Lyotard's notion of 'postmodernity' and Derrida's idea of 'deconstruction'. For if the pragmatics of 'phrasing' sustain a relation of exteriority between the subject and the legislative forms of reason, then we might suggest that the difference between (Lyotardian) postmodernism and (Derridean) deconstruction is the difference between an 'external' culture of criticism (the *sensus communis*) and a more modest – 'strategic' – account of what is possible within the 'substance' of reason. What Jameson has called Lyotard's 'embattled endorsement of the supreme value of aesthetic innovation' is instructive here, as it points up a tendency in his thought towards a kind of sublime transcendence of the feeling/affection.[96] I will argue that this 'transcendence' (of the *sensus*) maintains a quasi legislative priority in Lyotard's writing, and that it is the 'play' of collaboration, complicity and remission through which Derrida characterizes 'living in' the structures of reason that is most disquieting for the concept of ethical life (*Sittlichkeit*).

Lyotard's *Lessons on the Analytic of the Sublime* (1994), provides an extensive clarification of the relationship between the idea of the phrase and the faculty of reflective judgement which is at the core of Kantian aesthetics.[97] We have seen that, for Lyotard, the principal difficulty with the critical philosophy is the determination to present the ('noumenal', unconditioned) condition of agency in general through the rules of cognitive representation. Moral actions, for example, are schematized by an analogical relationship to the idea of serial causality; for the categorical imperative requires that I am able to represent the maxim of my will as if it were a universal law of action for all rational beings. Lyotard's explication of the third *Critique*, therefore, is concerned to show that Kant's idea of the sublime gestures towards an apprehension of 'the absolute' (i.e., of reason's ideal of unconditioned causality/initiation) which marks its resistance to cognition.

For Lyotard, the idea of 'absolute causality' (initiation which does not refer beyond the intelligible totality of its conditions) is presented negatively throughout Kant's critical philosophy. Reason's capacity to determine particular rights and duties, for example, depends upon the concept of a universal/unrestricted will, while the sensible causation of the first *Critique*, refers to a power which exceeds the 'mathematical' series of phenomenal events. As Lyotard puts it in the *Lessons*:

Several properties of the agent are thus determined negatively: the agent is an entity that is only intelligible (not presentable); it does not contribute to the knowledge of phenomena according to understanding; it is unconditioned; it is not sustained in succession.[98]

What is important here, is the affinity between Kant's notion of a 'dynamical' absolute and Lyotard's notion of the phrase. For Kant, the absolute – the noumenal condition of initiation – is categorically distinct from the determinations of particularity. Both the first and second *Critiques* presuppose the necessity of an 'intelligible' cause, but neither attempts to show that such an Idea is destined to appropriate the finitude (exteriority, succession, inclination, etc.) through which our experience is organized. It is this 'dynamical' heterogeneity of universal and particular, finite and infinite, that Lyotard attempts to transcribe in his idea of the phrase. For the 'fact' that the phrase, as the form of communicative initiation in general, cannot have its 'finality' determined in any particular genre means that every discourse is threatened by the condition of its own possibility.

Ultimately, Lyotard's reading of the 'Analytic of the sublime' is concerned with Kant's 'dynamical' re-presentation of reason as the faculty of 'pure desire'. We can briefly schematize his exposition. In the first *Critique*, imagination is conceived as the faculty of magnitude/spatiality. It is that which participates in the 'successive' acts of synthesis which sustain not only phenomenal experience (of objects), but also the Kantian sense of self-identity – the 'I think'. In the second *Critique*, Kant sets out the conditions under which the Idea of absolute causality 'rends' itself into particular rights and duties. It is through the notion of 'the type', in other words, that reason's capacity for ideas is brought into conformity with the demand that the moral will be active in the phenomenal world. Finally, in the third *Critique* (or more specifically in the 'Analytic of the sublime'), Kant sets out the conditions under which the faculties of reason and imagination 'signify' an 'affinity' which neither has the power to determine (realize). Reason's 'differend' with imagination, in other words, is sustained through the latter's powerful determination of 'duty'; a duty which imagination, in the presence of the sublime, feels not as 'respect' for the moral law, but as an obligation to extend itself beyond the limits of cognitive presentation.

The critical subject's encounter with the excessive ('almost too great') magnitudes, through which nature signifies its totality/infinity, produce a sense of 'terror' at the loss of the serial time which is imagination's transcendental principle. For the immediate, or 'reproductive', synthesis of magnitudes, which reason demands of imagination in the presence of the sublime, does violence to the successive ('compositional') time which is the condition of particular intuitions (and of the 'intuition of ourselves and of our state'). As Lyotard puts it:

'The subject' would be deprived of the means of constituting its subjectivity. For under the name of the 'I think', the subject is nothing more than the consciousness of the originary synthetic unity to which all representations are imputed. Without this imputation, called apperception, representations would not be those of a subject.[99]

Yet for Kant, this feeling of terror is not unmixed; for it is co-present with a sense of 'exultation' in reason's capacity to conceive the Idea of nature as a self-determining, self-related totality. Imagination, then, feels a certain terror at its 'reproductive' intuition; for serial time – the 'maximal power' attributed to imagination in the first *Critique* – is threatened by the simultaneity of discrete, compositional magnitudes. Reason, on the other hand, feels a certain exultation in the 'presence' of the absolute, an exultation which, according to Lyotard, stems from thinking's recovery of its own 'maximal power' of 'beginning a series without being bound to it'.[100]

It is the dynamical heterogeneity of reason and imagination in Kant's account of sublime affection which is of primary importance to Lyotard's idea of critical judgement. For Kant, the synthesis of terror and exultation that occurs in the presence of the sublime expresses a tension between the 'pure desire' of reason freed from the constraints of serial time (i.e., the power of pure conceptual 'initiation' which exceeds the limits of cognition) and the conditioned and determinate apprehensions of imagination. Thought, or rather the faculty of reason at its 'maximal extent', is final in the sense that the absolute (totality, infinite self-determination) always re-emerges from the realm of determinate forms, cognitions and interests. It is an idea that demands critical 'reflection' upon the finality (purposiveness) of nature, but which is impossible to 'restore' to the realm of cognition: 'Thus . . . the sublime feeling is the subjective state critical thought must feel in its being carried to its limits (and therefore beyond them) and its resistance to this impetus, or, conversely, what it must feel in its passion to determine and its resistance to this passion.'[101]

It should be clear by now that Lyotard's *Lessons on the Analytic of the Sublime* is concerned primarily with the relationship between Kant's specification of the possibility of reflective judgement and the radical contextualism of *The Differend*. We have seen that in the 'Analytic of the sublime', reason ('the thought that conceives') places imagination under an obligation to go beyond its 'norm' of presenting 'sensible' magnitudes. This is impossible, for no matter how imagination might extend itself, it remains the faculty of limited, spatial forms. Yet for Kant, the 'strenuousness' of the imagination's effort to go beyond its transcendental principle constitutes a kind of presentation of the infinite – although one which is 'negative' from the point of view of cognition. It is at this point that *The Differend*'s account of linkage, obligation and judgement begins to come more sharply into focus. As we saw in the previous section, Lyotard's idea of critical judgement depends upon an affective/aesthetic response to the conflicts that occur among (and between) genres of discourse and phrase regimen. The phrasing of differends, in other words, is demanded by the feeling of agitation – 'suspension over the void' – that springs from a particular moment of linkage. The 'I' is instantaneously abstracted from every generic (technical, moral, political) responsibility, and confronted with the necessity of initiating a phrase for what has been silenced. Thus, following Kant's account of sublime affection, the *sensus*, through which differends are received, is 'present' in elements of '*Absonderung*', or flashes of pure desire which consist in a 'putting apart and to the side, an "abstraction" [from the 'litigations in which the other is always embroiled']'.[102]

I began the section by suggesting that the difference between Lyotard and Derrida is best understood in terms of their respective conceptions of 'living in' the structures of reason, and that this difference can be specified through a certain transcendentalism which is sustained in Lyotard's transcription of Kant's aesthetics. The relationship we have attempted to sketch between Lyotard's *Lessons on the Analytic of the Sublime* and the notion of the phrase presented in *The Differend* is of particular importance here. For it seems clear that the structure of initiation/communication that Lyotard designates in the phrase finds a kind of telos in the 'negative presentation' of difference and differends. The 'affective' abstraction in which the 'I' is freed from the constraints of generic formation, in other words, determines a transcendent (non-serial) time, in which it is both 'obligated' (to phrase differends) and 'legislative' (as that which is not the law). By way of a brief conclusion, then, we will argue: (1) that Derrida's conception of writing specifies an unavoidable complicity of 'initiation' with the legislative power of reason; (2) that this 'complicity' is what differentiates deconstruction from Lyotard's critical aesthetic; and (3) that Derrida's account of the 'originary' violence of the law misrecognizes the ethical and political dynamic of *Sittlichkeit*.

I return to quasi-transcendental ideas. For Derrida, the legislative power of philosophical reason (the *logos*) is originally discursive. It is written in texts which conceal the events of transition and differal that are designated by the ideas of trace supplement and *différance*. These texts are written as the uninterrupted plenitude of the 'Said'; or what we might think of as the legislation of a monological voice, abstracted from the events of articulation/signification (the 'Saying' that addresses the other). The 'phonocentrism' of philosophical thought, in other words, consists in its breathless, monological pursuit of presence, which, seemingly, forbids the possibility of 'countersignature' – the reading and rereading of the trace in the text. Deconstructive writing, then, encourages a kind of ethical recognition of the other (the addressee of the text) as 'countersignatory'. For 'after' Derrida's disclosure of the quasi-transcendental resources of the *logos*, a certain obligation to allow the other to participate in the (necessary) contingency sustained within the Said becomes inevitable.

What is important here is that, for Derrida, it is impossible to establish a clean break between any of the 'stratagems' that deconstruction might encourage, and the metaphysical *logos* from which remission is sought. Each quasi-transcendental marks the possibility of a series of non-identical 'interruptions' (of the Said, the text); a series which itself marks an economic distribution of complicities and tensions with the strictures of presence. Thus, in remarking (Saying) the interruptions which occur in rational discourse, deconstructive writing always remains 'contaminated' by the residue of reason's legislative power (its ends, rules, categorizations, etc.). It is through this constantly (and unforeseeably) reformulated complicity that we must understand the ethical significance of deconstruction (i.e., its claims to articulate the possibility of justice in relation to law and community). For it is the perpetual risk that 'remarking' the dispersal inscribed in rational determination of any kind will fall back into the legislative discourse that is 'remarked', that opens a uniquely ethical responsibility. A responsibility which finds all of its conditions within the 'order of reason'.

At the beginning of the section I claimed that Lyotard's pursuit of 'pure desire' through Kant's remarks on the sublime ends up by specifying not a particular 'moment' of remission, but the condition of ethical responsibility in general. Lyotard's idea of critical judgement, in other words, describes a certain a priori spontaneity/instantaneity (the phrase) that is without substance or determination. Yet even if this 'pure desire' does not become morally legislative in *The Differend*, it is a moment of 'purity' (in the Kantian sense of an absence of 'interest' in the object) which feels and judges beyond/outside the established order of reason. For Derrida, such a reliance upon the aesthetic (the priority of feeling, sensibility, affection) would be misleading, and ultimately dangerous, in the sense that it would tend to mask the play of violence and dispersal inscribed in the law, and to encourage unrecognized attachments to the legislative power of established discourses. It is the discursiveness of reason that should command our attention; for it is through the economy of tensions, liaisons and strictures which it sustains that it is possible to discern the shifting, ontologically threatened space of responsibility. This is perhaps, as close as we can get to 'specifying' the difference between Lyotard and Derrida.

I am left, then, with the necessity of defending my speculative idea of ethical life against Derrida's quasi-transcendental ideas – trace, supplementarity and *différance*. I have tried to show that Hegel's philosophy is best understood as the point at which dialectical reason first confronts the dynamics of modernity, that is, the displacement of traditional structures of integration, the increasing dominance of utilitarian relations, the liberation of 'reflective' subjectivity. According to Derrida's reading, however, this encounter of the *logos* with 'modern' forms of differentiation assumes the violent determination of an 'inside' (the ethical community), in which the 'ends' of humanity are relieved of excess, anxiety and contingency. Hegel's notion of *Sittlichkeit*, in other words, is received into the 'general economy' of deconstructive writing, as a certain 'restricted' space of inscription. For the differentiation of ethical substance which Hegel presents in the *Philosophy of Right* has, according to Derrida, already acknowledged 'the law' (i.e., the law of sublation towards totality) as that which will maintain the interiority (life) of the concept against the intrusions of 'otherness'. This relationship of violence, rationality and community is crucially important, and I will return to it in a moment.

We have seen that Derrida acknowledges the complicity of deconstruction with the metaphysical *logos*, and that this complicity marks a certain 'ethical' responsibility to remark the violence of the law. For Derrida, then, Hegel's proposition '*What is rational is actual and what is actual is rational*' could only be taken as expressive of dialectical reason's inability to account for the space of its own inscription. The Hegelian *Aufhebung* (i.e., the overcoming of opposed and contradictory determinations which preserves both in a higher totality) is possible only within the legislative 'space' from which spirit has already excluded the possibility of loss and dispersal. Derrida's reading of *Hegel, la mort*, for example, attempts to show that Bataille's account of the relationship between death and subjectivity marks an unacknowledged condition of speculative dialectics.[103] For Bataille, it is the co-presence of death with the experience of ethical substance (mediation, identity etc.), which opens the possibility of autonomy (as a kind of creative/destructive excess beyond the recuperative power of the system). Thus, it is only by forcing the proximity of death to curb its excessiveness in the moment of enslavement,[104] that Hegel's speculative history – the history of 'exchanges within ethical substance' – can get under way. There is, in other words, something originally 'undialectical' presupposed in the law of dialectical exchange, a moment whose excess cannot be named as such in the system, and which, in its very subordination to 'exchange', remains an unsublatable possibility of dispersal within the substance of *Sittlichkeit*.[105]

This account of dialectical reason returns us to the question of the relationship of violence, rationality and community. We have seen that, for Derrida, the law is founded upon an originary violence. Deconstruction therefore determines that we think the complicities of heterogeneous discourses in the (re)determination of this originary violence – the violence of a law which, for Derrida, will always encourage mythological reactivations of its origins. (We might recall that, for Lyotard, the annihilation of ethical substance at Auschwitz is brought about through the conjunction of philosophical anxiety, racial mythology and technical efficiency in the 'law' of Nazism.) The possibility of justice – that is, the 'speaking against' reason from within its established order – therefore depends upon a 'differential contamination' of every possible discourse within the originary violence of the law. I would suggest, however, that Derrida's notion of the originary violence which is inscribed in the law (or more particularly in the law of dialectical recuperation) fails to acknowledge the 'space' (of violence and contingency) inscribed in Hegel's ethical substance.

This space is the lacuna which is always reopened between the ends/ promises postulated in formal law, and the 'social actuality' they pre-suppose and reproduce.[106] Speculatively conceived, every postulation of universal ends will ultimately demand judgement of the affective and mythological forms of representation which its (positive) legality has been inadequate to control (the violence of racism, sectarianism, national-ism, etc.). Perhaps, then, the relationship which Derrida expounds between the violence (originally) inscribed in the law and the idea of peace as an ever-receding horizon ends up by subordinating the (socio-historical) differences which sustain the conflict implicit in ethical life. Perhaps deconstruction tends to encourage us to judge the law as an originary violence, and to miss the actual (historical) complicities of violence and reason constituted in modern political life.

I am not claiming that the kind of 'hyper reflective'[107] reading of texts suggested by deconstruction is simply a powerful encouragement to nihilism with respect to the 'substance' of ethical life. Indeed, I have deployed Derrida's quasi-transcendental ideas of trace, supplement and *différance* in order to disclose the functionalism repressed in Foucauldian genealogy. Yet this deconstructive disclosure of Foucault's complicity with certain established forms of hegemony, fails to situate the develop-ment of instrumental reason within the ethical and political actuality of the law. In order to judge Foucault, in other words, we need to under-stand his relationship not simply to the violence implicit in carceral-hygienic society, but also to the way in which that 'community' has represented itself as the dominant 'end' of modernity. (A phenomenol-ogy of genealogy perhaps.) In any event, I would suggest that a specu-lative conception of *Sittlichkeit*, and of the critical judgements that this conception demands, presupposes the history of abstraction (of func-tionality, productivity, communicability, etc.) by which I have charac-terized the practice of social science. And so it is to the relationship between speculative thought and the concepts deployed in social theor-etical and analytical discourses that I must now turn.

Notes

1. K. Marx, 'Preface to the First German Edition' *Capital, Volume One*, trans. S. Moore and E. Aveling, Lawrence & Wishart, 1977a, p. 19.

2. M. Foucault, 'Two lectures', in *Power/Knowledge: Selected Interviews and Other Writings 1972–1977*, trans. and ed. C. Gordon, Harvester Press, 1986, p. 80.

3. J.-F. Lyotard, 'Hegel Notice', in *The Differend: Phrases in Dispute*, trans. G. Van Den Abbeele, Manchester University Press, 1988a, pp. 91–7.

4. J. Derrida, 'From restricted to general economy: a Hegelianism without reserve', in *Writing and Difference*, trans. A. Bass, Routledge, 1990b.

5. Ibid., p. 256.

6. J. Derrida, *Of Spirit*, trans. G. Bennington and R. Bowlby, University of Chicago Press, 1990a, pp. 24–30.

7. Derrida's conception of 'writing', as we will see, is the medium through which the legislative power of reason – or the *logos* – is both determined and dispersed.

8. See J. Derrida, 'Violence and metaphysics', in *Writing and Difference*.

9. See Derrida's famous note on Heidegger's notion of the question in *Of Spirit*, pp. 129–36.

10. M. Foucault, 'What is Enlightenment?', trans C. Porter, in *The Foucault Reader*, P. Rabinow ed., Penguin, 1991, p. 42.

11. Ibid., p. 42.

12. For Foucault's 'genealogies' of sanity and madness, sickness and health, sexuality and perversion, see: *Madness and Civilisation: A History of Insanity in the Age of Reason*, trans. R. Howard, Routledge, 1995; *Discipline and Punish: The Birth of the Prison*, trans. A. Sheridan, Vintage Books, 1979; *The History of Sexuality: An Introduction*, trans. R. Hurley, Vintage Books, 1980.

13. For an interesting account of the tension between the Kantian and Nietzchean strands in Foucault's thought, see J. Simons, *Foucault and the Political*, Routledge, 1995.

14. Foucault, *Power/Knowledge*, p. 121.

15. M. Foucault, *Discipline and Punish*, trans. A. Sheridan, Vintage Books, 1979, p. 221.

16. Ibid., p. 220

17. Ibid., p. 89.

18. Ibid., p. 29.

19. Ibid., p. 201.

20. Ibid.

21. Ibid., p. 204

22. M. Foucault, *The History of Sexuality: An Introduction, Volume One*, trans. R. Hurley, Vintage Books, 1980, p. 141.

23. Ibid., p. 123.

24. Ibid., p. 23.

25. Ibid., pp. 104–5.

26. Ibid., p. 70.

27. Ibid., p. 92.

28. Ibid., p. 93.

29. M. Foucault, 'Powers and strategies', in *Power/Knowledge*, pp. 134–45.

30. Foucault, *History of Sexuality*, trans. R. Hurley, Vintage Books, 1980, p. 94.

31. Foucault, *Discipline and Punish*, p. 29.

32. Foucault, 'Two lectures', p. 93.

33. M. Foucault, 'What is an author?', in *The Foucault Reader*.

34. Ibid., p. 120.

35. M. Foucault, 'On the genealogy of ethics', in *The Foucault Reader*, pp. 340–72.

36. Ibid., p. 351.

37. For example, Foucault's infamous remark that, regarding sex with minors, 'the child can be trusted to say whether or not he was subjected to violence'. Quoted in R. Boyne, *Foucault and Derrida: The Other Side of Reason*, Unwin Hyman, 1990, p. 140.

38. M. Foucault, *The Uses of Pleasure: The History of Sexuality, Volume Two*, trans. R. Hurley, Penguin Books, 1987.

39. See R. Boyne, *Foucault and Derrida*.

40. M. Foucault, 'Friendship as a way of life', in *Foucault Live*, S. Lotringer ed., trans. J. Johnston, Semiotext, 1993, p. 209.

41. Derrida, 'Violence and metaphysics'.

42. Ibid., p. 126.

43. See 'Sexual difference' in G. Bennington and J. Derrida, *Jacques Derrida*, trans. G. Bennington, University of Chicago Press, 1993, pp. 204–7.

44. J. Derrida, *The Post Card*, University of Chicago Press, 1987.

45. Derrida, 'Violence and metaphysics', p. 148.

46. J. Kristeva, 'Women's time', in Kristeva, *The Kristeva Reader*, T. Moi ed., trans. A. Jardine and J. Blake, Blackwell, 1992, p. 210.

47. Foucault, 'On the genealogy of ethics'.

48. Derrida's famous long footnote in *Of Spirit* is concerned to show that we are originally 'promised' to language in the sense that we cannot escape the 'economic' violence determined through its significations. It is this necessity of 'exteriority' which, for Derrida, precedes even the possibility of the Heideggerian 'question'.

49. Lyotard summarizes the idea of the differend as 'a case of conflict between (at least two) parties, that cannot be resolved for lack of rule of judgement applicable to both parties'. *The Differend*, p. ix.

50. J.-F. Lyotard, *Libidinal Economy*, trans. I. Hamilton Grant, Athlone Press, 1993.

51. J.-F. Lyotard, *Peregrinations: Law, Form, Event*, Columbia University Press, 1988b, p. 15.

52. Lyotard, *Libidinal Economy*, pp. 95–154.

53. Ibid., p. 24.

54. G. Deleuze, *Kant's Critical Philosophy: The Doctrine of the Faculties*, trans. H. Tomlinson and B. Habberjam, Athlone Press, 1995.

55. Lyotard, *The Differend*, §126.

56. Ibid.

57. Ibid., p. 123.

58. I. Kant, *The Critique of Judgement*, trans. J. Creed-Meredith, Oxford University Press, 1982b, p. 119.

59. Ibid.

60. The fundamental point Lyotard is making in *Libidinal Economy* is one that persists through all his later writings: the impossibility of determining a 'neutral space' from which to offer 'objective' criticism and evaluation.

61. J.-F. Lyotard, 'The desire named Marx', in *Libidinal Economy*, p. 141.

62. Lyotard, *The Differend*, 'Reading dossier', p. xvi.

63. J.-F. Lyotard, 'Narratives and the legitimation of knowledge', in *The Postmodern Condition: A Report on Knowledge*, trans. G. Bennington and B. Massumi, Manchester University Press, 1991a, pp. 31–7.

64. Lyotard, *The Differend*, §40.

65. Ibid., §40.

66. Ibid., §179.

67. Ibid., §180.

68. Ibid. See also T.W. Adorno, 'Meditations on metaphysics', in Adorno, *Negative Dialectics*, trans. E.B. Ashton, Routledge, 1990.

69. Lyotard, *The Differend*, §159.

70. Adorno's conception of Auschwitz as 'model' – rather than a dialectical form – is intended to signify the brute 'factuality' of the Holocaust. Speculative philosophy, in other words, is confronted by an evil which it can neither sublate nor erase.

71. Lyotard, *The Differend*, §97.

72. Ibid., §156.

73. J.-F. Lyotard, 'Discussions, or phrasing "after Auschwitz"', trans. G. Van Den Abeele, in *The Lyotard Reader*, A. Benjamin ed., Blackwell, 1991b, p. 379.

74. J.-F. Lyotard, *Heidegger and 'the jews'*, trans. A. Michel and M. Roberts, University of Minnesota Press, 1990, p. 22.

75. Lyotard, *The Differend*, §153.

76. Lyotard, *Heidegger and 'the jews'*, p. 29.

77. P. Levi, *The Drowned and The Saved*, trans. R. Rosenthal, Abacus, 1992, p. 19.

78. See 'After Auschwitz', in Adorno, *Negative Dialectics*, pp. 361–5.

79. Adorno, *Negative Dialectics*, p. 408.

80. Lyotard, *The Differend*, §23.

81. J.-F. Lyotard, '*Sensus Communis*', in A. Benjamin ed., *Judging Lyotard*, Routledge, 1992, p. 24.

82. Ibid., p. 22.

83. Lyotard, *The Differend*, p. 130.

84. See 'On the critical "post": Lyotard's agitated judgement', in Benjamin, *Judging Lyotard*, p. 74.

85. Kant, *Critique of Judgement*, p. 96.

86. See 'Contest of the faculties', in I. Kant, *Political Writings*, H. Reiss ed., Nisbet, Oxford University Press, 1991.

87. Ibid., p. 187.

88. Lyotard, *The Differend*, §238.

89. Ibid., §238–§239.

90. Ibid., p. 135.

91. Ibid., p. 167.

92. Ibid., §240.

93. Ibid., 'Reading dossier', p. xiv.

94. Ibid., §242.

95. Ibid., §263.

96. F. Jameson, *Postmodernism: Or the Cultural Logic of Late Capitalism*, Verso, 1995, p. 61.

97. J.-F. Lyotard, *Lessons on the Analytic of the Sublime*, trans. E. Rottenburg, Stanford University Press, 1994.

98. Ibid., p. 135.

99. Ibid., p. 144.

100. Ibid., p. 146.

101. Ibid., p. 150.

102. Ibid., p. 151.

103. J. Derrida, 'From restricted to general economy: a Hegelianism without reserve', in *Writing and Difference*, pp. 258–9.

104. G.W.F. Hegel, *Phenomenology of Mind*, trans. J.B. Baillie, Harper & Row, 1967a, pp. 228–40.

105. See the account of 'The gift', in G. Bennington and J. Derrida, *Jacques Derrida*, trans. G. Bennington, University of Chicago Press, 1993, pp. 188–204.

106. G. Rose, 'Of Derrida's Spirit', in Rose, *Judaism and Modernity: Philosophical Essays*, Blackwell, 1993, pp. 86–7.

107. P. Dews, 'Deconstruction and German idealism', in Dews, *The Limits of Disenchantment: Essays in Contemporary European Philosophy*, Verso, 1995, p. 143.

5

Truth and Modernity

The aim of this chapter is to explain what a social science is: the kind of knowledge it generates, and how that knowledge is related to the social ethical and political constitution of modernity. So far I have set myself the (apparently) negative task of expounding the theoretical difficulties that characterize structural and cognitivist sociologies – difficulties which I traced back to their origins in Kant's critical philosophy. I argued that in the case of the former, subjectivity tends to lack any spontaneous differentiation from, and independence of, the 'objective' structures of the totality. In general, Marxist and functionalist explanations have tended to marginalize the concepts of 'reflection' and 'subjective forma-tion'. Cognitivist sociologies, on the other hand, have reproduced con-ceptions of subjectivity which are abstracted from the 'actual' complexity of the ethical life. As we saw with Weber's idea of meaning, and Habermas's concept of communicative rationality, 'the subject' appears as transcendent of the concrete forms of law, productive activity, custom ('objective spirit'), etc., which have structured its self-recognition. Both meaning and the pragmatics of communication, in other words, fail to recognize the formative power inscribed in the temporality of objective spirit. Thus, if structural and cognitivist sociologies reproduce their own particular contradictions, how can they contribute to a positive under-standing of community, modernity and the social bond?

To begin to answer this question, I must recognize that the paradigms which comprise structural and cognitive sociologies are 'unified' by certain general themes. The first of these I will call alienation. Relieved of its strictly Marxist connotations, this term refers to a much more general set of ethical and theoretical issues than those circumscribed by the 'estrangement' of productive activity. Questions concerning an historical corruption of humanity and the ways in which modern structures and institutions complete (universalize) that corruption can be identified not only in Marx's presentation of 'capitalism', but also in Durkheim's account of the 'abnormal' forms of the division of labour (those which split the individual off from its 'true' articulation with the collective), Weber's notion of the 'iron cage' of bureaucratic organization (the systemic homogenization of subjective meaning and spontaneity), and Habermas's idea of the functional 'colonization' of the life world (the loss of dialogical competence). The second of these themes, I will call social solidarity. Again, this term has come to be identified with one particular perspective: Durkheim's understanding of the 'objective' forces which bind the individual to the social whole. Yet it must be acknowledged that the history of social cohesion (and its relationship to the concept of autonomy) is a theme which occupies every sociological perspective: for Marx, capitalist societies are necessarily repressive, yet prefigure the socialization/humanization of production, while for Weber, the progress bureaucracy determines a shift away from traditional forms of authority towards the administration of 'rational purposive' individuals. Finally, there is the question of the normative content articulated in different paradigms – what I will call moral sociology. Again, there are crucial theoretical differences regarding the origin and persistence of injustice and inequality – and indeed, with regard to their persistence in the future. However, I will argue that sociological/social scientific paradigms are, in general, characterized by their attempts to determine comprehensive 'moral' critiques of modern institutions and relations. (We do not have the time to conduct a lengthy discussion of whether or not T.S. Kuhn's notion of the 'scientific paradigm' is applicable to the established forms of sociological reason. His claim, however, that within the different regimes of 'normal science', the dominant theory 'is not the same paradigm for them all',[1] does at least admit that the practice of science demands a certain 'simultaneous' particularizing of universal principles. My argument is that within the discipline of social science, this 'particularizing' – of the moral, economic, functional elements of modernity – should be understood as the condition of 'speculative' judgements about actual social relations.)

This attempt to determine the universal themes articulated through different paradigms is necessarily abstract. In the first instance, it should be clear that the issues I have categorized under 'alienation', 'social solidarity' and 'moral sociology' all refer to one another. The idea of historical development cannot be divorced from the ethical critique of modernity; and we cannot understand the ideas of loss and alienation without reference to the injustice of contemporary social organization. In the end, then, it is perhaps best to understand sociological paradigms as discrete philosophical accounts of the history of ethical life, accounts which allow us to make judgements about how human sociality ought to be organized, and the way in which this 'truth' has been dominated and suppressed by contemporary structures and institutions.

The question I must address, then, is this: how is it possible to maintain that social scientific perspectives constitute a differentiated unity when their 'differentiation' appears to exclude any universal idea of community, or of the kind of formations and distortions that community would be subject to in general? It is a similar question which occupies Jean-François Lyotard's discussion of social science's relationship to the 'postmodern' form of the 'social bond' in *The Postmodern Condition* (1991a). He claims that Marxist and functionalist sociologies presuppose a totality of structures and institutions which are either entirely negative (capitalism) or productive of overall coherence and regulation (value consensus). As such, both paradigms are conceived as insensitive to the pluralization of knowledge which has emerged through traditional 'modernist' determinations of community (law, economy, culture, education, etc.), a pluralization which demands the abandonment of established 'narratives' of truth and identity. (We might recall that in Lyotard's more recent work, ethical and political judgement is conceived on an analogy with aesthetic feeling, rather than conceptual congruence.) I will argue, however, that the relationship between theory and ethical life is one in which the conflicts, satisfactions, desires and exclusions determined in the 'actual' expression of 'the good' are repeated – and reinforced – by the paradigmatic forms in which they are expressed. The 'complexity' of the social bond – that is, the totality of the conditions of its historical possibility – can only be disclosed through the limited conceptions of truth posited in different paradigms. Thus, while social theory cannot avoid repeating the contradictions of 'modernity', its 'abstraction' of different elements from the whole (*Sittlichkeit*) demands a 'judgement' which has at least recognized loss, exclusion, otherness, etc., as ethical strictures unavoidably imposed by reason.

The idea of a social science I am seeking to defend is founded ultimately upon the conceptions of community and social formation set out in Chapter 1. My fundamental claim is that the relationship between individual subjects and the 'objective' conditions of their social existence is such that the ideal of absolute ethical mediation remains historically unrealizable. The best that can be hoped for is an acknowledgement of the 'necessity' of the structures which have articulated the substance of ethical life (law, civil society, morality, etc.), of the domination and misrecognition which is produced, and reproduced, through these structures; and of the complicities into which theoretical discourse tends to enter with subjectivizing 'cultures' of liberation. In general, therefore, a sociology ought to respond to the changing relationship between the 'modern' institutions which form the individual and the recognition/ misrecognition through which (self-conscious) subjects participate in, and are differentiated from, the 'objectivity' of the social bond. Thus, the thematics by which I have characterized social scientific paradigms – alienation, social order and moral prescription – bear directly upon this relationship: each paradigm gives an account of social organization which, while abstractly privileging a particular element of the totality, allows us (as speculative theorists) to recognize the formative, suppressive, emancipatory and destructive potential of those elements which constitute the modern community.

So far, then, I have maintained that the concept of a sociology is constituted through distinct and heterogeneous paradigms, that those paradigms are related to certain Kantian assumptions about the social and its relationship to individual experience, and that these assumptions reproduce specific misrecognitions of community and social formation. In the first instance I saw how the structural determination of human work, desire and satisfaction is divided into the 'bourgeois' and 'radical' traditions of Marxism and functionalism. The work of Durkheim, Parsons and Luhmann, I argued, articulates a progressive exclusion reflective subjectivity from the instrumental reproduction of the whole, while the Marxist tradition tends to make the negativity of capital into the exclusive determinant of (pre-revolutionary) work, satisfaction and desire. In the end, neither approach can give an adequate account of the relationship between community and autonomy: functionalism because of its deployment of integration as determining the systemic/objective limits of individual action; Marxism because it proposes that it is only through absolute alienation and estrangement that productive humanity can bring about its historical fulfilment. Yet we have also seen that an abstract privileging of practico-cognitive spontaneity, reproduces its own contradictions and complicities. Weber's account of the evolution of socio-cultural 'meanings' has tended to depict 'modernity' as an inevitable shift towards the homogenization of culture, and the bureaucratic suppression of moral spontaneity. Habermas's attempt to reformulate the legislative power of practical reason, on the other hand, has tended towards a decidedly Kantian loss of particularity – that is, towards the postulation of a purified discourse of consensus and universal equity (the 'ideal speech situation').

Chapters 2 and 3 sought to develop the idea that the theoretical assumptions of structural and cognitivist sociologies reproduce their own particular misrecognitions of the social bond. I am not, however, suggesting that these sociologies are simply wrong, or that the paradigmatic assumptions through which they are articulated can only obscure the truth of community and social formation. What I am saying is that each paradigm prioritizes a particular category – self-determining subjectivity, institutional integration, productive humanity, etc. – and posits that element as the foundation of its moral, ethical and political critique. The universal themes I have identified as characteristic of social scientific perspectives, therefore, are always expressed through this abstract priority: Marx's concept of 'estrangement', for example, is determined through the exploitation (and commodification) of *homo faber*, of an essentially productive humanity; Durkheim expounds the idea of 'anomie' as the violent release of individualism from the restraint of established restraints; while Weber's idea of domination of capitalism refers to the loss of individual spontaneity/diversity determined by bureaucratic organization. Each paradigm, in other words, proposes that a distinctive category has emerged as the determining element of 'modernity', a category which has yet to fulfil its 'true' moral, ethical and political significance. For Marx, capitalism's 'objective' socialization of the means of production had yet to bring about the end of bourgeois property and the humanization of labour; for Durkheim, the modern individual had yet to recognize fully the 'organic' mediation of its (ontological) dependency; while for Weber, the 'iron cage' of bureaucracy has yet to complete its organization of worldly asceticism.

These disparate propositions about a future in which modernity 'fulfils' what it currently promises (or threatens) are fundamental to our understanding of a social science. Our claim is that different paradigms attempt to articulate comprehensive descriptions of modernity, and that it is these descriptions which allow us to recognize the logic of emancipation, domination and conflict inscribed in contemporary social relations. Each proposes that the development of human sociality cannot be properly understood unless the primacy of a particular element is acknowledged. For Marx, it is the violence inherent in the commodity production which informs his ideal of freely associative labour;[2] for Durkheim, it is the 'organic' differentiation of the totality which promises the fulfilment of a rational, socially regulated freedom;[3] while for Weber, the continued dominance of bureaucractic reason threatens to produce a final renunciation of individual spontaneity.[4] Thus, it is through their respective representations of the future that each paradigm discloses a formative potential which is present in, yet unfulfilled by, the contemporary form of ethical life.

The respective futures which Marx, Durkheim and Weber propose for contemporary social organization, therefore, are postulated through discrete and exclusive categories. The prioritization of productive activity in Marx's account of social justice, for example, tends to exclude the possibility that human 'estrangement' could have sources which transcend the commodity form of production (or that the 'unity' engendered by 'capitalist' societies is not entirely repressive/ideological). Durkheim's idea of organic solidarity, on the other hand, tends to suppress acknowledgement of the processes – of domination, exclusion, exteriorization – through which 'the whole' (society, the group) comes to achieve its 'objective', morally regulative significance for the individual. (Indeed, the same can be said for 'functionalist' sociologies in general.) Each paradigm, in other words, postulates a specific realization of the dominant category it 'discovers' in the complexity of the social bond. My claim is that by prioritizing one particular element of ethical life, sociological paradigms articulate a certain maximal and intensified disclosure of that element. A disclosure that is most clearly determined in the moral, ethical and political prescriptions through which 'the future' (of modernity) is presented. Thus, it is the 'abstractness' inscribed in each paradigm which informs our idea of the relationship between sociology and speculative thought. For it is by recognizing the intensity and concentration with which sociological paradigms present the 'truth' of modernity that it becomes possible to judge (speculatively) their relationship to ethical life, and to each other.

What I am claiming about the way in which truth is deployed in social scientific paradigms is neatly expressed in a phrase of Adorno's: 'Truth is always an exaggeration.'[5] The general themes of alienation, social cohesion and moral prescription, which appear in each of the paradigms I have examined, determine the necessity of a certain aspect of modernity – something which I cannot simply ignore or refuse to acknowledge in my understanding of community and social formation. Consequently, I am not denying that Marx, Weber and Durkheim all recognize something which is essential to the constitution of modern relations. Yet by making (capitalist) expropriation, or anomie, or bureaucratic rationality the determining characteristic of modernity, they also misrecognize the complexity, differentiation and conflict that is 'actualized' in ethical life. It is this misrecognition which informs their respective claims about the moral, ethical and political 'ends' which are being realized through contemporary social relations. Thus, in order to understand the relationship of speculative judgement to the project of a social science, I need to examine the way in which 'abstraction' (the limitation, concentration and exclusiveness of particular paradigms) is related to the 'concept' of ethical life (i.e., to the historical negativity of 'spirit's' relationship to its temporal/secular forms).

Marx and Weber: utopic and dystopic ends

The fundamental tendency I have sought to expound in Marxism is its reduction of ethical life to a set of originally agonistic categories: capital and labour, use value and exchange value, truth and ideology, etc. From an orthodox Marxist point of view, in other words, the continued existence of capitalism can only be explained through its ability to represent the dehumanizing and exploitative nature of its relations, through new 'ideologies' of identity, autonomy and achievement. Thus, there is no social institution or practice which can enter into the (orthodox) Marxist equation without being judged in terms of its significance either for the cause of proletarian justice or for the continuation of the commodity form of production. Thus, by denying any 'formative' influence to the (legal, political, religious, aesthetic, philosophical, etc.) institutions which comprise 'capitalist' society, Marxist critique tends to become a self-fulfilling activity which presupposes a universal condition of alienation.

At its worst, this blindness to the autonomy and differentiation sustained in modern communities takes a terroristic form: the 'law' of historical necessity is violently imposed upon those individuals and institutions deemed 'reactionary' or 'pre-revolutionary'. What has yet to be accomplished through the dialectics of historical evolution, in other words, it is up to 'The Party' – as the organ of Marxist science – to bring into being.[6] In a sense, then, this Stalinist deployment of historical materialism – as legitimizing every act of barbarism by the state – is the political form of an orthodoxy which insists on constantly re-forming the 'negativity' of capitalist relations and institutions. For once the iniquity of private ownership has been abolished, the reformative action of the state tends constantly to search for the 'vestiges' of pre-revolutionary decadence and corruption. Vestiges which it is relatively simple to identify with certain out groups – like the Jews – who become the subject of a continuous 'revolutionary' violence. This historical complicity of abstract reason (i.e., the promises of 'socialized' production, the transcendence of greed and acquisitive desire, etc.) and political terror, therefore, demand that we treat Marx's originary denunciation of 'capital' as a kind of radical idealism which constantly threatens the more 'speculative' insights of his critique. We saw in Chapter 2, how the most interesting developments of Marxist theory have attempted to articulate the social and political consequences of mass consumerism and popular culture. Thus, while Theodor Adorno and Fredric Jameson might not share some of the more celebratory contentions of 'postmodern' cultural theory (the infinite 'good' of plurality, diversity and particular experience), they both recognize the power of new subjective formations in the history of 'late-capitalism'.[7] In the end, then, it is Marx's attempt to write the history of capitalism as the progressive estrangement of humanity's natural essence which makes Marxism both interesting and problematic. For while it is true that the Marxist paradigm remains rooted in an essential suspicion of moral, political and aesthetic 'spontaneity' within the commodity form of production, it has continually reopened the need to evaluate the relationship between productive activity and subjective autonomy.

What I am claiming, therefore, is that although Marx's presentation of productive activity in the early writings produces a somewhat naïve account of the social formation of self-consciousness, his critique demands that we acknowledge the influence of 'capital' – its formation of self-seeking individuals, the culture of acquisitiveness, the morality of independence and self-determination – on the development of modern ethical life. What must be recognized, in other words, is that the comprehensiveness of Marx's critique of capital does disclose certain persistent forms of social domination and control: the colonization of cultural and aesthetic practices by corporate capital, the presentation of 'autonomy' as a realm originally dissociated from restraints of material production, etc. However, what is distinctive about the broadly 'Marxist' approaches I have looked at is a willingness to acknowledge that orthodox ideas of proletarian identity, class consciousness, alienation and ideology can no longer be uncritically applied to modern – or 'late' – capitalism. If the texture of everyday life is increasingly determined by the productions of 'the culture industry', or if the experience of commodification is one of increasing evanescence, diversity and contingency, then these effects suggest that we would be wrong to consider 'capitalism' (i.e., the persistence of private ownership and expropriation) as a form which must systematically exhaust all of its social, cultural and political potential. Critical Marxism, therefore, while it is still concerned with the basic issues of historical materialism – the frustration of human creativity, the ethics of commodification and the economic conditions of political control, etc. – retains a certain scepticism about the 'unity' of socialized production and the transcendence of capitalism's 'pre-revolutionary' institutions.

Although I have sought to characterize Adorno's (and Jameson's) remarks on 'late-capitalist' culture as critical/reflective modifications of Marxist theory, it must be remembered that Adorno's relationship to Hegel is very far from being one of straightforward approbation. In his later work, particularly *Negative Dialectics* (1990), he attempts to expound a relationship between the 'reified' concept of totality which attributes to Hegel's thought and the constitution of totalitarian political ideals.[8] For Adorno, in other words, it is the yearning for a pure speculative immediacy which fulfils itself in the constitution of the state – a yearning which informs Hegel's recuperative history of universal self-consciousness/humanity – that is implicated in Nazism's determination to destroy the 'other' (the Jew) who corrupts the experience of universal self-identity. Yet Adorno's attempt to expound a 'negative dialectics', in which the 'metaphysical' presuppositions of synthesis, mediation and (universal) identity have become subject to the strictures of 'micrology' (i.e., to an acute sensitivity to the particularities which cannot be included in the determination/reification of identity), has misrecognized speculative history – the history of *Sittlichkeit*. For it fails to acknowledge that the universal – through its necessary embodiment in ethical life – has already 'gone over' into non-identity and contradiction. The work of speculative judgement, in other words, is 'satisfied' in the sense that it has acknowledged the necessity of its mediations, yet 'transformative' in the sense that their identity must remain speculative (i.e., inscribed in the aporias of ethical life). Thus, while Adorno's account of a 'late-capitalist' modernity does gesture towards a more 'critical' recognition of 'the subject' within the edifice capital, it must be acknowledged that this recognition (of cultural homogenization, of trivialization, of lack of spontaneity) is ultimately determined as a kind of dogmatic anti-Hegelianism, which keeps it tied to a distinctively Marxist conception of *Sittlichkeit*.

I am not, therefore, suggesting that Marxism – through the deployment of certain Kantian ideas of subjectivity and judgement – begins to determine a 'synthesis' with speculative thought. As an explanatory form, it repeats a number of distinctive oppositions (between the negative/reified 'being' of the universal and the formation of the particular; between the law posited – or 'determinately existent' – in ethical life and the possibility of a transformative labour of re-cognition; and between the comprehension of 'necessity' and the recognition of 'freedom') which present the 'totality' (the mode of production) as the subject of an infinitely judgemental reflection. Adorno's 'negative dialectic', for example, cannot free itself from the pursuit of 'non-dialectical' particularities, a pursuit which fails to re-cognize that 'micrology'[9] is possible only through the abstractness of the law and the positedness of the universal within *Sittlichkeit*. For Jameson, on the other hand, the 'experience' which has come to determine modern culture requires that we attend to the processses of commodification which characterize late capitalism, processes which, in their hyperextension, globalization and intensification of the commodity form, determine the universal feeling of evanescence that is theorized in 'postmodern' conceptions of ethics, politics and aesthetics. Yet this attempt to 'ground' the experience of modernity in the development of commodification again attributes a kind of 'givenness' to the 'objective' structures that control the cultural reproduction and recognition of ethical life. Jameson's 'cultural logic', in other words, ends up by ignoring the processes of mediation, conflict and recognition, through which the 'objectivity' of *Sittlichkeit* constituted.

At the beginning of this chapter, I defined social scientific paradigms as philosophical accounts of the history of modernity, which provide the basis for judgements about how human sociality ought to be, and the way in which this truth is dominated or suppressed by contemporary social structures and relations. Marx's insights into a 'capitalist' modernity are expounded through a set of abstract oppositions (transformative activity and external necessity; self-consciousness and ideology; alienation and humanity; commodification and spontaneity) which determine the necessity of socialized production and the realization of human/proletarian justice. These oppositions, however, begin to lose their absolute stricture even in Marx's own work; for we have seen that in his remarks on commodity fetishism, he begins to question the relationship between (subjective) representation and the constitution of (objective) social and economic necessity. It is this acknowledgement of the subject as re-presenting and re-producing the conditions of its activity which is developed in the social and cultural theory of 'critical' Marxism.[10] Adorno's 'culture industry' thesis, for example, develops the idea that it is the power of mass culture to conceal the conditions of its production – that is, to appear as 'given' in the moment of consumption – that is crucial to the exercise of social control. While Jameson's presentation of late-capitalism attempts to show that it is the hyperintensive, globalized nature of commodity production which informs the 'postmodern' dissociation of experience from the 'objective' conditions of its production. Thus, in order to understand the formation of the individual in late-capitalist culture, we need to recognize that the concepts of plurality, fragmentation and dispersal deployed postmodern ethics, aesthetics, politics, etc., have obscured the 'real' moral issues which are determined through the commodity form (i.e., the consequences of automation and computerization, changes in the international division of labour, relations betweeen 'First' and 'Third world' economies, etc.). This 'critical' strand of Marxism, then, is significant because it begins to acknowledge that if there is a peculiarly 'capitalist' form of social necessity, then this has developed through moral, cultural and political representations, whose dynamics cannot be reduced to the simple reproduction of 'ideology'.

Weber's idea of social formation, we have seen, attempts to expound the relationship between the meaningful actions of rational subjects and the socio-economic structures in which those actions are performed. The idea of history which emerges from Weber's thought, therefore, is one in which the category of 'subjectivity' (volition) must be respected as independent of the structures and relations which presuppose it: as 'sociologists', in other words, we must describe ideal-typically the cultural, religious, moral and political forms through which individual actors understand the 'meaning' of their actions. It is this form of historical understanding which informs Weber's critique of modernity. For according to *The Protestant Ethic and the Spirit of Capitalism* (1978a), it is Protestantism's establishment of a 'worldly asceticism' which allows the emergence of 'capitalism' as a distinctively rationalized form of economic activity. The functioning of the corporations which come to dominate capitalist economies, the legitimacy of political parties and institutions; the 'consensual' necessity of the law, all of these presuppose a subject which has renounced the plurality and spontaneity of its formation, and accepted limitation and efficiency in their stead. Fundamentally, then, Weber's account of the relationship between Protestantism – particularly Calvinism – and the rise of capitalism is an attempt to set out the historical fate of this kind of ascetic subjectivity: its progressive rejection of religious and cultural ideals, the limitation of its creativity to profitable forms of production; and its creation of, and submission to, the 'iron cage' of bureaucratic rationality.

Concluding the *Protestant Ethic*, Weber remarks that:

> [no] one knows who will live in this cage in the future, or whether at the end of this tremendous development entirely new profits will arise, or there will be a great rebirth of old ideas and ideals, or, if neither, mechanised petrification, embellished with a sort of compulsive self-importance.[11]

What this amounts to, I would suggest, is an admission that the voluntarism, which Weber has made essential to historical explanation, is becoming increasingly subject to the demands of bureaucratic rationality, and that the only way out of the 'iron cage' is through the theoretically unaccountable intervention of charismatic individuals. For Weber, then, the central problem of modernity is not the continued existence of 'capitalist' relations of production, but rather the general tendency towards homogenization and suppression of moral, religious, cultural, etc. meanings within the limits of bureaucratic rationality.

We have seen that, for Marx, the transition from feudalism to capitalism is achieved through the violent uprooting of traditional forms of obligation, exchange, tutelage etc., by the increasing power of mercantile capital. It is, in other words, the productive forces liberated by the influx of wealth into the cities which determines the class constitution of the capitalist mode of production. 'Capitalism', therefore, is conceived as the highest form of exploitation, a form which originates in the violent coercion of those displaced by the collapse of the feudal system. (Such is the basis of Marx's 'moral' demand for the 'socialization' of production.) For Weber, on the contrary, such a massive socio-historical transformation cannot be explained purely in terms of economic necessity. There must, according to this analysis, have been fundamental changes in the way that individuals – in general – understand the significance of their secular existence (their work, satisfaction and desire) which predate the establishment of a 'capitalist' economy. It is this 'volitional' element which is provided by the rise of Protestantism in Western Europe. Thus, Weber is able to claim that the concept of bureaucratic reason has theoretical primacy over the Marxist model, in the sense that without this instrumental organization of the ascetic individual, the edifice of 'bourgeois' civil society would have no volitional/meaningful foundation. The difficulty with this analysis, however, is that the idea of subjective meaning which Weber deploys in his sociology is a descriptive, rather than a legislative concept. Thus, the increasingly powerful influence of bureaucratic reason upon the moral and political ends of ethical life appears as the inevitable fate of rational self-consciousness (a fate to which 'the subject', stripped of its practical/moral authority, can only acquiesce).

To return to Marxism for a moment, we have seen that the reflective strand I tried to identify in the critique of late-capitalism involves a certain recognition of 'the subject' within the culture of commodification. Yet both Adorno's attempt to describe the cultural forms through which the evaluative ('synthetic') capacities of 'the masses' are suppressed, and Jameson's account of the 'postmodern' confusion of the economic conditions of subjective re-formation, produce a sense that the 'capitalist' character of modernity still determines a kind of 'external' (objective, inhumane) necessity. Indeed, the Adornian conception of 'negative dialectics' demands that we attend to the complicities which late-capitalism tends to produce between political terror and metaphysical/ dialectical conceptions of totality. The action theoretical accounts of social relations I examined in Chapter 3, therefore, in general determine a move away from the 'objective' (coercive, negative) necessity reproduced by historical materialism. On Weber's understanding, for example, Marxism's constant recourse to the primacy of productive forces fails to acknowledge the autonomously formative power of moral and religious ideas in the constitution of modernity, while for Habermas, the categories of historical materialism are to be understood as establishing the parameters of a certain necessity (i.e., the material reproduction of society – or rather of the 'life world'), which must be mediated through the rule of rational/dialogical communication. As we have seen, however, both the Weberian and Habermasian versions of action theory determine their own particular forms of abstraction and opposition, forms which, in general, present the cognitive activity of the subject as (originally) independent of the objective determinations of ethical life.

So far, then, I have argued that the powers of Marx's account of 'capitalism', and Weber's notion of bureaucratic reason, are specified through their respective conceptions of historical development and completion. We have seen that Marx's attempt to disclose the universal character of capitalist exploitation determines a set of distinctive oppositions, which are repeated, in different forms, throughout the 'culture' of Marxist thought.[12] Crucially, it is these oppositions which have formed the 'critical' acknowledgement of subjectivity within the processes of late-capitalist commodification, an acknowledgement which, while it gestures towards an idea of rational self-recognition, still preserves the negative power of totality. This theoretical closure, or rather enclosure, of *Sittlichkeit* within the negativity of the commodity form, however, should not be conceived simply as a misrecognition of the substance/differentiation of ethical life. First, such an understanding would obviously neglect Marxism's construction of 'capital' as a powerfully 'objective' determinant of the moral, cultural and political life of modernity. For although this objectivity is constituted through the contradictory formations, desires and mediations sustained in ethical substance, it must be recognized that the commodity form has developed beyond the 'institutional' mediations suggested by Hegel in *Philosophy of Right*,[13] and constitutes a persistent reformative potential for self-conscious individuality. Secondly, the negative necessity of 'structure' maintained in historical materialism redetermines the Kantian demand that the rational subject should be acknowledged as primary in the constitution of 'civil community'.[14] Thus Weber and Habermas have both attempted to establish the conditions under which the commodity form has become the 'object' of rational volition. Yet both, we have seen, reproduce the abstractness of Kant's critical ethics: Weber by completing the complicity between (moral) formalism and utilitarian ends (in the iron cage of bureaucracy), and Habermas by attributing a 'consensual' necessity to the universal 'pragmatics' of language.

What is unrecognized by both Marx and Weber is the limitation (closure) which their respective ideas of 'capitalism' and 'bureaucratic rationality' set upon the concept of the social: a limitation that excludes acknowledgement of how the (present) conflict and mediation of social categories could produce 'unrecognized' forms of autonomy, domination and violence. Thus, what Marx and Weber contribute to our understanding of modernity are determinate socio-historical categories, whose (abstract) truth must be acknowledged as requiring moral, ethical and political judgements. The 'phenomenology' of social thought that I have expounded shows that the paradigmatic forms – Marxism, functionalism, action theory, etc. – are part of a 'differentiated unity', and that as such, certain 'modifications' are possible within their basic explanatory categories. 'Critical' Marxism, for example, begins to acknowledge the formation of rational subjectivity as essential to the cultural reproduction of capital. Yet we have seen that such acknowledgement tends to subsume the 'other' categories under the essential configuration of the appropriative paradigm. The 'speculative' judgements which are demanded by sociological forms of abstraction, therefore, are in the end concerned with recognizing contemporary forms of authority (exclusion, restriction, omission, forgetting) as part of a 'history' in which self-consciousness inevitably suffers limitation and contradiction of its freedom. This relationship – between the discourse of abstraction and speculative judgement – needs to be examined further.

Community, modernity and speculative judgement

In the previous two sections, I have attempted to define the universal characteristics of sociological paradigms, and to show how these opposed and contradictory forms contribute to a 'speculative' recognition of ethical life. In the first case, I argued that each paradigm articulates a social ethic, in which abstract ideas of alienation, integration and emancipation are imposed upon the 'modern' social relations. In the second case, I claimed that although the 'truth' of these perspectives is always partial, each remains necessary to the concept of community (i.e., to the forms identity, subjectivity and freedom which are realized in the modern form of *Sittlichkeit*). My idea of the relationship between sociological reason and speculative thought, in other words, concerns the recognition of the contradictions determined in each (paradigmatic) reconstruction of social relations. Thus, the kinds of judgement characteristic of a sociology (i.e., evaluations the inclusiveness and exclusiveness of particular social institutions; of the social construction of difference; of the possibility of social justice and equality) bear upon an historical present which is constantly reconstructed in relation to the idea of rational/universal human existence. It is this notion of a unique, and (necessarily) misrecognized 'present', which is fundamental to my understanding of the relationship between truth and the discourse of social science.

I began my account of this relationship in the first chapter, by suggesting that a 'speculative'[15] reading of Hegel's *The Science of Logic* and *Phenomenology of Mind* allows us to articulate a concept of truth which is neither transcendentally determined nor violently suppressive. What is emphasized in this reading is the 'spirit' of the Hegelian universal (idea, concept), that is, the attempt to expound the aporias and contradictions through which the 'substance' of ethical life has become the object of autonomy and reflection. A speculative reading of Hegel's thought, therefore, acknowledges that the 'concrete' universal (i.e., the absolute mediation, recognition and fulfilment of rational subjectivity) is a 'spiritual' form, which, because it can never be realized in any historical configuration of *Sittlichkeit*, demands the labour of judgement and reflection. The 'present' (modernity, ethical life) is always 'thrown down': it is constituted through categories which *remain to be* recognized in their 'true' moral, ethical and political significance. For Hegel, in other words, the history of humanity is the history of the limitation which spirit must suffer in the temporal/finite forms of expression (a limitation which demands that we – as speculative thinkers – attend to the ethical and political complicities into which the categories of sociological reason have already entered).

So, at the risk of reproducing the 'abstractness' which his philosophy attempts to criticize, I will recapitulate the main elements of Hegel's theory of social formation. First, every determinate social, ethical or political category must be conceived as belonging to a finite/secular totality, that is, as part of a concrete historical expression of *Sittlichkeit*. It is important to recognize here that the 'substance' of each historical form of ethical life cannot be expounded simply in terms of its structural/objective determinations, and that, conceived speculatively, moral, religious aesthetic and cultural forms of representation participate in the 'actuality' of each particular epoch.[16] Secondly, it must be acknowledged that the evolution of ethical life takes place through the production of historically specific contradictions.[17] For Hegel, every epoch, considered as a finite expression of the idea of universal subjectivity, is an attempt to bring particular forms of work, satisfaction and desire into an ethical totality of mediation, recognition and fulfilment. As we have seen, however, all such attempts are afflicted with the finitude which constitutes historical time: the forms of subjective presentation and objective necessity which constitute 'the present' always contradict the idea of universal autonomy. Finally, then, we must acknowledge that the 'true' significance of modernity – that is, the historical present of self-consciousness within ethical life – is never recognized until a new form of *Sittlichkeit* has already begun to emerge. Thus, while speculative thought is able to make out a certain 'prowess' in history, such judgement always proceeds from the 'fate' (violence, misrecognition, separation, exclusion) which self-consciousness has suffered in 'this particular' epoch. 'The owl of Minerva', with which Hegel famously identifies self-consiousness' 'reflective' recognition of the age, 'spreads its wings only with the falling of dusk'.[18]

Speculatively conceived, the objective and subjective forms which constitute the historical present – law, productive relations, moral and religious sensibilities etc. – are misrecognized by sociological theorizations of structure, functionality, integration and conflict. The ideas of estrangement, solidarity and ethical realization articulated within the discrete, paradigmatic forms of sociological reason, in other words, reproduce a certain Kantianism, in the sense that 'difference' and 'identity' remain the product of a determinate priority: either that of 'structure' (over autonomy and self-recognition) or rational action (over social formation and objectivity). I concluded the previous section by suggesting that what Marx and Weber contribute to our understanding of modernity are determinate social categories, whose explanatory power must be acknowledged as requiring speculative judgements. Such judgements, I have maintained, do not aim at disclosing the uncondi- tional truth of social existence; but rather at recognizing contemporary forms of domination as part of a history in which the 'substance' of ethical life is always already determined through conflict and contra- diction. The kinds of reflection determined through sociological paradigms (evaluations of justice, equality, difference, etc.) are therefore 'reconstructions' of ethical life. Each paradigm presents modernity through abstract separations of the subjective and objective forms which constitute *Sittlichkeit*, and as such, each is complicit with the epoch's mediation and contradiction of the idea of universal freedom.

The universal feature of these sociological reconstructions of ethical life is what Hegel refers to in his logical writings as 'reflection': 'the form of equality-with-self and therefore of being unrelated to another without opposition'.[19] Hegel's original references here are to the Kantian and Fichtean oppositions of pure moral spontaneity to the 'objective' (i.e., social) conditions of action. What I am suggesting is that sociological paradigms reproduce this abstraction of 'the essential' from concrete social relations, and that as such, they generically misrecognize the moral, ethical and political aporias constituted in the modern form of *Sittlichkeit*. Yet it is these discourses of abstraction which constantly reformulate the necessity of speculative judgements upon the determina- tions of the historical present (law, productive relations, moral recog- nition, etc.). For it is only through their isolation of particular 'essential' characteristics from the concept of ethical life that sociological paradigms can provide theoretically and methodologically coherent responses to questions of difference, justice and domination. Each of these paradigms attempts to expound the concept of community through its relationship to an abstractly essentialized form (Marx's *homo faber*, Weber's norma- tively spontaneous individual, Habermas's communicative pragmatics), and it is this form which is reproduced in their respective accounts of how modernity estranges, emancipates or excludes what is originally 'human' (or at least that which opens the possibility of universal humanity). Thus, 'daring to know'[20] the nature of the present always involves the misrecognition of the 'rational' determinations of commu- nity; for without the abstract categories of sociological reason, specu- lative judgement would lack the limiting conditions of 'empirical' (i.e., particular) contents.

What is most important to recognize here is that the 'content' (particularity, existential determinations), which is assumed by specu- lative thought, is not something which it can ever 'have done with'. As Hegel puts it in the *Phenomenology of Mind*: '[t]he movement of what is [i.e., *Sittlichkeit*] partly consists in becoming another to itself, and thus developing into its own content; partly again it takes this evolved content, this existence it assumes, back into itself, i.e., makes it into a moment, and reduces it to simple determinateness'.[21] Thus, the speculative conception of *Sittlichkeit* is not a 'metaphysical' construction which systematically violates every form of difference:[22] its concept originally includes difference and finitude (the defining characteristics of reflection) as forms which both express and contradict the idea of universal autonomy. Speculative judgements of the categories presented in sociological paradigms, then, do not attempt to 'synthesize' each reconstruction into a comprehensive account of the historical present. What they do is to acknowledge the difference of each paradigm (i.e., its limitedness) as something whose 'truth' demands preservation in the 'concept' of sociality. For it is through these paradigmatic reconstructions that we are able to judge ethically the contradictions determined between law and subjectivity, reason and desire, work and satisfaction (that is, to judge the lacunae which *Sittlichkeit* always opens between the universal and the particular).

In the end, my attempt to expound the powers of sociological reason is an attempt to describe the relationship between the substance of ethical life (law, morality, custom, transformative activity, etc.) and its representation through the paradigmatic forms of reflection. The speculative judgements, whose necessity I have tried to establish, therefore do presuppose a certain inner-relatedness of reason: the 'logical' dialectics make it clear that the categories of 'pure thought' are, for Hegel, inseparable from the 'concept' of rational autonomy (i.e., action which would know and re-cognize the totality of the conditions which have produced it). Yet it is the *speculative* nature of this proposition which is crucial. For while *The Science of Logic* can be read simply as an exercise in 'Platonic' dialectics (an exercise which would demand that the 'actual' be brought under the legislative power of a purely formal rationality), it is obvious from Hegel's historical-phenomenological writing that the import of his logic is speculative, rather than ('metaphysically') legislative. His deployment of the categories of 'Being' and 'Essence' in the *Phenomenology of Mind*, for example, takes the form of showing how their concrete determination within the 'substance' of ethical life is always (empirically, temporally) 'differentiated' from the pure conceptual necessity of the logic. Ultimately, then, the type of judgement I have described aims not at closing the lacunae (between law and subjectivity, reason and desire, etc.), but rather at recognizing the complicities into which 'abstract' reason enters with actual forms of domination.

This notion of the complicity' between (abstract) reason and domination returns me to the Derridian question with which I concluded the previous chapter: what is the relationship between violence and metaphysics? To conclude, then, I will try to specify how speculative thought can judge the moral, aesthetic and cultural categories through which racist politics in general, and Nazism in particular, have attempted to 'found' (or rather 're-found') the totality of ethical life, and to show how this judgement acknowledges the 'concept' of humanity, without determining the kind of 'metaphysical' (dialectical) violence which Derrida attributes to Hegelian thought.

Hegel, Derrida and the metaphysics of race

The question of racial difference – of its construction, re-construction and judgement – is one which bears directly upon the ethical and political strictures articulated in deconstructive and speculative thought. Thus, in order to understand why I have chosen to expound the idea of community as a 'substantive' form (in relation to the 'abstraction' of sociological reason), and to preserve the concept of law as the 'finality' of ethical life (a finality which is, however, never realized), I need to determine pricisely the difference between deconstructive and speculative conceptions of 'responsibility' to the other. In the previous chapter, I gave a brief account of the relationship of deconstruction to the concept of gender. We saw that Derrida's idea of a non-essentialized feminine schematizes not only the undecidability of 'phallogocentric' power, but also a more generalized conception of the relationship between reason and autonomy. For it is through the acknowledgement of the 'general text', and its 'economic' production of violence, that we are able to judge the ways in which different discourses deploy the necessity of 'presence'. In order to evaluate Derrida's deconstruction of racial politics, therefore, it will be necessary to pay close attention to specify the involvement of Hegel's spirit (*Geist*) in the historical phenomenon of Nazism. I need, in other words, to examine the way in which the 'ghost' of Hegel is woven into the text of *Of Spirit* (1990a), and to analyse the notion of (metaphysical/dialectical) violence which Derrida seeks to distinguish from the 'spirit' of Heidegger's philosophy.

Briefly, the intention behind Derrida's exposition of spirit in Heidegger's thought is to show that it signifies a more originary, more disquieting relation to Being than 'the question' through which Heidegger characterizes the history of *Dasein* in *Being and Time* (1983). This project famously encounters the problem of Heidegger's membership of the Nazi party during the years leading up to World War Two. Such an obvious alignment with the *Volksgeist* of German nationalism, coupled with his remarks about the eminent superiority of German language and culture in the tasks of 'spiritual' revelation (of Being), would seem to pose a profound difficulty for any work of 'ethical' reappropriation. Yet by the end of Derrida's exposition, it is Hegel's 'spirit', not Heidegger's, which has emerged as the 'obsessing ghost',[23] whose recuperations are inevitably associated with racist nationalism and the annihilation of the other. For Derrida, Heidegger's notion of *Geist*, despite its entanglement with the hierarchies of cultural and linguistic 'Germanism', gestures towards a deconstructive stricture. By suggesting that the very questioning of Being – the questioning whose structures are expounded in *Being and Time* – presupposes a certain 'promise' of *Dasein* to the conditions of language (i.e., exteriority, partiality, non-identity with 'the Said'), Heidegger's thought encourages us to recognize that 'the text' cannot reserve its necessity within the presence of the Said.[24] For Derrida, every legislative discourse includes a priori the 'ghost' of its 'remarking', and so deconstruction becomes the discourse of justice, in the sense that it is the remarking of this unavoidable 'doubling' (i.e., the impossibility of a pure, non-textualized 'presence'). And so according to *Of Spirit*, Heidegger's later recourse to the notion of *Geist*, is the philosophical condition of his Nazism, that is, a prioritizing of the German language with regard to the 'spiritual' questioning/revelation of Being.

The question which concerns me at the moment, however, is not the significance of Heidegger's pre-war politics; nor is it directly the detail of Derrida's relationship to the body of Heidegger's thought. What I am concerned with is the way in which Derrida represents Hegel's notion of spirit as something which is clearly implicated in the combining of different discourses into the ideology a law of Nazism. I need, then, to look at the final lecture in *Of Spirit* in some detail. Derrida remarks:

> . . . we have been speaking of nothing but the 'translation' of these thoughts and discourses [regions, philosophies, political regimes, economic structures, etc.] into what are commonly called the 'events' of 'history' and of 'politics'. . . it would also be necessary to 'translate' what an exchange of places would imply in its most radical possibility [the 'flame' of the Final Solution]. . . . We have here a programme and a combinatory whose power remains abysmal. In all rigour it exculpates none of the discourses which can thus exchange their power. It leaves no place for any arbitrating authority. Nazism was not born in the desert. We all know this, but it has to be constantly recalled. And even if, far from any desert, it had grown like a mushroom in the silence of a European forest, it would have done so in the shadow of big trees, in the shelter and silence of their indifference but in the same soil.[25]

A number of important points emerge from this final lecture. (1) The emergence of Nazism (and its determining project of racial purification) from the philosophical, religious, economic and political ideals of European culture should be conceived as a possibility sustained by discourses which proceed from the a priori restriction of linear/teleological history. For Derrida, then, 'universal' ideas of subjectivity, identity and humanity, circulate through texts whose general settlement is the accumulation of meaning in social and political institutions. Thus, it is through these texts that the power, extent and exclusiveness of the law is determined (i.e., its 'presence' in the community of rational citizens). (2) The 'combinatory' of which Derrida speaks in relation to the Final Solution, 'exculpates none of the discourses which can thus exchange their power. It leaves no place open for an arbitrary authority.'[26] In view of the remarks with which Derrida begins the final lecture of Of *Spirit*, it seems clear that the 'arbitrating authority' he has in mind is Hegel's philosophy of spirit. For by suggesting that the movement of *Aufhebung* – spirit's preserving transcendence of its natural (i.e., finite) conditions[27] – is like the evolution of gas from the putrefaction of the dead, Derrida clearly implicates the 'synthetic' (integrating, combinatory) necessity of the dialectic in the constitution of Nazism as a political ideology. Derrida's example of the Hegelian spirit's need to gather existing determinations of 'otherness' into its movement towards the realization of the concept – that is, Hegel's account of the transcendence of Judaic consciousness of the infinite through the philosophical rigour of the German nation[28] – therefore refers us to the 'most radical possibility' of metaphysical thought – the 'flame and ashes' of the Final Solution. (3) Finally, Derrida is claiming that the 'translation' of the 'thoughts and discourses' that have organized the history of Western civilization into the ideology of Nazism demands that we attend carefully to the formation of 'the other' within each particular discourse. Given the dangerous necessity inscribed in Hegel's philosophy of spirit, 'we' – as practitioners of deconstruction – cannot have recourse to 'higher' syntheses of religious, economic and political discourses. We must instead attempt to follow the 'striction' imposed by the 'general text': that of 'remarking' the deployment of trace, supplement and *différance*, through which the law (of 'this' particular discourse) is announced (Said) as 'present'.

It has now become urgent that I return to the difference between 'speculative' and 'dialectical' thought. For Derrida, Hegel's philosophy – which he characterizes through the operation of the *Aufhebung* on every conceivable content – is incapable of taking account of the 'exteriority' through which its law (of determinate/productive negation) is originally given. Thus, the 'history', which Hegelian Phenomenology articulates, is 'metaphysical' in the sense that it is governed by a 'restricted economy' of categories which depict a linear, teleological, eschatological development towards the realization of the concept. Derrida's concern, then, is to distinguish his own proximity to the discourses in which trace, supplement and *différance* articulate the possibility of non-metaphysical stricture (i.e., responsibility towards 'the other' constituted in 'the Said') from Hegel's 'spiritual' reproduction of presence (totality, mediation, iteration, etc.). Yet this account of Hegel's philosophy as a kind of disordered machine, in which the 'spiritual' community (*Sittlichkeit*) can be regenerated from every form of violence, terror and persecution, has misrepresented the imperative inscribed in speculative thinking. For as we have seen, (Hegel's) *Phenomenology* does not seek to impose the formal necessity of dialectical logic on the historical configurations of ethical life. Rather, it demands that the violence which afflicts the totality is comprehended through the lacunae between the law (the formal postulation of the rights, duties, freedoms and satisfactions for which the community exists) and the 'substance' of ethical life (the forms of work, satisfaction and desire consititued in actual social relations). Such a comprehension, I will argue, requires the abstract reconstructions of community, identity and subjectivity, which are postulated in the paradigms of sociological reason.

It is obvious that if we are to understand the significance of racist politics for modern forms of ethical life, we need to comprehend the relationship of racial difference to the economic structures of capitalism. The orthodox Marxist account of this relationship is not difficult to rehearse. Capitalist economies develop through the increasing capitalization of all areas of production, a development which inevitably causes the average rate of profit to fall in the domestic economy. The history of enslavement, colonization and immigration which has unfolded with the expansion of capitalism is therefore a necessary consequence of the need to find new sources of raw materials, new markets to exploit and new sources of cheap labour power. Thus, the ideologies of racial difference, which become enshrined in the culture and politics of the nation state, are reducible ultimately to demands constituted in the mode of production (the need to reduce labour costs, the fracturing of unities within 'the proletariat', etc.). Leon Trotsky's account of the rise of fascism in Germany,[29] for example, attempts to show that Nazism's encouragement of violent anti-Semitism was in fact 'capitalism's' final response to the collapse of the economic base, and of the values sustained in the ideologies of civil society (formal equality before the law, equitable distribution of rewards, the work ethic, etc.). In the end, the appeal to 'blood and soil', to the community of the *Volksgeist*, is conceived as a strategy designed to preempt the formation of a revolutionary class identity, a strategy which is reproduced – perhaps with more cynicism, or more 'legality' – in every 'political' deployment of race within the capitalist mode of production.

We have seen, however, that the 'culture' of Marxism includes a rather more critical understanding of the relationship between race and capital than the one which is formulated in Trotsky's writings. Adorno's *Negative Dialectics* presents the relationship between the crises which afflict late-capitalism (crises which include the 'spiritual' determinations of 'productive forces' – universal 'objectification' and 'commodification' – as well as unemployment, hyperinflation, etc.) and the success of Nazism as attesting to the inability of 'culture' to bring about a transcendence of humanity's 'scatological' obsession with death, corruption and violence. The 'fact of Auschwitz', in other words, functions as a 'model', as an historical moment which jams the dialectical mechanisms of cultural development and the accumulation of meaning in the institutions of *Sittlichkeit*. As Adorno memorably puts it:

> That this [Auschwitz] could happen in the midst of the traditions of philosophy, of art, and of the enlightening sciences says more than that these traditions . . . lacked the power to take hold of men and work a change in them . . . all post-Auschwitz culture, including its urgent critique, is garbage.[30]

Once this recuperative power of civilization is demonstrably and irretrievably lost in the destructive necessity of Auschwitz, Adorno contends that it is the modern complicities of capitalism with the metaphysics of totality (the political deployment of a *Volksgeist* into the moral, economic and political destitution of the nation state; the encouragement of a limitless 'idealism' which supplants the satisfactions of civil society) which should become the focus of critical reflection. Such complicities demand a 'micrological' sensitivity to the violence that is suffered, or may be suffered, by the other in the name of 'immanence', a sensitivity which ought to invoke the particular exclusions and deprivations to which 'this' deployment of totality is addressed. (According to *Negative Dialectics*, Hegel's account of particularity as the bare determinations of 'Existenz' constitutes a violent secondarization of what originally differentiates the universal from its diversified forms: the 'indefinite something' that resists subsumption under totality.)[31]

Adorno's conception of the relationship between the 'metaphysics' of totality (i.e., the claims of a 'spiritual' history in which culture expresses an autonomous civilizing power) and the exigencies of late-capitalism therefore clearly marks a sophistication of Marxism's relationship to the politics of race. The critique of capitalism expresses neither a simple faith in the negativity of bourgeois property relations; nor in the eventual transcendence of racial ideologies in the constitution of a revolutionary class identity. For while Adorno acknowledges that there are certain fundamental necessities which animate capitalist modes of production (the 'objectifying' power 'unleashed' by forces of production, the spread of cultural commodification, etc.), the processes through which 'the other' (of autonomy, of freedom, of right) is determined have no 'essential' relationship to the redemption of humanity (in the law of proletarian justice). Thus, 'critical' thought must seek to identify the violence which the political deployment of 'immanence' does to the particular, a violence which serves no historical destiny beyond the immediate (legal, ethical, economic, etc.) exclusions which it determines.

For both Adorno and Lyotard, Auschwitz is the name which marks the end of metaphysical recuperation. The law of the SS which demands of the Jewish deportee 'that you should die, that is my law' formalizes a violence which cannot be taken into the dialectical machine and made into a moment in the evolution of *Sittlichkeit*. The difference between Adorno's conception of the relationship between racial violence and dialectical thought and that which Lyotard presents in *The Differend*, however, returns us to the questions of abstraction, reconstruction and judgement which have informed our account of ethical life and modernity. Lyotard's reading of Adorno, we have seen, maintains that his critique of Hegel's philosophy of spirit produces a negative fixation of thought with 'immanence', which ultimately fails to articulate what is unnameable in the particular – the unique, the heterogeneous, the incommensurable. According to *The Differend*, Adorno's admiration for

Kant's refusal to allow the law (of the intelligible world of moral ends)
inscription in the historical forms of human sociality, fails to acknowledge the most urgent expression of this (disturbing, productive) absence
in Kant's critical philosophy – the 'Analytic of the sublime'. If we are to
judge ethically that which is unnamed in the transactions between the
law (the formal/universal expression of community) and those who are
subject to its necessity, we must recognize that the 'silence' – the lack of
any language through which to appeal to the established 'tribunal' of
litigation – is received through unforeseen events of incommensurability
(differend). We are, like Kant's critical subject in the presence of the
sublime, 'suspended over the void', forced to judge in the absence of any
moral or theoretical concept. Thus, the necessity which a post-
Auschwitzian ethics places upon all of us (as members of the *sensus
communis*, the community of judgement) is to sustain a vigorous
'aesthetic' productivity of thought; of originating new literary, artistic
and philosophical 'phrasings', through which to subvert the totalizing
discourses of the law (the race, the nation, the people, etc.).[32] Ultimately,
negative dialectics is too preoccupied with setting out a (Kantian)
critique of the relationship between (Hegelian) 'immanence' and the
dynamics of productive forces to acknowledge the breaks, silences and
gaps (the 'unpresentable') which, for Lyotard, are the conditions of
ethical responsibility.

In the previous chapter, I attempted to mark the difference between
Derridean and Lyotardian thought through the latter's attempt to
abstract a certain specifying, particularizing sensitivity to the 'unpresentable' (the heterogeneous, the incommensurable), from Kant's *Critique of
Judgement* (1982b). We argued that if poststructuralism does represent a
challenge to speculative thought, this challenge is expressed in Derrida's
attempts to articulate a disquieting proximity to the Hegelian *logos*,
rather than in Lyotard's transcription of evanescent, aestheticized apprehensions of responsibility. *The Differend* therefore opens the way for
an exposition of Nazism as a 'premodern' (savage, occultic) narrative,
which is founded upon the troubling antithesis of Judaism (that which
eschews representation, the 'graven image' of God and the law) to
the categories 'Occidental thought'. What is important here is that the
concept of racist politics which Lyotard expounds in *Heidegger and 'the
jews'* (the lower case form of 'the jews' is used by Lyotard to mark not
only the victims of the Nazi genocide, but all the 'minorities' excluded by
the 'inclusiveness' of 'Occidental' reason) is founded upon a dynamic of
memory and forgetting constituted through the 'architectonics' of the
ethical community. For by comprehending Nazism as an attempt to
'"terminate" the interminable'[33] otherness which haunts this community,
Lyotard's analysis tends crucially to underplay the significance of economic, bureaucratic and functionalist powers, in the formation of racist
law and the success of racist political movements. Adorno's thought, I
would argue, does at least articulate a theory of how productive forces

are related to the 'spiritual' life modernity (culture, philosophy, ethics, artistic creativity, etc.), and how this relation can determine 'spirit' as a terrible destructive idealism. Lyotard's version of 'capitalist' economic necessity (i.e., the determination of a 'temporal economy' in which every 'transaction' presupposes a distribution of 'goods' – information, services, etc. – equivalent in terms of the amount of time expended in their production), however, fails to recognize the violence which is inscribed in the concept of a productive 'force', and so is unable to reconstruct a crucial part of the social reality from which racist politics are born. Thus, as speculative thinkers, we need to attend to the 'actual' relations of ethical life: relations whose aporetic constitution is always already determined *in relation to* the formal finalities of the law.

For Derrida, as we have seen, the determination of the law through the multiple discourses of community demands that we acknowledge an 'economic' distribution of violence, and that the idea of peace (universally mediated coexistence) is something which must remain on the 'horizon' of legislative interventions. The ethical stricture of difference, in other words, demands that we register the deployment of 'presence' in the discourses of economics, religious belief and political authority, a stricture which, from the beginning, proceeds from the 'violence' of legislation/determination. The relationship of speculative thought to the relations and structures of modern community, however, acknowledges the law and its substantive determinations as maintaining a certain potential for violence and exclusion. This potential, I have argued, is recognized (or rather re-cognized) through the forms of sociological reason; for it is through these 'abstract' reconstructions of community that we are able to comprehend the complicities of functionalism, bureaucratic order, commodification, etc. with the violent idealism of racist 'culture' (i.e., the 'lawless' reformation of the law whose finalities – rights, duties, freedoms – are threatened by the powers of instrumentalism, homogenization, totalization, etc.). If, therefore, the law is *not* originarily violent (as Derrida claims it is), and if the stricture of ethical responsibility is not to remain outside of the rational determinations of community, we must provide an example of the reconstructive potential inherent in the modernist sociologies.

The moral sociology expounded in Zygmunt Bauman's book *Modernity and the Holocaust* (1991), is interesting in this respect, as it represents the classic Weberian critique of bureaucratic authority through Emmanuel Levinas's idea of a pre-societal relation of ethical responsibility – the relation of 'being with others'. Bauman's claim is that 'functionalist' conceptions of morality are unable to register the distantiating and divisive tendencies of modern social organization. According to these systemic accounts of society, normative distinctions cannot, and ought not, to be made between different moral codes. The most that we, as social scientists, can maintain is that 'evil' is invariably associated with a lack of social integration, and the infringement of (chaotic, unregulated) 'nature' upon the social system. Weber's critique of bureaucratic authority, on the other hand, makes it clear that we cannot simply assume that the negative consequences of modernity are a result of a lack of social integration, and that they are contingent 'dysfunctions' that can be put right by appropriate adjustments to the system. The suppression of moral spontaneity and the homogenization of experience which occurs through bureaucratic structures is something about which Weber expresses a deep sense of foreboding. For we have seen that *The Protestant Ethic* concludes that, in the absence of charismatic revitalizations of 'old ideals', we can expect only 'mechanized petrification [of society], embellished with a sort of convulsive self-importance'.[34] What Bauman's account of the Holocaust does, therefore, is to introduce an ethical dimension into Weber's critique of the 'iron cage' bureaucracy. He attempts to show that the 'worldly asceticism' which Weber presents as the subjective counterpart of bureaucratic ends (efficiency, economy, impersonality) is crucially important in the 'de-moralization' of modernity, and that it is the generalized substitution of moral ends for instrumental tasks which allowed the emergence of the Final Solution as a legitimate (and accomplishable) end.

Thus, instead of starting from the assumption that it is only the enculturated individual embedded in 'the system' who can be considered a moral being, Bauman takes the position that there is a relation of moral responsibility which is existentially prior to 'the societal'. This relation is what Bauman, following Levinas, calls 'being with others'. According to Levinas, the origin of the ethical commandment is the proximity of the face, a proximity in which each feels 'himself' (although we have seen that Levinas attributes neither race nor gender to the infinite 'resemblance' of the face to God) unconditionally responsible to the plight of 'the Other'. According to Bauman, this originary relation of moral proximity is increasingly displaced by four essentially bureaucratic processes. The first of these is 'the social production of distance', a distance between decision and execution which progressively excludes the moral authority of the face. The second is 'the substitution of technical for moral authority', which effectively conceals the significance of action. Thirdly, Bauman talks about 'the technology of separation' which promotes indifference to the plight of the other which would otherwise be subject to moral evaluation and morally motivated response. Finally, there is the 'usurpation' of ethical authority by 'the principle of sovereignty of state powers': each individual recognizes only the 'legitimate' demands of the state.[35] Thus for Bauman, 'The point made . . . is that powerful moral drives have a pre-social origin, while some aspects of modern societal organisation cause considerable weakening of their constraining power; that, in effect society may make the immoral conduct more, rather than less, plausible.'[36]

Bauman's sociology therefore articulates an acute recognition of the way in which bureaucratic rationality can participate in the transformation of racist mythologies into a programme of systematic persecution. However, Levinas's account of the face as the moment of infinite and unconditional responsibility to the other, is ultimately unable to determine an 'actual' connection of the moral commandment with the conditions of modernity, that is, with the aporias constituted in the world of civil society, productive relations, particular satisfactions and desires. Thus, while Bauman's critique of modern 'distantiated' communication does disclose a powerful de-moralizing potential in bureaucratic organization, it fails to recognize that the violence of racial exclusion cannot be attributed simply to the exteriority of 'the same' (i.e., the law of the totality of inclusive categories) to the originary source of ethical responsibility – the infinity of the face. His understanding of the relationship between the Holocaust and modernity, in other words, reproduces the estrangement of the ethical relation (being with others) from the substance of *Sittlichkeit*, the estrangement which both sustains and nullifies the infinity of the Levinasian commandment. Ultimately, then, modernity and the Holocaust are unable to determine any more substantive responses to the violence that remains potential in functional and bureaucratic order than to suggest: 'An ethics that would reach over the socially erected obstacles of mediated action and the functional reduction of the human self'.[37] Such an account of the preservation of moral proximity, however, seems to return us to the abstract ideals of neo-Kantianism, that is, to the privilege of a 'transcendent' procedural rationality over the actual substantive conditions of action, legislation and desire.

In order to understand the political deployment of race as a legislative force within ethical life, therefore, we must recognize that it is the disjunctive relationship of actual social institutions to the formal finality of the law which sustains the racist imagination. If we are to comprehend the 'combinatory' of discourses through which the racial 'other' is constituted, therefore, we must grasp that the 'millennial' ideologies of fascism are founded upon the yearnings of individuals who are caught between the promises inscribed in the law (freedom, equality, liberty) and the substance of ethical life – a 'substance' which is, from the beginning, prone to impoverish the individual before the law. Nazism, for example, could only become such a powerfully destructive 'culture' of racial persecution because the nation state was unable to maintain any semblance of an approximation between the formal concept of community inscribed in the law and the moral, political and economic destitution of *Sittlichkeit*. Thus, if the idea of spirit was involved in the historical phenomenon of Nazism, it was not, as Levinas's (and Bauman's) arguments suggest, because of its external 'synthetic' necessity (i.e., the reduction of my likeness–semblance–infinity to the categories of sameness–totality–exclusion); nor is it because, as Derrida has argued, it cannot be articulated as an ethical necessity which remains independent of the hierarchical organizations (of race, culture, etc.) in which it is expressed.[38] Rather, the 'necessity' inscribed in Hegelian spirit derives from its dispersal into the contradictory relations which constitute ethical life, a dispersal which demands that we attend to the moral, economic and political differentiations of *Sittlichkeit*, and their relationship to its posited ideals.

Levinas's thought is particularly important here, as *Totality and Infinity* (1994) opens a dialogue with Hegel which refuses the simple Marxist 'inversion' of spiritual primacy. For Levinas, dialectical thinking – whether 'materialist' or 'idealist' in origin – necessarily presupposes the (possible) accomplishment of a rationalized whole in which the ethical life of humanity would be realized. Such presuppositions, however, fail to recognize the ground of their own possibility: they fail to acknowledge that it is the 'uncontainable' resemblance of the human face to God which founds the original human relationship of moral proximity. Thus, that the other can become the object of racial violence is explained ultimately by the reduction of moral proximity – the 'being with' of being with others – through the categories of the same (the 'being' of the totality). We saw in the previous chapter that Derrida's objections to the absolute alterity of the face are founded upon Levinas's 'critique' of Hegelian metaphysics. For Derrida, such an attempt to specify the absolute neutrality and alterity of the origin (i.e., of ethical responsibility in its relation to the social) cannot escape the dialectical mechanism: the absolute 'other' must always be drawn back into the absolute, non-coercive identity of spirit. In the end, Levinas's account of the infinite strangeness of the face only serves to conceal the 'economic' distribution of conflicts which occur through the rationalizations of race (and of gender). That which claims absolute/infinite transcendence, in other words, cannot acknowledge the violence of its interventions in the structures and discourses of reason. All this, however, wrongly assumes that Levinas's critique of Hegel – his presentation of the philosophy of spirit as a forced recuperation of 'the same' (or the 'iterable', to use Derrida's term) – is true to the necessity acknowledged in speculative thought. What this means, then, is that we must examine Derrida's assumption that what is wrong with Levinas's ethics of care is its unacknowledged complicity with Hegel's dialectic, a complicity which, by presenting the face as infinite likeness–resemblance–non-identity, obscures the ethical stricture of difference.

Yet Levinas's thinking, in its radical disengagement of 'the infinite' (the ethical commandment inscribed in the face) from the categories of 'the same', is closer to Kant's critical morality than to a speculative recognition of the law in its relations with the state and civil society. Ultimately, Levinas's ethics of care hold the law aloof from the difficulties of social actuality: it demands that we do the right thing, as it is disclosed to us through the plight of the other, without concern for the wider consequences of our actions. This radical alterity of the moral commandment, however, is not, as Derrida claims, identical with a 'non-violent' unity which repeats itself as 'spirit' in Hegel's philosophy. Speculative thought demands that we attempt to grasp the aporetic constitution of ethical life (the modern organization of work, satisfaction and desire) in relation to the formal promises of freedom, equality and protection enshrined in the law. Thus, we can distinguish speculative critique from Levinas's presentation of Hegel, and from Derrida's attempt to identify the ethics of care with the 'Hegelian' necessity of absolute mediation, by the fact that speculative thinking begins with the actual, aporetic relations through which the individual is formed. If we want to comprehend the pervasive injustice determined through racial mythologies, in other words, we cannot proceed from the assumption that these are the result of the violence originally inscribed in the totality of social relations. Neither Levinas's attempt to make the undeterminable revelation of God (in the face of the other) the foundation of moral responsibility, nor Derrida's account of rational legislation as the reproduction of difference within the 'economy of violence' are able to reconstruct the ethical difficulty of living under a law whose promises (of freedom, respect, recognition) must remain abstract and unrealized.

Ultimately, Derrida's conception of difference, through its inscription in the originary inclusiveness of the law and its legislations, becomes the unspecifiable 'object' of a ceaseless 'hyper-reflection'. The other, to whom we, as rational subjects, are responsible, is always 'excluded', rather than 'formed': it never receives anything from the 'actuality' of ethical life, in the sense that the condition of its difference (i.e., the opacity and unreflectiveness which is inscribed in the law as such), is originally violent in its determinations of the universal (the community). In other words, by making 'peace' and 'justice' ideas which are beyond any rational determination of *Sittlichkeit*, racial difference is abstracted from its formation in the lacunae between the finality of the law and the particularity inscribed in actual forms of work, satisfaction and desire. The violence associated with the 'racializing' of the other (i.e., the determination to coercive social practices which, through the limitation of 'humanity' to a certain set of 'genetic' characteristics, appear as moral), therefore, should be conceived in terms of the ways in which the law (the formal inscription of the promise of ethical life, the mediation of universal autonomy and particular satisfactions) becomes increasingly estranged from actual social relations. Hannah Arendt's account of Nazism, for example, draws attention to the ways in which the mythology of a 'millennial' Aryan destiny (the hegemony of German culture, the purifying of 'Nordic' humanity, etc.) come to fill the void left by the collapse of established class structures and the edifice of bourgeois legality.[39] Thus, speculative thought (that is an Hegelianism not 'without reserve',[40] but without the strict dialectical 'iteration' which Derrida attributes to the activity of spirit) approaches the idea of race, not as a 'striction' which presupposes reason's differential reproduction of an original violence, but rather as that which is prone to become embroiled in destructive 'cultures' of social and political re-formation.

As we have seen in Hegel's account of the French Revolution, where the law appears as the 'other' of justice and humanity, the violence produced is 'absolute' rather than 'economic' (in the deconstructive sense of 'economy'). There is no possibility of ethical recognition of the other, precisely because the 'origin' of such a recognition (the laws, relations and institutions established in *Sittlichkeit*) is obscured and undermined by the constant pursuit of an abstract and exclusive essence – the 'bad infinite' of pure, uncorrupted humanity. The labour of speculative thinking in relation to modernity, therefore, has accepted both the necessity of the law (i.e., the formal postulation of rights, duties and freedoms) and the 'unrealized' nature of its relationship to the differentiated forms of satisfaction and desire constituted in ethical life. Thus, if we are to judge the political significance of race, we must recognize that mythologized constructions of the other, take place through the adventitious deployment of certain discourses (genetics, ethnology, anthropology – to cite a few Foucauldian examples) to supplement the 'absence' of the law – or rather, the absence of the freedoms it promises from actual social relations. Unlike deconstruction, speculative thought attempts to comprehend the violence produced by the law; not just posit its formality as an abstract originary violence. If we are to understand the dynamics of racist and nationalist politics – 'those epistemological and political practices which exclude the other in a multitude of subtle and not so subtle ways'[41] – we must understand what 'living in' the law actually means: we must recognize that the recourse to racial mythology – such as the 'Aryanism' which precipitated the rise of National Socialism, or the white supremacist ideals enshrined in Apartheid – is precipitated by strains which 'modernity' places upon the moral and political ideals of the law. If we are to respect the general principle that social philosophy should continue to address the rights of the other, then the violence which is done to him or her through the construction (and re-construction) of race demands the kind of historical-phenomenological comprehension of community, law and ethical life which is excluded by the deconstructive postulate of an originary violence (the violence inscribed in the foundation of the law as such). For it is only through such a comprehension that it is possible to judge the potency of race in its particular national, cultural, ethnic and political contexts.

Notes

1. T.S. Kuhn, *The Structure of Scientific Revolutions*, University of Chicago Press, 1970, p. 50.

2. See K. Marx, 'Private property and communism', in Marx, *Economic and Philosophical Manuscripts of 1844*, Progress Publishers, 1977b, pp. 93–108.

3. See E. Durkheim, 'The progress of the division of labour and of happiness', in Durkheim, *The Division of Labour in Society*, trans. G. Simpson, The Free Press, 1964, pp. 233–55.

4. See M. Weber, *The Protestant Ethic and the Spirit of Capitalism*, trans. T. Parsons, George Allen & Unwin, 1978a, p. 182.

5. See T.W. Adorno, *Minima Moralia*, trans. E.F.N. Jephcott, Verso, 1996.

6. See J.-F. Lyotard, 'Judiciousness in dispute, or Kant after Marx', in *The Lyotard Reader*, A. Benjamin ed., Blackwell, 1991b, pp. 324–59.

7. See M. Horkheimer and T.W. Adorno, *The Dialectic of Enlightenment*, trans. J. Cummings, Continuum, 1986, and F. Jameson, *Postmodernism: Or the Cultural Logic of Late Capitalism*, Verso, 1995.

8. See T.W. Adorno, 'Meditations on metaphysics', in Adorno, *Negative Dialectics*, trans. E.B. Ashton, Routledge, 1990, pp. 361–408.

9. Ibid.

10. See especially in the work of the Frankfurt School: Adorno, Horkheimer, Marcuse and, latterly, Habermas.

11. Weber, *The Protestant Ethic and the Spirit of Capitalism*, p. 182.

12. See G. Rose, 'The culture and fate of Marxism', in Rose, *Hegel Contra Sociology*, Athlone Press, 1981, pp. 214–20.

13. See 'The system of needs', 'The administration of justice' and 'The police and the corporation', in G.W.F. Hegel, *Philosophy of Right*, trans. T.M. Knox, Oxford University Press, 1967b, pp. 122–55.

14. In general, Kant's political writings are informed by the idea that, ultimately, the utilitarian determinations of 'community' are constituted for the 'purpose' of bringing about a universal recognition of rational sovereignty – a recognition which ought to be perpetuated in an international confederation of states. See especially 'Idea for a universal history with a cosmopolitan purpose', in I. Kant, *Political Writings*, H. Reiss ed., trans. H.B. Nisbet, Cambridge University Press, 1991, pp. 41–60.

15. See especially 'Rewriting the Logic', in Rose, *Hegel Contra Sociology*, pp. 185–203.

16. There is a particularly concise exposition of the concept of 'actuality' in G.W.F. Hegel, *Hegel's Logic: Encyclopaedia of the Philosophical Sciences, Volume One*, trans. W. Wallace, Oxford University Press, 1982, pp. 200–22.

17. See 'The realization of spirit in history', in G.W.F. Hegel, *Lectures on the Philosophy of World History, Introduction: Reason in History*, trans. H.B. Nisbet, Cambridge University Press, 1980, pp. 44–124.

18. Hegel, *Philosophy of Right*, p. 13.

19. G.W.F. Hegel, *The Science of Logic*, trans. A.V. Miller, George Allen & Unwin, 1969, p. 411.

20. See Kant's essay 'What is Enlightenment?', in Kant, *Political Writings*.

21. See Hegel's Preface to the *Phenomenology of Mind*, trans. J.B. Baillie, Harper & Row, 1967a, p. 111.

22. See 'The result' in J.-F. Lyotard, *The Differend: Phrases in Dispute*, trans. G. Van Den Abeele, University of Manchester Press, 1988a, pp. 86–106.

23. J. Derrida, *Of Spirit*, trans. G. Bennington and R. Bowlby, University of Chicago Press, 1990a, p. 99.

24. Ibid., footnote 3, pp. 132–6.

25. Ibid., p. 109.

26. Ibid.

27. Ibid., p. 99.

28. Ibid., footnote 3, pp. 132–6.

29. See Leon Trotsky, *The Struggle Against Fascism in Germany*, Pathfinder Press.

30. Adorno, *Negative Dialectics* , p. 367.

31. Ibid., pp. 173–4.

32. Lyotard, *The Differend*, §208.

33. J.-F. Lyotard, *Heidegger and 'the jews'*, trans. A. Mitchel and M. Roberts, University of Minnesota Press, 1990, p. 22.

34. Weber, *The Protestant Ethic and the Spirit of Capitalism*, p. 182.

35. Z. Bauman, *Modernity and the Holocaust*, Polity Press, 1991, p. 199.

36. Ibid., p. 198.

37. Ibid., p. 221.

38. Derrida, *Of Spirit*, p. 109.

39. See 'A classless society' and 'The totalitarian movement', in H. Arendt, *The Origins of Totalitarianism*, Harvest/HJB, 1979, pp. 305–88.

40. See 'From restricted to general economy: a Hegelianism without reserve', in J. Derrida, *Writing and Difference*, trans. Alan Bass, Routledge, 1990b, pp. 250–77.

41. R. Boyne, *Foucault and Derrida: The Other Side of Reason*, Unwin Hyman, 1990, p. 158.

Bibliography

Adorno, T.W. (1990) *Negative Dialectics*, trans. E.B. Ashton, London, Routledge.

Adorno, T.W. (1996) *Minima Moralia*, trans. E.F.N. Jephcott, London, Verso.

Althusser, L. (1971) *Lenin and Philosophy, and Other Essays*, trans. B. Brewster, London, NLB.

Althusser, L. (1983) *Reading Capital*, London, Verso.

Althusser, L. (1986) *For Marx*, trans. B. Brewster, London, Verso.

Arendt, H. (1979) *The Origins of Totalitarianism*, New York, Harvest/HJB.

Arendt, H. (1982) *Lectures on Kant's Political Philosophy*, R. Beiner ed., Chicago, University of Chicago Press.

Avineri, S. (1980a) *The Social and Political Thought of Karl Marx*, Cambridge, Cambridge University Press.

Avineri, S. (1980b) *Hegel's Theory of the Modern State*, Cambridge, Cambridge University Press.

Bauman, Z. (1991) *Modernity and the Holocaust*, Cambridge, Polity Press.

Benjamin, A. (ed.) (1992) *Judging Lyotard*, London, Routledge.

Bennington, G. (1988) *Lyotard, Writing the Event*, Manchester, Manchester University Press.

Bennington, G. (1994) *Legislations: The Politics of Deconstruction*, London, Verso.

Bennington, G. and Derrida, J. (1993) *Jacques Derrida*, trans. G. Bennington, Chicago, University of Chicago Press.

Boyne, R. (1990) *Foucault and Derrida: The Other Side of Reason*, London, Unwin Hyman.

Burke, E. (1973) *Reflections on the Revolution in France*, Harmondsworth, Penguin Books.

Cassirer, E. (1981) *Kant's Life and Thought*, trans. J. Haden, New Haven, CT, Yale University Press.

Couzens Hoy, D. (ed.) (1986) *Foucault: A Critical Reader*, Oxford, Blackwell.

Deleuze, G. (1995) *Kant's Critical Philosophy: The Doctrine of the Faculties*, trans. H. Tomlinson and B. Habberjam, London, Athlone Press.

Derrida, J. (1976) *Of Grammatology*, trans. G. Spivak, Baltimore, MD, Johns Hopkins University Press.

Derrida, J. (1982) *The Margins of Philosophy*, Brighton, Harvester Press.

Derrida, J. (1987) *The Post Card*, Chicago, University of Chicago Press.

Derrida, J. (1990a) *Of Spirit*, trans. G. Bennington and R. Bowlby, Chicago, University of Chicago Press.

Derrida, J. (1990b) *Writing and Difference*, trans. Alan Bass, London, Routledge.

Dews, P. (1995) *The Limits of Disenchantment: Essays on Contemporary European Philosophy* , London, Verso.

Durkheim, E. (1964) *The Division of Labour in Society*, trans. G. Simpson, New York, The Free Press.

Durkheim, E. (1982) *The Rules of Sociological Method*, trans. W.D. Halls, London, Macmillan Press.

Durkheim, E. (1992) *Suicide: A Study in Sociology*, trans. G. Simpson and J.A. Spalding, London, Routledge.

Foucault, M. (1979) *Discipline and Punish: The Birth of the Prison*, trans. A. Sheridan, New York, Vintage Books.

Foucault, M. (1980) *The History of Sexuality: An Introduction*, vol. 1, trans. R. Hurley, New York, Vintage Books.

Foucault, M. (1986) *Power/Knowledge: Selected Interviews and Other Writings 1972–1977*, C. Gordon ed., Brighton, Harvester Press.

Foucault, M. (1987) *The Uses of Pleasure: The History of Sexuality, Volume Two*, trans. R. Hurley, Harmondsworth, Penguin.

Foucault, M. (1991) *The Foucault Reader*, P. Rabinow ed., trans. C. Porter, Harmondsworth, Penguin.

Foucault, M. (1993) *Foucault Live*, trans. J. Johnson, ed. S. Letringer, New York, Semiotext(e).

Foucault, M. (1995) *Madness and Civilization: A History of Insanity in the Age of Reason*, trans. R. Howard, London, Routledge.

Gadamer, H.-G. (1976) *Hegel's Dialectic: Five Hermeneutic Studies*, trans. C.P. Smith, New Haven, CT, Yale University Press.

Giddens, A. (1980) *Capitalism and Modern Social Theory: An Analysis of the Writings of Marx, Durkheim and Max Weber*, Cambridge, Cambridge University Press.

Habermas, J. (1976) *Legitimation Crisis*, trans. T. McCarthy, London, Heinemann.

Habermas, J. (Spring 1979) 'History and evolution', trans. D.J. Parent, in *Telos*, 39, pp. 127–43.

Habermas, J. (1987) *Theory of Communicative Action* (2 vols), trans. T. McCarthy, Boston, Beacon Press.

Habermas, J. (1994) *The Philosophical Discourse of Modernity*, trans. F. Lawrence, Cambridge, Polity Press.

Habermas, J. (1995a) *Postmetaphysical Thinking*, trans. W.M. Hohengarten, Cambridge, Polity Press.

Habermas, J. (1995b) *Justification and Application: Remarks on Discourse Ethics*, trans. C. Cronin, Cambridge, Polity Press.

Hegel, G.W.F. (1967a) *Phenomenology of Mind*, trans. J.B. Baillie, New York, Harper & Row.

Hegel, G.W.F. (1967b) *Philosophy of Right*, trans. T.M. Knox, Oxford, Oxford University Press.

Hegel, G.W.F. (1969) *The Science of Logic*, trans. A.V. Miller, London, George Allen & Unwin.

Hegel, G.W.F. (1975) *Natural Law. The Scientific Ways of Treating Natural Law, Its Place in Moral Philosophy, and Its Relation to the Positive Sciences of Law*, trans. T.M. Knox, Philadelphia, PA, University of Pennsylvania Press.

Hegel, G.W.F. (1980) *Lectures on the Philosophy of World History, Introduction: Reason in History*, trans. H.B. Nisbet, Cambridge, Cambridge University Press.

Hegel, G.W.F. (1982) *Hegel's Logic: Encyclopaedia of the Philosophical Sciences, Volume One*, trans. W. Wallace, Oxford, Oxford University Press.

Heidegger, M. (1983) *Being and Time*, trans. J. Macquarrie and E. Robinson, London, Blackwell.

Horkheimer, M. and Adorno, T.W. (1986) *The Dialectic of Enlightenment*, trans. J. Cumming, New York, Continuum.

Hume, D. (1975) *A Treatise on Human Nature*, Oxford, Oxford University Press.

Hyppolite, J. (1974) *Genesis and Structure of Hegel's Phenomenology of Spirit*, trans. S. Charniak and J. Heckman, Evanston, IL, Northwestern University Press.

Jameson, F. (1995) *Postmodernism: Or the Cultural Logic of Late Capitalism*, London, Verso.

Jay, M. (1984) *Marxism and Totality: The Adventures of a Concept from Lukács to Habermas* , Berkley, CA, University of California Press.

Kant, I. (1956) *Critique of Practical Reason*, trans. L. White Beck, New York, Bobbs-Merrill.

Kant, I. (1982a) *Critique of Pure Reason*, trans. N. Kemp-Smith, London, Macmillan.

Kant, I. (1982b) *Critique of Judgement*, trans. J. Creed-Meredith, Oxford, Oxford University Press.

Kant, I. (1983) *Prologomena to any Future Metaphysics*, trans. P. Carus (revised by W. Ellington), Indianapolis, IN, Hackett.

Kant, I. (1985) *Foundations of the Metaphysics of Morals*, trans. L. White Beck, New York, Macmillan.

Kant, I. (1991) *Political Writings*, H. Reiss ed., trans. H.B. Nisbet, Cambridge, Cambridge University Press.

Keat, R. and Urry, J. (1975) *Social Theory as Science*, London, Routledge.

Kojeve, A. (1969) *Introduction to the Reading of Hegel: Lectures on the Phenomenology of Spirit*, A. Bloom ed., trans. J.H. Nichols Jr., Ithaca, NY, Cornell University Press.

Kristeva, J. (1992) *The Kristeva Reader*, T. Moi ed., trans. A. Jardine and J. Blake, Oxford, Blackwell.

Kuhn, T.S. (1970) *The Structure of Scientific Revolutions*, Chicago, University of Chicago Press.

Levi, P. (1992) *The Drowned and the Saved*, trans. R. Rosenthal, London, Abacus.

Levinas, E. (1994) *Totality and Infinity: An Essay on Exteriority*, trans. A. Lingis, Pittsburgh, PA, Duquesne University Press.

Lichtheim, G. (1967) *Marxism*, London, Routledge.

Luhmann, N. (1984) *Soziale Systeme*, Frankfurt.

Lukács, G. (1975) *The Young Hegel: Studies in the Relations between Dialectics and Economics*, trans. R. Livingstone, London, Merlin Press.

Lukes, S. (1981) *Emile Durkheim. His Life and Work: A Historical and Critical Study*, Harmondsworth, Penguin.

Lyotard, J.-F. (1988a) *The Differend: Phrases in Dispute*, trans. G. Van Den Abeele, Manchester, Manchester University Press.

Lyotard, J.-F. (1988b) *Peregrinations: Law, Form, Event*, New York, Columbia University Press.

Lyotard, J.-F. (1989) *Just Gaming*, trans. W. Goldzich, Minneapolis, MN, University of Minnesota Press.

Lyotard, J.-F. (1990) *Heidegger and 'the jews'*, trans. A. Mitchel and M. Roberts, Minneapolis, MN, University of Minnesota Press.

Lyotard, J.-F. (1991a) *The Postmodern Condition: A Report on Knowledge*, trans. G. Bennington and B. Massumi, Manchester, Manchester University Press.

Lyotard, J.-F. (1991b) *The Lyotard Reader*, A. Benjamin ed., Oxford, Blackwell.

Lyotard, J.-F. (1993) *Libidinal Economy*, trans. I. Hamilton Grant, London, Athlone Press.

Lyotard, J.-F. (1994) *Lessons on the Analytic of the Sublime*, trans. E. Rottenburg, Stanford, CA, Stanford University Press.

MacRae, D. (1976) *Weber*, London, Fontana.

Mandel, E. (1977) *Marxist Economic Theory*, London, Merlin Press.

Marcuse, H. (1968) *Reason and Revolution: Hegel and the Rise of Social Theory*, London, Routledge.

Marx, K. (1976) *The Poverty of Philosophy: Answer to 'Philosophy of Poverty' by M. Proudhon*, Moscow, Progress Publishers.

Marx, K. (1977a) *Capital, Volume One*, trans. S. Moore and E. Aveling, London, Lawrence & Wishart.

Marx, K. (1977b) *Economic and Philosophical Manuscripts of 1844*, Moscow, Progress Publishers.

Marx, K. (1977c) *The German Ideology*, C.J. Arthur ed., London, Lawrence & Wishart.

Marx, K. (1977d) *Karl Marx: Selected Writings*, D. McLellan ed., Oxford, Oxford University Press.

Mommsen, W.J. (1974) *The Age of Bureaucracy: Perspectives on the Political Sociology of Max Weber*, Oxford, Blackwell.

Nietzsche, F. (1990) *The Birth of Tragedy* and *The Genealogy of Morals*, trans. F. Golfing, New York, Doubleday.

Parsons, T. (1951) *The Social System*, London, Routledge.

Parsons, T. (with E. Bates and R. Shils) (1953) *Working Papers in the Theory of Action*, London, Collier-Macmillan.

Parsons, T. (1968) *The Structure of Social Action*, London, Collier-MacMillan.

Pippin, R.B. (1989) *Hegel's Idealism: The Satisfactions of Self-consciousness*, Cambridge, Cambridge University Press.

Popper, K.R. (1966) *The Open Society and Its Enemies (Volumes One and Two)*, London, Routledge.

Ritzer, G. (1996) *The McDonaldization of Society*, Thousand Oaks, CA, Pine Forge Press.

Rose, G. (1978) *The Melancholy Science: An Introduction to the Thought of Theodor W. Adorno*, London, Macmillan.

Rose, G. (1981) *Hegel Contra Sociology*, London, Athlone Press.

Rose, G. (1993) *Judaism and Modernity: Philosophical Essays*, Oxford, Blackwell.

Rosen, S. (1974) *G.W.F. Hegel: An Introduction to the Science of Wisdom*, New Haven, CT, Yale University Press.

Rouseau, J.-J. (1988) *The Social Contract and Discourses*, London, J.M. Dent.

Rundell, J. (1987) *Origins of Modernity: The Origins of Modern Social Theory from Kant to Hegel to Marx*, Cambridge, Polity Press.

Simons, J. (1995) *Foucault and the Political*, New York, Routledge.

Smith, A. (1976) *The Theory of Moral Sentiments*, Indianapolis, Liberty Classics.

Steinberger, P.J. (1988) *Logic and Politics: Hegel's Philosophy of Right*, New Haven, CT, Yale University Press.

Taylor, C. (1979) *Hegel and Modern Society*, Cambridge, Cambridge University Press.

Taylor, C. (1983) *Hegel*, Cambridge, Cambridge University Press.

Thompson, J.B. and Held, D. (eds) (1986) *Habermas: Critical Debates*, London, Macmillan.

Trotsky, L. (1971) *The Struggle Against Fascism in Germany*, Introduction, E. Mandod, London, Pathfinder Press.

Weber, M. (1949) *The Methodology of the Social Sciences*, trans. E. Shils and H. Finch, Chicago, Free Press.

Weber, M. (1978a) *The Protestant Ethic and the Spirit of Capitalism*, trans. T. Parsons, London, George Allen & Unwin.

Weber, M. (1978b) *Weber Selections*, W.G. Runcimen ed., Cambridge, Cambridge University Press.

Weber, M. (1978c [1921]) *Economy and Society*, trans. G. Roth and C. Widdith eds, Berkeley, CA, California University Press.

Yovel, Y. (1980) *Kant and the Philosophy of History*, Princeton, NJ, Princeton University Press.

Index